Robert Geffner, PhD, ABPN
Mark Braverman, PhD
Joseph Galasso, MA
Janessa Marsh, BS
Editors

Aggression in Organizations: Violence, Abuse, and Harassment at Work and in Schools

Aggression in Organizations: Violence, Abuse, and Harassment at Work and in Schools has been co-published simultaneously as *Journal of Emotional Abuse*, Volume 4, Numbers 3/4 2004.

Pre-publication
REVIEWS,
COMMENTARIES,
EVALUATIONS . . .

"**V**ALUABLE. . . . INSIGHTFUL. . . . TIMELY. . . . VERY READABLE. This edited book will benefit those who seek to make the work environment a just and safe place. It is useful to management and their staff, to employers and their employees, and to school administrators, teachers, and their students. It also has a place for those who work with 'workplace abused' employees–those involved in workplace safety, in workplace equity, in workplace policy, and in counseling."

Peter A. Newcombe, PhD, BEd
Senior Lecturer in Behavioral Studies
School of Social Work
and Applied Human Sciences
The University of Queensland, Australia

More Pre-publication
REVIEWS, COMMENTARIES, EVALUATIONS . . .

"**C**UTS TO THE HEART OF THE
ISSUE. . . . A comprehensive
and in-depth analysis of violence
and its complexity, and then guides
the reader through prevention strategies and treatment guidelines for
those most affected by workplace or
school violence. This book examines
the issues that impact the places
where a variety of people spend the
majority of their time–the workplace
and schools. Bullying, sexual harassment, and emotional abuse are
among the many issues explored.
Professionals in disciplines such as
psychology, women's studies, and
child development will find selected
chapters to be critical readings.
Overall, this edited work is MOST
APPROPRIATE FOR GRADUATE
STUDENTS IN ADVANCED SOCIAL
WORK, EDUCATION, AND BUSINESS
COURSES."

Ira Colby, DSW
Dean and Professor
Graduate School of Social Work
University of Houston

HMTP

The Haworth Maltreatment & Trauma Press®
An Imprint of The Haworth Press, Inc.

New York • London • Victoria (AU)
www.HaworthPress.com

Aggression in Organizations: Violence, Abuse, and Harassment at Work and in Schools

Aggression in Organizations: Violence, Abuse, and Harassment at Work and in Schools has been co-published simultaneously as *Journal of Emotional Abuse*, Volume 4, Numbers 3/4 2004.

The *Journal of Emotional Abuse*[TM] Monographic "Separates"

Below is a list of "separates," which in serials librarianship means a special issue simultaneously published as a special journal issue or double-issue *and* as a "separate" hardbound monograph. (This is a format which we also call a "DocuSerial.")

"Separates" are published because specialized libraries or professionals may wish to purchase a specific thematic issue by itself in a format which can be separately cataloged and shelved, as opposed to purchasing the journal on an on-going basis. Faculty members may also more easily consider a "separate" for classroom adoption.

"Separates" are carefully classified separately with the major book jobbers so that the journal tie-in can be noted on new book order slips to avoid duplicate purchasing.

You may wish to visit Haworth's website at . . .

http://www.HaworthPress.com

. . . to search our online catalog for complete tables of contents of these separates and related publications.

You may also call 1-800-HAWORTH (outside US/Canada: 607-722-5857), or Fax 1-800-895-0582 (outside US/Canada: 607-771-0012), or e-mail at:

docdelivery@haworthpress.com

Aggression in Organizations: Violence, Abuse, and Harassment at Work and in Schools, edited by Robert Geffner, PhD, ABPN, Mark Braverman, PhD, Joseph Galasso, MA, and Janessa Marsh, BS (Vol. 4, No. 3/4, 2004). *A review of current statistics, interventions, and examples of past and future programs that help prevent or alleviate the stress of being terrorized at work or in school.*

The Effects of Intimate Partner Violence on Children, edited by Robert A. Geffner, PhD, ABPN, Robyn Spurling Igelman, MA, and Jennifer Zellner, MS (Vol. 3, Nos. 1/2 and 3/4, 2003). *Examines short- and long-term developments/problems facing children exposed to domestic violence.*

Bullying Behavior: Current Issues, Research, and Interventions, edited by Robert A. Geffner, PhD, ABPN, Marti Loring, PhD, LCSW, and Corinna Young, MS (Vol. 2, No. 2/3, 2001). *Shows how to stop schoolyard terror before it escalates to tragedy with timely intervention strategies and up-to-date reports on the dynamics of bullying.*

Aggression in Organizations: Violence, Abuse, and Harassment at Work and in Schools

Robert Geffner, PhD, ABPN
Mark Braverman, PhD
Joseph Galasso, MA
Janessa Marsh, BS
Editors

Aggression in Organizations: Violence, Abuse, and Harassment at Work and in Schools has been co-published simultaneously as *Journal of Emotional Abuse*, Volume 4, Numbers 3/4 2004.

HMTP

The Haworth Maltreatment & Trauma Press®
An Imprint of The Haworth Press, Inc.

New York • London • Victoria (AU)
www.HaworthPress.com

Published by

The Haworth Maltreatment & Trauma Press, 10 Alice Street, Binghamton, NY 13904-1580 USA

The Haworth Maltreatment & Trauma Press is an imprint of The Haworth Press, Inc., 10 Alice Street, Binghamton, NY 13904-1580 USA.

Aggression in Organizations: Violence, Abuse, and Harassment at Work and in Schools has been co-published simultaneously as *Journal of Emotional Abuse*™, Volume 4, Numbers 3/4 2004.

Cover design by Kerry Mack.

Library of Congress Cataloging-in-Publication Data

Aggression in organizations: violence, abuse, and harassment at work and in schools/Robert A. Geffner et al., editors.
     p. cm.
     "Co-published simultaneously as Journal of Emotional Abuse, Volume 4, Numbers 3/4, 2004."
     Includes bibliographical references and index.
     ISBN 0-7890-2841-7 (hard cover: alk. paper)–ISBN 0-7890-2842-5 (soft cover: alk. paper)
     1. Violence in the workplace–United States–Prevention. 2. School violence–United States–Prevention. 3. Harassment–United States–Prevention. 4. Bullying in schools–United States–Prevention. 5. Bullying in the workplace–Ireland–Prevention. 6. Psychological abuse United States–Prevention. 7. Aggressiveness–Prevention. I. Geffner, Robert.
  HF5549.5.E43A33 2004
  658.4'73–dc22
                                                 2004027873

Indexing, Abstracting & Website/Internet Coverage

This section provides you with a list of major indexing & abstracting services and other tools for bibliographic access. That is to say, each service began covering this periodical during the year noted in the right column. Most Websites which are listed below have indicated that they will either post, disseminate, compile, archive, cite or alert their own Website users with research-based content from this work. (This list is as current as the copyright date of this publication.)

Abstracting, Website/Indexing Coverage . . . . Year When Coverage Began

- *Applied Social Sciences Index & Abstracts (ASSIA) (Online: ASSI via Data-Star) (CDRom: ASSIA Plus) <http://www.csa.com>* 1998

- *Business Source Corporate: coverage of nearly 3,350 quality magazines and journals: designed to meet the diverse information needs of corporations; EBSCO Publishing; <http://www.epnet.com/corporate/bsource.corp.asp>* 1998

- *Cambridge Scientific Abstracts is a leading publisher of scientific information in print journal; online databases, CD-ROM and via the Internet <http://www.csa.com>* 1998

- *Criminal Justice Abstracts* 1998

- *e-psyche, LLC <http://www.e-psyche.net>* 1998

- *EBSCOhost Electronic Journals Service (EJS) <http://ejournals.ebsco.com>* 1999

- *Educational Research Abstracts (ERA) (online database) <http://www.tandf.co.uk/era>* 2002

- *EMBASE.com (The Power of EMBASE + MEDLINE combined) <http://www.embase.com>* 1999

(continued)

*Exact start date to come.

(continued)

ABOUT THE EDITORS

Robert Geffner, PhD, ABPN, is Founder and President of the Family Violence and Sexual Assault Institute located in San Diego, CA. Dr. Geffner is a Clinical Research Professor of Psychology at the California School of Professional Psychology, Alliant International University in San Diego, and is also a Licensed Psychologist and a Licensed Marriage and Family Therapist in California and in Texas. He was Clinical Director of a large private practice mental health clinic in East Texas for over 15 years. Dr. Geffner is Editor-in-Chief of Haworth's Maltreatment and Trauma Press, which includes being the Editor of the *Journal of Child Sexual Abuse* and *Journal of Aggression, Maltreatment, & Trauma*, and co-editor of *Journal of Emotional Abuse*, all internationally disseminated. He also is Senior Editor of the Maltreatment, Trauma, and Interpersonal Aggression book program for The Haworth Press. He has a Diplomate in Clinical Neuropsychology from the American Board of Professional Neuropsychology. He served as an adjunct faculty member for the National Judicial College from 1990-2000, and was a former Professor of Psychology at the University of Texas at Tyler for 16 years. Dr. Geffner has published extensively and given presentations and workshops world-wide in the areas of family violence, sexual assault, child abuse, family and child psychology, custody issues, forensic psychology, neuropsychology, aggression, trauma, and diagnostic assessment. He has served on several national and state committees dealing with various aspects of family psychology, family violence, child abuse, and family law. In addition, he has served as a con- sultant for various agencies and centers of the federal government, including the Department of Health & Human Services, National Center for Child Abuse & Neglect, Department of Defense and different branches of the military.

Mark Braverman, PhD, is National Practice Leader for Human Impact with Marsh Crisis Consulting. Dr. Braverman has provided training, case management, and acute crisis response to Fortune 500 companies and to numerous Federal Agencies, including the U.S. Postal

Service. He has designed workplace violence prevention programs and provided threat assessment and case management to corporations and institutions, including higher education, in the public and private sector, since 1988. In 1992, he testified before the U.S. Congress on the causes of violence in the U.S. Postal Service. Dr. Braverman is the author of *Preventing Workplace Violence: A Guide for Employers and Practitioners*, Sage Publications, 1999.

Joseph Galasso, MA, received his undergraduate degree from Quinnipiac University in Hamden, CT. He is a recent graduate of Fairleigh Dickinson University (Madison, NJ), where he received a Master's degree in Industrial/Organizational Psychology. The scope of his expertise has expanded to team building, coaching, and helping people define and maintain a balance between life and work. At present, Mr. Galasso is a doctoral candidate in Clinical Psychology, with an emphasis on Child and Family Systems, at the California School of Professional Psychology (Alliant International University, San Diego, CA). He is also the co-founder and lead consultant for Educational Coaching Solutions, LLC which is based out of New Jersey.

Janessa Marsh, BS, is currently pursuing her Master's degree in Industrial-Organizational Psychology at the California School of Organizational Studies at Alliant International University in San Diego, CA. She received her BS in Psychology from Louisiana State University. Ms. Marsh is Assistant Editor for the *Journal of Aggression, Maltreatment, & Trauma*, the *Journal of Child Sexual Abuse*, the *Journal of Emotional Abuse*, and the *Journal of Child Custody* and is on staff at the Family Violence and Sexual Assault Institute in San Diego. Her current research interests include human resource management, specifically selection, individual differences, and feedback.

Aggression in Organizations: Violence, Abuse, and Harassment at Work and in Schools

CONTENTS

About the Contributors

Nancy J. Amick, PhD, is Manager in the Employee Assistance Program of a national financial services company. Dr. Amick received a PhD in Clinical Psychology from the California School of Professional Psychology. She is a licensed psychologist in Phoenix, AZ.

Shawn M. Bergman, MA, is a doctoral student in the Industrial and Organizational Psychology program at The University of Tennessee. Mr. Bergman's research interests include the integration of implicit and explicit personality, statistical methodology, and academic performance.

Jo Blase, PhD, is Professor of Educational Leadership at the University of Georgia. Her primary research interests include administrator-teacher interaction vis-à-vis school reform and supervisory discourse in education and medicine, leadership preparation, and democratic school leadership. Recent publications include *Handbook of Instructional Leadership: How Successful Principals Promote Teaching and Learning*, 2nd ed. (with Joseph Blase, Corwin, 2004) and "The Micropolitics of Instructional Supervision: A Call for Research" (with Joseph Blase) in *Educational Administration Quarterly* (2002).

Joseph Blase, PhD, is Professor of Educational Leadership at the University of Georgia. His primary research interests include principal-teacher relationships, school-level micropolitics, democratic school leadership, and principal mistreatment. Recent publications include *Breaking the Silence: Overcoming the Problem of Principal Mistreatment of Teachers* (with Jo Blase, Corwin, 2002) and "The Phenomenology of Principal Mistreatment" (with Jo Blase) in the *Journal of Educational Administration* (2003).

Robert J. W. Clift is a Forensic Psychology PhD student at the University of British Columbia.

Patty Dulle, APRN, Intermountain Health Care, specializes in the evaluation of long-term and cumulative effects of traumatic events. She has more than twenty years of clinical experience in assisting individuals in their recovery from traumatic events.

Donald L. Gault, MA, is Manager of the Healthy Communities Section with the St. Paul-Ramsey County Department of Public Health. He has worked in The Initiative for Violence-Free Families and Communities since 1990. His violence prevention work has focused on working with local school systems (K-12 and higher education), faith communities, workplaces, and the media. He has a Bachelor of Arts degree in Political Science from Northeastern Illinois University and a Master of Arts degree in Public Policy from the Hubert Humphrey Institute of Public Affairs at the University of Minnesota.

Thomas M. Green, PhD, is Interim Dean of the School of Business and Information Management. Prior to joining National University in 1996, Dr. Green served as Chief of Research and Statistics at the Hawaii Department of the Attorney General, as well as Director of the State Uniform Crime Reporting Program. His research interests include domestic violence, sexual assault, and victimology.

Marsha Hammond, PhD, received her doctorate in Clinical/Health Psychology. She is a member of the American Psychological Association, a Division 32 Board member, and member of the National Academy of Neuropsychology. She currently works in private practice in Asheville, NC.

Nikki A. Hawkins, PhD, is currently affiliated with the Centers for Disease Control and Prevention, Atlanta, GA. She was a PhD Candidate in the Department of Psychology and Social Behavior at the University of California, Irvine when completing work on her article. Her research examines decision-making and coping with significant life events.

Nancy J. Heacox, PhD, is a Senior Scientist with Pacific Science & Engineering Group, Inc., a human factors research and development company in San Diego, CA. She focuses on the influence of environmental, organizational and personal factors on the outcomes of work processes, both positive-productivity and negative-aggressive employee behavior. Dr. Heacox received a BA in Psychology from Chapman College, an MS and a PhD in Industrial-Organizational Psychology from the California School of Professional Psychology. She is a licensed Psychologist in the State of California. She is a member of the American Psychological Association, the Society for Industrial-Organizational Psychology, Sigma Xi, Psi Chi, and the Human Factors and Ergonomics Society.

E. Alison Holman, PhD, FNP, is Staff Research Associate at the Health Policy and Research Unit, University of California, Irvine. A health psychologist and family nurse practitioner with clinical experience with children and their families, she has studied coping in various traumatized populations. Her research addresses interactive effects of cognitive, social, emotional, and physical responses on adaptation to traumatic stress. In 2001, she received the Chaim Danieli Young Professional Award from the International Society of Traumatic Stress Studies.

Lawrence R. James, PhD, is Pilot Oil Professor in the Industrial and Organizational Psychology program at The University of Tennessee. Dr. James' contributions have been designed to make possible tests of new models in areas such as organizational climate, leadership, personnel selection, and personality.

Michele Koonin, LCSW, MBA, is Founder and Director of American Continuing Education and Workplace Training Institute. Ms. Koonin has been in private practice in San Diego since 1990 dealing with the areas of trauma and abuse. She has authored and co-authored curriculums on treating female and male perpetrators of domestic violence, a program for child abuse offenders, and a book on the recognition, intervention, and prevention of workplace violence. Her current interest is in the area of prevention and wellness for individuals and organizations.

James N. Madero, PhD, is Professor of Psychology in the California School of Professional Psychology at Alliant International University, San Diego. He was the Director of the Doctoral Program in Clinical Psychology at United States International University, San Diego, for over 20 years. Dr. Madero has 35 years of experience as a teacher, administrator, and practicing clinical psychologist. He is an expert in psychological testing, threat assessment, and workplace and school violence prevention. Dr. Madero has conducted over 800 threat assessments of potentially violent employees for public and private sector companies and organizations. He has developed workplace violence prevention training programs and materials and has trained numerous Workplace Violence Prevention Teams in companies and organizations across the United States. Dr. Madero is a graduate of the Doctoral Program in Clinical Psychology at Catholic University, Washington, DC, and a licensed psychologist in the state of California.

Anne Maloney practices law in Squamish, British Columbia.

Daniel N. McIntosh, PhD, Associate Professor of Psychology at the University of Denver, is a social psychologist who studies adjustment to negative life events, emotion, and the psychology of religion. His work examines social and cognitive responses to stressful and low control situations, the role of religion in coping, and basic interpersonal emotional processes.

Michael D. McIntyre, PhD, is Research Assistant Professor in the Industrial and Organizational Psychology program at The University of Tennessee. Dr. McIntyre's research interests include personality measurement and employee selection.

Angelea Panos, PhD, Intermountain Health Care, is a consultant and researcher in the area of workplace violence prevention and response. Dr. Panos has consulted nationally and internationally to more than a hundred organizations affected by many types of workplace violence and trauma, including terrorism, kidnapping, robbery, war, homicide, and suicide.

Patrick Panos, PhD, Brigham Young University, is a researcher that evaluates treatment outcomes in populations affected by trauma and violence. He has a special interest in the needs of multicultural and diverse populations.

Sandra Rasmussen, PhD, received her doctorate from Harvard University in 1973, MA from the University of Minnesota in 1960, MSN from Anna Maria College in 1984, and BSN from the University of Minnesota in 1957. She is currently Program Faculty Mentor in the Psychology and Public Health programs at Walden University, Addition Therapist at The Williamsburg Place, Psychiatric Nurse at Eastern State Hospital in Williamsburg, and Senior Instructor at Cambridge College Graduate Programs in Counseling Psychology and School Nursing.

Elizabeth A. Rock, PhD, is currently a School Psychologist at Park County School District #1 in Powell, WY. She is also the trainer for staff, parents, and students in the "No Bullying Allowed Here" program. Her research interests include bullying prevention, relational aggression, and peer relations in the elementary school setting. She received her MA in Psychology from San Francisco State University in 1978 and her PhD in Academic/Clinical Psychology from Walden University in 2002.

Jeff Schanowitz, PhD, recently graduated with his PhD in Clinical and Industrial/Organizational Psychology from the California School of Professional Psychology at Alliant International University, San Diego. Dr. Schanowitz has completed his internship in workplace and school violence prevention programs and continues to consult for schools and corporations in assessments and violence prevention programs. He has assisted in developing workplace violence prevention programs and materials.

Almon Shumba, PhD, MEd, Dip Ed, BScEd, has taught at Morgenster Teachers' College for 12 years, where he rose from Lecturer to Principal Lecturer, and at Bindura University College of Science Education in Zimbabwe for 3 years, where he was appointed member of the University of Zimbabwe Senate and Academic Staff Representative to the Research Board. He worked at the University of Botswana for 4 years and rose from Lecturer to Senior Lecturer in Educational Psychology, has published a book with two other colleagues and published more than 15 articles on child abuse in refereed international journals. He is currently Senior Lecturer and Visiting Scholar at the University of the North, South Africa and has a very strong interest in Child Abuse by Teachers in Schools.

Roxane Cohen Silver, PhD, is Professor in the Department of Psychology and Social Behavior and Department of Medicine at the University of California, Irvine. An expert in stress and coping, she is a Fellow of the American Psychological Association and the American Psychological Society. In December 2003, Dr. Silver was appointed by U.S. Department of Homeland Security, Secretary Tom Ridge, to the Academe and Policy Research Senior Advisory Committee of the Homeland Security Advisory Council.

Richard C. Sorenson, PhD, is Professor in the Department of Psychology at National University in San Diego, CA. He teaches graduate courses in Human Behavior and Industrial-Organizational Psychology and is involved in the development of novel measurement approaches in organizational assessment, telework, and leadership. Dr. Sorenson earned a MS and PhD in Psychology from the University of Washington, Seattle. He is a licensed Psychologist in the State of California and is a member of the American Psychological Association, American Psychological Society, International Association of Applied Psychology and several other professional organizations.

Jason Winters is a Forensic Psychology PhD student at the University of British Columbia.

Preface

As our nation huddles together after the 9/11 attacks and ongoing bombings around the world, we focus on the inhumane actions by those we have labeled terrorists, or outsiders, not people whom we have contact with on a daily basis. However, one of our biggest "battles" on the home front is eliminating acts of violence and abusiveness that occur within the sanctity of our homes, schools, and our places of business. The problem of violence in society has become one of the most pressing social issues in the United States, especially as it is becoming more and more prevalent in our institutions and places of employment. In many organizations, concerns about violence have become the highest priority for reform and intervention. No longer are the days of academic success in school or financial personal gain in business on the top of every headline; now, we are struck by images of metal detectors in our doorways and security personnel on our grounds. However, the focus of the nation and homeland security continues to only be on outside threats and acts. It is time we spend equivalent efforts on those situations that do not necessarily make the headlines but affect numerous people daily.

When violent acts occur in the workplace or in schools, the problem becomes the utmost concern for the community at large, especially those charged with the duty of understanding the nature of violence, how to predict it, and how to treat its effects. What is under attack with each new incident of violence is our sense of safety, our sense that the world as we once knew it has become something new, something indefinable, and something unsafe. The most overt results are a push toward the increased presence of security officials, mandatory attendance in training workshops, and the sense of anxiety and disorder that this creates. What we don't see, however, are the countless people who are affected by the abuse and violence in local settings, those studying the nature of violence and aggression as it exists today, and the various techniques being utilized to remediate or prevent the abuse and violence.

[Haworth co-indexing entry note]: "Preface." Geffner, Robert, Janessa Marsh, and Joseph Galasso. Co-published simultaneously in *Journal of Emotional Abuse* (The Haworth Maltreatment & Trauma Press, an imprint of The Haworth Press, Inc.) Vol. 4, No. 3/4, 2004, pp. xxv-xxvi; and: *Aggression in Organizations: Violence, Abuse, and Harassment at Work and in Schools* (ed: Robert Geffner et al.) The Haworth Maltreatment & Trauma Press, an imprint of The Haworth Press, Inc., 2004, pp. xxi-xxii. Single or multiple copies of this article are available for a fee from The Haworth Document Delivery Service [1-800-HAWORTH, 9:00 a.m. - 5:00 p.m. (EST). E-mail address: docdelivery@haworthpress.com].

http://www.haworthpress.com/web/JEA

This volume is our move toward achieving the feelings of safety again and dealing with the less noticed forms of abuse and harassment that many people are experiencing. This is the third in a series of special publications in the *Journal of Emotional Abuse* that focus on issues of importance that are not sufficiently highlighted in the media. The first two issues were *Bullying Behavior: Current Issues, Research and Interventions* (Geffner, Loring, & Young, 2001) and *The Effects of Intimate Partner Violence on Children* (Geffner, Igelman, & Zellner, 2003). The current volume provides a clearer, more defined picture of what violence and harassment in our schools and workplaces looks like and attempts to offer an integrated framework for types of abuse and aggression seen in these environments. Finally, we try to offer some insight into what can be done to prevent a future filled with violence in our organizations as well as a set of guidelines for treating people previously affected by such acts of violence, aggression, and maltreatment.

This volume includes articles from people in different organizational sectors, some from educational institutions and some from the workplace. This unique look helps us to integrate the needs of organizations in general, not only from a general wellness perspective, but also from a perspective of increasing safety and preventing acts of aggression on every level of our society. There is a general feeling among the people in our society, and abroad, that we are not safe in the places where we spend the majority of our time: the workplace and/or school. This volume offers current statistics, interventions, and examples of past and future programs to help alleviate the stress of being "terrorized" in these contexts.

Robert Geffner
Janessa Marsh
Joseph Galasso

REFERENCES

Geffner, R., Igelman, R. S., & Zellner, J. (2003). *The effects of intimate partner violence on children*. Binghamton, NY: The Haworth Press, Inc.
Geffner, R. A., Loring, M., & Young, C. (2001). *Bullying behavior: Current issues, research, and interventions*. Binghamton, NY: The Haworth Press, Inc.

FOUNDATIONS AND OVERVIEW

Abuse and Violence
in the Workplace and School:
Toward a Systems-Based Model

Mark Braverman

SUMMARY. Workplace violence covers a wide range of phenomena. There is a need for a definition that establishes boundaries between violence and other injurious behaviors while still encompassing a continuum of behaviors related directly to violence, from verbal abuse to institutionalized harassment, to fatal violence itself. Although the articles in the current volume attest to the fact that there is a continuum of phenomena that may lead to violence, and that personality factors are important in the development of preventative approaches, the articles make the equally powerful argument that system-level factors, such as the use of power and the level of communication and collaboration between stakeholders, are of crucial importance in the genesis and preven-

Address correspondence to: Mark Braverman, PhD, 6819 Selkirk Drive, Bethesda, MD 20817 (E-mail: Mark.Braverman@Marsh.com).

[Haworth co-indexing entry note]: "Abuse and Violence in the Workplace and School: Toward a Systems-Based Model." Braverman, Mark. Co-published simultaneously in *Journal of Emotional Abuse* (The Haworth Maltreatment & Trauma Press, an imprint of The Haworth Press, Inc.) Vol. 4, No. 3/4, 2004, pp. 1-11; and: *Aggression in Organizations: Violence, Abuse, and Harassment at Work and in Schools* (ed: Robert Geffner et al.) The Haworth Maltreatment & Trauma Press, an imprint of The Haworth Press, Inc., 2004, pp. 1-11. Single or multiple copies of this article are available for a fee from The Haworth Document Delivery Service [1-800-HAWORTH, 9:00 a.m. - 5:00 p.m. (EST). E-mail address: docdelivery@haworthpress.com].

1

tion of destructive behaviors. A system level of analysis is proposed through which implications for policy and practice can usefully be derived. *[Article copies available for a fee from The Haworth Document Delivery Service: 1-800-HAWORTH. E-mail address: <docdelivery@haworthpress.com> Website: <http://www.HaworthPress.com> © 2004 by The Haworth Press, Inc. All rights reserved.]*

KEYWORDS. Workplace violence, harassment, violence prevention, profiling, continuum of abuse

The articles collected in this volume represent a wide range of approaches to violence in the workplace. Given the timeliness of this topic, and the urgency with which it arises with every high-profile instance of workplace violence, there exists the ongoing risk of typical discourse about this topic: The search for simple causes and unitary solutions. The very multiplicity of approaches presented here is the best argument against such a tendency. Approach the contents as if you are looking at pieces of a puzzle. Taken together, the articles in the first section of this volume will help us move toward a more complete picture of this complex issue.

DEFINITIONS

The first and fundamental issue that we must consider is that of the definition of workplace violence. The articles contained in this volume present a range of perspectives. The title of the volume itself raises the question: What is the relationship between workplace violence and the range of abusive behaviors often named "harassment"? It can be argued that there is a need, from both a practical and a theoretical standpoint, to establish boundaries around the definition of workplace violence. If every phenomenon, from the most indirect forms of harassment and intimidation to fatal violence itself, falls within the category of workplace violence, then the category loses its meaning and becomes of limited usefulness. On the other hand, how the workplace deals with the full range of victimization phenomena is, as I will suggest further on, the central policy issue that emerges from the work presented here. As several research studies suggest, including those looking at schools as well as workplaces (e.g., Blasé & Blasé's study of abuse of teachers by school principals in this volume), a key issue is power: On the one hand, the power differentials that are inherent in authority relationships, and on the other the responsibility of the organization to protect rights, health, and safety of workers. The issue of power has another central meaning in this discussion: Its relevance to the phenomenology of victimization. Several of the articles in this volume specifically touch on the importance of powerlessness and sense of helplessness in the clinical and psychosocial outcomes of victimization, including Gault's report on the Ramsey County initiative; the study by Shumba of emotional abuse of students; Koonin and Green's summary of the emotionally abusive workplace; Hawkins, McIntosh, Silver, and Holman's report on the Columbine shootings; and Blasé and Blasé's study of maltreatment of teachers by school principals referenced above. Interestingly, this same issue underlies our understanding of what motivates the perpetrator of workplace abuse and violence. Bergman, McIntyre, and James in this volume present a new tool to screen violence-prone individuals in the hiring process. This is based on a theory of aggression as motivated by the individual's sense of powerlessness. The apparent fact of this inextricable relationship between the dimension of power in organizations (work or school), the effects of victimization on the individual victims, and the contribution of victimization to aggressive behavior means that we must apply a system-level analysis to properly understand the phenomena described in this volume and to usefully derive implications for policy and practice.

In popular parlance, workplace violence is often associated with fatal worker-on-worker assault: The so-called "disgruntled worker" or "postal" scenario. The selection of articles in this volume makes short work of this distorted and overly restrictive definition. Koonin and Green, in this volume, utilize a particularly broad construct, "the emotionally abusive workplace," beginning from a victim-centered perspective and proposing a continuum of abuse behaviors along a wide range of behaviors and situations, including sniping, work sabotage, and patterns of consistent rudeness. Although comprehensive in scope and based on a coherent theory with a foundation in victim studies, such a construct might invite the criticism, referenced above, that it is too broad to be useful. In contrast, Madero and Schanowitz, in the following overview article in this volume, propose a definition for workplace violence as "crimes of violence that occur at work." About this definition one might ask: Is it too narrow to restrict workplace violence to crime? Would it not, in fact, exclude the various types of harassment covered here? The definitions, existing at these two poles, in fact set out the issue nicely. It is good to set some boundaries; as suggested above, if the term covers everything from murder to harassment, then does it not lose its meaning as a concept? On the other hand, in limiting the definition to crime we run the risk of short-circuiting a crucial set of issues, since violence at work, as evidenced by the range of situations documented in this volume, is a multifaceted and multi-leveled phenomenon.

In his article, Gault makes the point that most workplace violence involves non-physical forms of violence, and furthermore that the majority of violence affecting the workplace originates from outside its walls. For example, domestic violence is an important and chief example of this. Thus, we have to look beyond simple, unitary definitions and remember that it is the individual workplace's analysis of its own "profile" of vulnerability that should motivate its search for solutions. The fact that "bullying" and "mobbing" are referenced in many of the articles makes this point for us: What begins as gossip can turn into scapegoating and may end in organized, wholesale destruction of an individual in the workplace or school environment. Rock, Hammond, and Rasmussen, in their report in this volume of a school-wide bullying prevention program, point out that although the incidence of bullying in United States schools may be as high as 15%, and often manifests as organized, systematic abuse directed at specific groups, it is often not identified as such by authorities at any organizational level. Indeed, bullying may not be recognized by adults at all, who instead see even this form of "conflict" among children as a "normal part of growing up" (Rock et al., p. 228). Amick and Sorenson's study of women's perception of a sexually hostile workplace reported in this volume also emphasizes the need for education about behaviors that may be offensive to women. The findings reported in these articles should alert us to the fact that: (1) a useful definition of workplace violence will transcend categories of what constitutes crime in society at large, although it will certainly include these phenomena, and (2) it will begin with an assessment of the quality of interpersonal relations in each workplace or school along multiple dimensions and organizational systems.

Should the definition of workplace also include such other environments as schools? Abuse and violence in schools presents us with further examples of the need for broader definitions geared to the workplace context. The two studies on abuse of students highlight this issue. In their report in this volume of university students' experience of sexual harassment by teachers during their high school years, Winters, Clift, and Maloney note that most of their subjects did not understand what sexual harassment was, relating this to their finding of very low rates of reporting of the harassment to adults. Shumba's study of emotional abuse of students by teachers in the classroom ends with an urgent call to government authorities to establish clear definitions of what constitutes abuse in the classroom (as well as for public actions to support enforcement and for education of teachers and administrators.) Blasé and Blasé's study also raises awareness of what may be the "hidden problem" of the abuse of authority in the school setting where (unlike other work settings where awareness is higher) insufficient controls are present and where school districts, Boards of Education, and unions appear ineffective in protecting staff from severe abuse. When the problem is identified and named for what it is, however, the possibility exists for remediation.

Finally, and fundamental in its implications for policy, is the issue of the relationship between stress and violence. The authors in this volume are not the first to posit a direct connection between workplace conditions causing stress and workplace violence. With respect to practical application, the relevance of this connection is clear: If we can identify those conditions, we can modify them and reduce the incidence of some forms of workplace violence. Heacox and Sorenson's study reported in this volume represents an advance in the attempt to refine one theory based on this connection and to test hypotheses generated by the theory. Drawing on the construct of organizational frustration leading to aggression, they hypothesize that workplace conditions such as work constraints, role ambiguity, and social support, in interaction with personality variables (chiefly external locus of control), will increase the frequency of aggressive behaviors. Theoretically, this connection is important in view of other studies in this volume, which draw a connection between violence and the experience of helplessness. This concept has support from earlier work concerned with occupational health and burnout, which draws clear connections between the degree of personal control at work in constructs such as Decision Latitude (Karasek & Theorell, 1990) and Hardiness (Mardi & Kobasa, 1984). The connection between frustration and violence also calls to mind again the work of Bergman et al., in this volume, in which helplessness is seen to relate directly to certain forms of aggressive and antisocial behavior at work. Continued work in this area as it relates specifically to violent behavior is important as it applies to practical approaches to prevention. To the extent that those responsible for the workplace understand the destructive effects of conditions that create stress and frustration, they can create safer, healthier, and more productive work environments.

However, caution is advised as we attempt to apply these findings to practical approaches to prevention. Antisocial and aggressive behaviors may indeed be the precursors of actual violence in some cases. Even if these behaviors do not lead to overt violence, they may create an unhealthy climate in the workplace or school, and, if tolerated, create implicit norms that allow more dangerous behavior to manifest. However, personality characteristics and behaviors linked to violence, even through the most rigorous of scientific method, should not be used to create "profiles" of individuals who, when exhibiting these behaviors or shown to possess these personality features, are then presumed to be potentially violent. Workplace policy is seldom applied in a fashion respectful of scientific principles or rigor. Policy makers and those who carry out and enforce the policies seek simple solutions and uncomplicated models. As evidenced in the studies contained in this volume, human behavior is complex and can only be understood in the context of organizational and social settings. Policy related to the prevention of violence must be based more on sociological principles and not merely on forensic or clinical models that can be used to target individuals displaying particular characteristics.

The importance of this principle is demonstrated in what is generally advocated as best practice in the assessment of dangerousness in a workplace threat context (Braverman, 1999). When we evaluate a potential for workplace violence, we look in particular for those aspects of the stressor that relate to the individual's connection to interpersonal and organizational supports and those who have an impact on that individual's sense of effectiveness in the world. It is precisely when such people feel *powerless* that they are at risk for violent or threatening behavior. To understand why this is, we must remember that violence is related to an overwhelming sense of desperation and isolation and a growing sense that *nothing I can do seems to help or change my situation.* The type of person who is most at risk for violent or self-destructive behavior is someone who is poorly equipped to maintain positive supports when things begin to go wrong. Because they cannot easily understand their own contributions to the problems, and instead blame other people or "the system" for misfortunes, they progressively alienate the people around them and use up the resources and good will of the systems designed to support them. In these situations, one will often hear managers or coworkers declare, "He's burned us out! There is nothing more we can do for him." This is where the interaction between personal and organizational factors becomes critical for an understanding of the causes of workplace and school violence and where the articles in this volume are useful as we continue to assemble important pieces of the puzzle.

THE CRISIS-PREPARED ORGANIZATION

Pauchant and Mitroff (1991), writers in the field of management, coined the terms "crisis prone" and "crisis prepared" to differentiate between companies that have recognized the reality of crisis, and those which, at their peril, have not. At the center of their analysis is the importance of early detection of and response to warning signals. The ability to listen and take action is the difference between *reactive* and *proactive* crisis management. Crisis-prone organizations face a "double jeopardy": First, the lack of systems thinking allows for poor risk management because no one is looking at the whole picture. It is as if all the pieces of the puzzle are lying on the table, but no one thinks to assemble them. Mounting evidence of unacceptable risk or explosive conditions can literally be rendered invisible in this way. Second, this same lack of coordination allows even the clearest, most alarming signals to be silenced, since there is little communication or accountability. This model has direct application to the issue of workplace and school violence in its implications for policy. Senge's (1990) description of the learning organization provides a closely related model that is useful to this discussion. Senge argues that systems break down and crises occur precisely because those responsible for planning and decision-making do not recognize or understand the complexity that underlies any event or phenomenon. Senge would agree that attempts to resolve crises based on non-systems thinking leads to an often disastrous worsening of the crisis. In Senge's view, faulty, non-system level approaches on the part of managers lead directly to business crises. These principles bear directly on the issue of violence in the workplace.

Every act of violence is the result of a series of events. As suggested by several of our authors, threats or acts of violence may be preceded by early signs of trouble. The signals are as varied as the systems and levels that make up every workplace or school. A crisis-prone organization will allow these early signs of possible violence or conflict to go undetected. Thus, a fragmented approach to decision-making and crisis management plays a major role in a wide range of workplace violence phenomena. Multiple systems, such as discipline, occupational health and disability, security, or labor relations fail to respond effectively to reports of violence-related threats. The sources of frustration and stress leading to violence are not considered when developing plans or policies to prevent violence in the workplace or school. Impaired or innocent employees are hurt or victimized as a result of systems that overreact or respond with well-intentioned but deeply flawed actions. If the company leadership responds at all to danger signals, they will typically allow such situations to be handled by standard disciplinary, labor relations, security, or occupational health procedures. Only when the crisis has blown up will leadership take direct action. Herein lies the point: Abusive working conditions may not cause violence, certainly not in every (or most) cases. However, these flawed organizations are the very ones that will most likely fail to properly identify potential violence hazards or abusive conditions and will most likely fail to intervene effectively. A recent analysis of the issue of violence in the United States Postal Service emphasizes this point (Braverman, 1999).

INTERVENTION

The issue of effective intervention for individuals who have been traumatized or subjected to severe or chronic abuse is one that has achieved great, and greatly overdue, attention since the 9/11 attacks. At that time, because of widespread and relatively unexamined assumptions about the efficacy and even necessity of clinical intervention in the aftermath of mass disasters, huge amounts of resources, both private and public, have been expended on "critical incident debriefing" or other forms of trauma counseling. Very properly, questions are now being raised: What do we know about the efficacy of these mass interventions? Who is providing them, and where are the standards for the protocols employed?

Two of the studies in this volume directly deal with this topic. In their 10-year case study, Panos, Panos, and Dulle evaluate the different types of support and inter- vention offered to hospital employees who were present at a hostage situation/homicide. A significant minority (15%) of their sample who felt the debriefings to be unhelpful blamed the timing of the intervention, saying that meetings held two months later were more effective. One wonders whether the nature of the intervention itself was a factor, and if retelling modalities may be contra-indicated for some people. Hawkins et al., in this volume, also speak to this subject in their report on interviews they conducted with students and parents in the aftermath of the Columbine High School shootings. They specifically call for further research in evaluating which types of intervention are useful, for which groups, and under what circumstances. Those of us in the field who agree with them in this regard are grateful that the authors chose to let one of the Columbine students speak eloquently to this point:

> That [counseling] activity and that day was so structured and everybody is telling everybody what to do and how to handle everything, it just doesn't work, especially when so many kids are in so many different spots recovering. Kids who weren't even there aren't taking it as hard as the kids who were in the cafeteria–like my friend [who was] watching [the shooters] reload. It's not helping. They're trying to treat everyone necessarily the same way . . . (Hawkins et al., p. 216)

One wonders whether timing is the issue here as much as modality and approach. The authors also return several times to the issue of social support and interpersonal connection, bringing to mind Panos et al.'s findings that put group rituals, such as memorial services, at the top of the list for efficacy. These studies remind us that as we consider what goes into healing and recovery from abuse and trauma, we will do well to consider the natural, endogenous organizational and social mechanisms that need to be facilitated by professional intervention for healing to occur.

IMPLICATIONS FOR POLICY

Managers, elected officials, and public administrators are faced with several clear realities with respect to workplace violence and abuse:

- Acts of violence and abuse in the workplace exist on a continuum.
- Some may reach the level of violence but many may fester under the surface.
- Some may be governed by laws or policies and for some there may be insufficient or non-existent controls or definitions.
- Some individuals are more prone to violence than others are, but these tendencies may surface only under some conditions at work. These same conditions will not evoke violence in most people.

Faced with these realities, each workplace must determine its own range of concerns and determine its own rules. The function of policy is to set guidelines for behaviors and for the control of conditions that affect workers. This includes preserving rights in accord with statutes and regulations, promoting or enforcing behaviors in accord with societal norms, promoting the values of the organization through consistent enforcement of internal codes and procedures, and responding to conditions and needs specific to the particular organization. At its core, and certainly from the perspective of management, workplace violence and abuse is a health and safety issue, with direct implications for policy and procedure. Recognition of this leads directly to issues of organizational policy: Leadership must determine what are the signals of possible trouble or policy violation, how to create systems that reliably detect these signals (including how to maximize reporting), and how to deal with them when they are identified. With respect to the kinds of knowledge available as a result of the work represented in this volume, the workplace and school can be cognizant of work conditions that have been shown to create frustration and hostility and make efforts to recognize the signs of these conditions in order to minimize them. Doing so will help leaders create crisis-prepared workplaces that translate these findings into policies and programs which enhance the sense of individual control and maximize systems for early detection of violence and abuse. With respect to violence in particular, workplaces are well advised to develop specific policies for the assessment of risk and management of potential perpetrators, rather than relying on standard disciplinary and occupational health procedures. Good policy is a living, changing thing: It must be directly responsive to what is observed and felt throughout an organization. We all know how counterproductive, wasteful, and even harmful it can be when policies become rigid and disconnected from its proper source and function.

CONCLUSION: THE NEED FOR AN INTEGRATIVE MODEL

What does it mean when norms, societal and organizational, can be violated by the behavior of peers and even more seriously, by people in authority? It means that the structure of leadership and governance is impaired, damaged, or inherently faulty. The proper function of research in this area is to provide direction and tools for the remediation of this condition. That is why it is crucial that researchers and practitioners, collectively as a group taking on this broad issue, transcend traditional categories. We must understand that although clinical knowledge gained from treating victims can be useful, this is not an issue that can be fully understood through diagnosis and treatment of clinical phenomena, regardless of how comprehensive and interactive our clinical models are. Similarly, we must understand that although identifying perpetrators and developing effective controls on behavior are important components for the development of public and corporate policy, this is much more than a forensic issue. Ignoring these cautions will lead to bad practice and bad policy. Limiting ourselves to only a clinical perspective tends to produce reactive, narrow responses, a model that leads to stigmatizing victims (and in some cases, the perpetrators), and to policies that ignore broader issues of organizational climate and governance. Limiting ourselves to only a forensic model leads to "bad apple" approaches, expressed in the narrow use of screening on the one end or in punishment or expulsion of identified perpetrators on the other. Procedures to prevent or control workplace and school violence, even when the threat originates from outside of the workplace (for example in the case of domestic violence), must be based on a system-wide understanding of the organizational and cultural contexts in which it takes place.

This volume presents state-of-the-art/science approaches to prevention and intervention based on sound theory and solid scholarship. These include: Screen out potentially violent employees before they are hired; train supervisors to recognize the signs of abuse (physical or emotional) and take appropriate and timely action; train employees and students in non-violent dispute resolution; and create a coalition of public and private entities dedicated to education about violence and abuse in the public and private sectors. These all have value in the context of an approach that integrates multiple modalities within a program guided from the top of the organization. However, any one of them alone, whether intended to prevent the occurrence or fix the problem, can be of limited value and even hazardous, because it can create the illusion that the problem has been handled. It comes down to a matter of responsible leadership and sound governance. It means leadership asking itself: What do I need in order to make my place of work or learning a place: Of safety and health; that values people's dignity; that encourages their growth and creativity; that supports interpersonal connections and social support; and that ensures a voice to all, especially when those rights and guarantees are violated or threatened? Gault's description in this volume of Ramsey County's community-wide initiative to promote respectful, violence-free workplaces is an example of an approach based on prevention, multiple stakeholders bridging public and private sectors, and a multi-source, multi-solution approach. One hopes that this initiative is not an isolated phenomenon, but represents a growing movement in this direction.

REFERENCES

Braverman, M. (1999). *Preventing workplace violence: A guide for employers and practitioners.* Thousand Oaks, CA: Sage Publications.

Karasek, R., & Theorell, T. (1992). *Healthy work: Stress, productivity, and the reconstruction of working life.* New York: Basic Books.

Mardi, S., & Kobasa, S. (1984). *The hardy executive: Health under stress.* Homewood, IL: Dow Jones-Irwin.

Pauchant, T. C., & Mitroff, I. A. (1992). *Transforming the crisis-prone organization.* San Francisco, CA: Jossey Bass.

Senge, P. M. (1990). *The fifth discipline.* New York: Doubleday.

An Overview of Workplace
and School Violence Prevention

James N. Madero
Jeff Schanowitz

SUMMARY. The safety of the American workplace began to change in the 1980s. The killings of 14 postal workers by a co-worker at the U.S. Postal Service in Edmond, Oklahoma, in 1986, and numerous other similar homicides in the early 1990s, resulted in workplace violence being one of the greatest concerns of employers in the United States. Considerable attention and research has involved the causes of workplace violence, the types and characteristics of the perpetrators, and the presence of warning signs. A number of comprehensive programs are now available, and are designed to prevent violence in the nation's workplaces and schools. Although workplace homicides have declined by approximately thirty percent over the past decade, the need for further research continues. *[Article copies available for a fee from The Haworth Document Delivery Service: 1-800-HAWORTH. E-mail address: <docdelivery@haworthpress.com> Website: <http://www.HaworthPress.com> © 2004 by The Haworth Press, Inc. All rights reserved.]*

Address correspondence to: James N. Madero, PhD, Professor of Psychology, California School of Professional Psychology, Alliant International University, 10455 Pomerado Road, San Diego, CA 92131 (E-mail: jmadero@alliant.edu).

[Haworth co-indexing entry note]: "An Overview of Workplace and School Violence Prevention." Madero, James N., and Jeff Schanowitz. Co-published simultaneously in *Journal of Emotional Abuse* (The Haworth Maltreatment & Trauma Press, an imprint of The Haworth Press, Inc.) Vol. 4, No. 3/4, 2004, pp. 13-22; and: *Aggression in Organizations: Violence, Abuse, and Harassment at Work and in Schools* (ed: Robert Geffner et al.) The Haworth Maltreatment & Trauma Press, an imprint of The Haworth Press, Inc., 2004, pp. 13-22. Single or multiple copies of this article are available for a fee from The Haworth Document Delivery Service [1-800-HAWORTH, 9:00 a.m. - 5:00 p.m. (EST). E-mail address: docdelivery@ haworthpress.com].

http://www.haworthpress.com/web/JEA
Digital Object Identifier: 10.1300/J135v04n03_02

KEYWORDS. Workplace violence, workplace violence prevention, school violence, school violence prevention, workplace homicide

Technology and innovation in the workplace have developed at an extremely rapid pace over the past 20 years. Personal desk computers, laptops, laser printers, fax machines, cell phones, PDAs, satellite conferencing, e-mail, the Internet, and World Wide Web have dramatically changed the way people work and how business is conducted. The future promises even more exciting developments over the next several decades. Unfortunately along with these exciting developments has come a problem relatively unheard of 20 years ago: The problem of workplace violence.

In the early 1980s, most people saw their workplace as a safe haven from the troubles and ills of the "outside world." But on August 20, 1986, this perception changed when Patrick Henry Sherrill stole some weapons from a local National Guard armory and went to the U.S. Postal Service office in Edmond, Oklahoma where he had been employed for 18 months. He then opened fire on the workers there. By the time he completed his killing rampage, 14 of his co-workers were dead and six were wounded. We'll never know his real motives, since Patrick Henry Sherrill then took his own life at the scene of the horrible carnage he had created.

Although there had been other past incidents of employee violence, even homicides, the Edmond, Oklahoma post office incident was different. This incident initiated feelings and concerns about workplace safety that have continued to the present. As word of the killings in Oklahoma spread, it started a process that culminated with the perception that, for most U.S. workers, the workplace was no longer safe. Since 1986, over 40 people have been killed and more than 20 people have been injured in U.S. Postal Service shootings. In the early 1990s, over 1,000 workers per year became victims of the fastest growing form of murder in the United States, workplace homicide. Homicides became one of the leading causes of occupational injury death (U.S. Department of Labor, 1995). In addition, the terrorist bombings at the World Trade Center in New York in 1993, the Murrah Federal Building in Oklahoma in 1995, and the horrible events of September 11, 2001, have further led to the erosion of the belief that America's workplaces were immune from acts of violence.

DEFINITION OF WORKPLACE VIOLENCE

Although there is some controversy regarding the exact definition of "workplace violence," there is consensus in that it involves crimes of violence that occur in the workplace while the victim is at work or on duty (Jenkins, 1996). According to the National Crime Victimizations Survey, workplace violence is considered to be all "violent acts, including physical assaults and threats of assault, directed toward persons at work or on duty" (Jenkins, 1996, p. 1). Essentially this covers all crimes of violence, including homicide, rape, robbery, and simple and aggravated assault that occur at work.

UNITED STATES POSTAL SERVICE

From 1990 to 1994 there was extensive media coverage of a number of workplace violence incidents, particularly those perpetrated by United States Postal Service employees. The term "going postal" entered our vocabulary and still resonates in daily conversations. Although some of the first major incidents of workplace violence covered extensively by the media occurred in post office facilities, the problem reaches well beyond that particular workplace. An analysis of National Traumatic Occupational Fatalities (NTOF) surveillance system data (U.S. Department of Health and Human Services, 1994) showed that neither the Postal Service industry nor postal occupations were among the groups at highest risk. For the periods 1983-1993, the workplace homicide rate for the Postal Service, 0.63 per 100,000 workers, was just under the average workplace homicide rate for all occupations from the NTOF. There were far more dangerous occupations, such as being a taxicab driver, working in retail sales establishments, and being a member of law enforcement.

CAUSES OF WORKPLACE VIOLENCE

Because the problem of workplace violence seemed to develop overnight, the greater focus to date has been on what to do about it in order to lessen or eliminate its impact. Less effort has been directed towards understanding the root causes of this type of violence. However, understanding the causes is a key element in developing practical solutions to the problem. Among the causes discussed to date are emotional abuse, media glamorization of violence, autocratic work environments, "disposable employees," domestic violence, anger, and alienation.

Patterns of emotional abuse are sometimes passed down from one generation to the next. Many parents believe they are satisfactorily disciplining and training their children as long as they do not hit the children. Yet there are many forms of behavior that are equally ineffective. These include belittlement, denigration, neglect, cruelty, humiliation, and verbal abuse. Adults who have been emotionally abused in childhood sometimes bring the trauma with them into the workplace and express the abuse in several ways: They may project past feelings on current co-workers and supervisors; they may take on the old roles played in their family as either rule-breakers or rule-enforcers as they interact with the new "work family"; they may see the boss as the good/bad parent; they may replay old historic developmental issues with co-workers; and during times of organizational crisis (mergers, downsizing, plant closings, consolidation, etc.), they may be overwhelmed by stress and act out against a boss or co-worker by committing an act of violence.

An old rule in journalism is, "If it bleeds, it leads," meaning that stories containing images of injury, violence, or death will have a good chance to appear at the top of any newscast or on the front pages of most newspapers. Our media sources continue to use violence as the focus of many of their top stories and special reports. The impact of these saturation techniques serves to help desensitize many people, including young children and adolescents, to the realities of violence. The tremendous availability of weapons adds to the risk. Recent studies conducted by the office of Senator Daniel Patrick Moynihan suggest we have at least a 200-year supply of guns in this country (and yet only an eight-year supply of ammunition). Even with stricter ownership requirements and regulations barring sales to certain people like convicted felons and people with admitted mental problems, those who really want a gun find little difficulty getting one. There are also many other forms of weapons available, ranging from knives and swords to pipe bombs and explosives. In June 2003, an employee of Albertsons grocery store in Irvine, California, used a samurai-like sword to kill two co-workers and injure several customers.

The "disposable worker" is another important causal factor. Thousands of American workers have been laid off in the past couple of years with no end in sight. The concept of lifelong employment that was once a major element in many assembly, production, and manufacturing firms, is now a thing of the past. As more firms outsource certain high-tech or product-creation tasks, the impact on the average U.S. worker is felt most often in the pay envelope or the pocketbook. The business pages are filled with stories of leaner and meaner organizations and the lean and mean men who run them. Examples include "Chainsaw Al" Dunlap, unabashed corporate rescuer, who as the CEO of Sunbeam, closed factories and slashed over 60% of the firm's workforce. The scandals at Enron, Arthur Anderson, and World Com have not only cost people their jobs, but also a good portion of their life savings and retirement.

Some highly visible firms, like Ben & Jerry's Ice Cream, Apple Computer, Starbucks, and Hewlett-Packard, have created a nourishing, employee-friendly company. The leaders of these companies have decided to place emphasis on the needs and goals of the employees. From the executive level on down to the least-senior hourly worker, the message is, "You count and your contribution is important to our success."

Unfortunately some other firms have an autocratic approach to the leadership model for success. In this view, the employees are simply interchangeable, just like the parts of an automobile. With little concern for their needs or the contributions they can or want to make, these companies risk creating deep-seated hostilities in their employees. The results of this kind of toxic culture appear in high turnover, low morale, and threats and/or incidents of employee sabotage or violence.

Speak to any personnel manager in the retail or fast-food industries, and he or she is likely to admit that employee turnover is a significant concern. Turnover rates as high as 300% are not uncommon, especially with firms who put little effort into hiring more than just marginal employees or providing them with the type of training necessary to make them feel as if they are valuable to the company. This approach creates an odd paradox: The more the leadership in a company follows this belief, the more they seem to hire inappropriate, transient, or downright unacceptable employees.

In years past, domestic problems tended to stay at home and not cross the boundary line of the workplace. Domestic violence and the related problems it creates have now entered the workplaces of many U.S. companies and organizations, making the workplace less safe than it once was. In 2001, over 50 women were the victims of domestic violence-related homicides at their place of work (Bureau of Labor Statistics, 2001).

Alienation is another source of concern in the workplace. Individuals who are involved in private stressful situations, such as a divorce or death in the family, may feel alone and depressed, frequently angry, and sometimes paranoid. For them, their job is the one source of security, an anchor to help the feeling of alienation, depression, and loss from getting out of hand. When their job security is threatened, they may feel all hope is lost and that they have little if anything to live for. At this stage, they can become extremely dangerous to unsuspecting people in the organization.

PREVENTION PROGRAMS

U.S. companies and organizations have developed a number of tools and techniques to meet the challenge of workplace violence. When crafted into a comprehensive program, these can help reduce an organization's chances of being devastated by an act of violence. The key to using these tools and techniques is to integrate them into a system that is comprehensive, yet logical and strategically planned.

There are a number of books, manuals, videos, and audiocassettes on workplace violence. The best approach is one that is comprehensive but not overbearing; one that contains all the needed elements presented in a clear and concise manner, so that it can be effectively implemented without leaving out essential components and without creating in the user the feeling of being overwhelmed. Performance strategies and best practice standards have been developed through the combined efforts of workplace violence prevention specialists, mental health professionals, and security experts. The efforts of these groups, along with the steps taken by the first companies to implement programs, have led to the standard of performance that presently exists in the country. A comprehensive workplace violence program includes the following: (1) a workplace violence prevention policy, (2) a workplace violence prevention team, (3) training for all managers, supervisors, and employees, as well as for each workplace violence prevention team member, (4) a workplace security audit, (5) procedures for responding to, and safely managing potentially violent incidents, and (6) processes for evaluating the effectiveness of these initiatives.

Among the more detailed and comprehensive approaches is that of the California Occupational Safety & Health Administration (Cal-OSHA, 1994). In 1994 Cal-OSHA released a series of "Guidelines for Workplace Security." These guidelines include information on compliance, communication, hazard assessment and correction, incident investigation, training, and record keeping. Although Cal-OSHA did not mandate that the guidelines be implemented, they strongly urged all employers to assess the potential for violence within their organization and implement measures to prevent the violence from occurring.

These initiatives, along with numerous media reports of workplace violence, place employers who ignore the guidelines and suggestions in a tenuous position. Should an act of violence occur in their workplace, they could be susceptible to claims of negligent training. The argument can be made that workplace violence prevention training programs are readily available and have already been implemented by many public and private sector employers. By failing to initiate such a program and then experiencing an act of workplace violence, the allegation could be made that the training program could have prevented the workplace violence act from occurring.

Business leaders can prepare themselves for this responsibility by establishing policies that define actionable behavior in the workplace and the procedures and sanctions to be used in dealing with these behaviors. Company policies should include effective pre-employment screening, threat reporting and response procedures, stress management assistance, improved employee communication, risk tracking and assessment, referral for psychological counseling, comprehensive planning and preparation for downsizing, crisis prevention and intervention, and management awareness and intervention procedures.

EFFECTIVENESS OF PROGRAMS

While there are some differences in the quality of various workplace violence programs, there is some evidence to suggest they are working. The Bureau of Labor Statistics reports that since 1994, workplace homicides have decreased annually, except for the year 2000, which showed a minor increase from the previous year (Bureau of Labor Statistics, 2001). The most recent data available indicates over a 30% decline in workplace homicides over the past 10 years. In addition, from 1990 to 1994 the U.S. Postal Service experienced a number of multiple homicide incidences. Toward the end of 1994, the U.S. Postal Service developed and began implementing a national workplace violence prevention program. Since 1995, there have been only a few homicides involving postal workers.

SCHOOL VIOLENCE

For the past several years, there has been considerable concern in the United States regarding school violence (Kaufman et al., 2000). This concern developed as a result of several incidents of school violence, the most notorious of which occurred at Columbine High School in the Denver, Colorado area. The Columbine High School tragedy was the work of two disgruntled seniors at the school. Dylan Klebold and Eric Harris, who were determined to kill as many teachers and fellow students as possible, first planted and detonated two 20-pound propane bombs in the school cafeteria and then shot survivors fleeing the inferno they hoped to create. Klebold and Harris killed 10 students and wounded a number of other persons, one of them seriously.

The U.S. Department of Education and Department of Justice annually publish Indicators of School Crime and Safety, which details episodes of school violence, including school-related deaths (homicides and suicides), rape, fighting, battery, injuries, robbery, and theft (U.S. Department of Education [DOE] and U.S. Department of Justice [DOJ], 1999). In the 1998-1999 school year (July 1, 1998 through June 30, 1999), there were 47 school-related violent deaths. Homicides accounted for 38 of the deaths, while six deaths were due to suicide, two people died from law-enforcement gunfire, and one death was unintentional (Kaufman et al., 2001). Two additional adults were killed by law enforcement in the line of duty (Small & Tetrick, 2001).

Since 1994, the number of school-related student homicides has varied between 30 and 38 (U.S. Department of Education & Justice, 2000). Of the 38 homicides in the 1998-1999 school year, 34 were student deaths (Small & Tetrick, 2001). The number of incidents where either a child or an adult were killed or committed suicide while at school has varied between 34 and 49 over the last five years (Small & Tetrick, 2001).

PREVENTION PROGRAMS IN USE

Many school safety and violence prevention programs and guidelines agree that any good plan will be comprehensive and multifaceted. A comprehensive safety plan will involve numerous components, such as security measures, new disciplinary policies, strategies for responding to violent situations, crisis response guidelines, a school-wide action plan, and training in the area of warning signs and risk factors of violence. Additionally, students, parents, teachers, administrators, the community, and many others will be called on to participate in various aspects of the program.

NEEDED RESEARCH

Workplace and school violence prevention programs have been developed and implemented at a number of companies, organizations, and schools. There are some indications that these programs have been effective. However, research into workplace and school violence is a relatively recent undertaking. There have been some promising studies that have gathered data on the incidence of workplace and school violence, particularly involving perpetrators and victims, factors associated with violence, and what individuals, organizations, employers, employees, schools, and communities can be doing in response to this problem. However, there is still more that needs to be done (Kellam, Prinz, & Sheley, 2001).

One important area of research involves outcome studies involving the extent to which these programs are able to prevent or diminish the incidence of homicide, as well as the non-fatal forms of violence, such as harassments, threats, and physical attacks. Since many programs are still relatively new, there needs to be evaluation research conducted to assess not only the effectiveness of the programs, but which programs work better than others and which programs would benefit from revisions in order to make them more effective.

Investigation into the differences between violent and non-violent employees and students needs to continue, specifically in terms of creating more distinct and effective violence perpetrator profiles. This research might include ongoing efforts to more effectively isolate precipitating factors of perpetrators, as well as strategies to avoid mislabeling or stereotyping particular people should they show some of the warning signs. It is also important to assess a person's potential for violence, particularly once they have made a threat. The areas of threat assessment and risk potential are critical to any violence prevention program. Research related to the ability of standardized tests and procedures hopefully will yield improved methods for determining who is likely to engage in a serious act of violence. Research is also needed in order to investigate mediating factors of violence, such as drug and alcohol use and student peer pressure.

Another area of research involves the most effective ways to create and implement a system-wide safety and violence prevention program. There are various sets of guidelines available for such programs, yet implementation of them is still a relatively recent event. Research is needed in developing the most effective ways for the workplace and schools that have not done so already to begin implementing comprehensive safety programs and policies.

The research articles contained in this journal are an important part of the attempt to understand workplace and school violence and prevent and diminish their occurrence. Hopefully as the years go by, the research that is conducted will help make school and workplace violence less and less of a problem in the United States.

REFERENCES

Bureau of Labor Statistics, U.S. Department of Labor. (2001). *National census of fatal occupational injuries.* Washington, DC: Government Printing Office.

California Division of Occupational Safety and Health (Cal-OSHA). (1994). *Guidelines for workplace security.* Sacramento, CA: California State Department of Industrial Relations.

Dwyer, K., Osher, D., & Warger, C. (1998). *Early warning, timely response: A guide to safe schools.* Washington, DC: U.S. Department of Education.

Erickson, W. H. (2001). *The report of Governor Bill Owens' Columbine Review Commission.* Denver, CO: State of Colorado.

Kaufman, P., Chen, X., Choy, S. P., Ruddy, S. A., Miller, A. K., Fleury, J. K. et al. (2000). *Indicators of school crime and safety, 2000* (NCES 2001-017/NCJ-184176). Washington, DC: U.S. Departments of Education and Justice.

Kaufman, P., Chen, X., Choy, S. P., Peter, K., Ruddy, S. A., Miller, A. K. et al. (2001). *Indicators of school crime and safety, 2001* (NCES 2002-113/NCJ-190075). Washington, DC: U.S. Departments of Education and Justice.

Kellam, S. G., Prinz, R., & Sheley, J. F. (2000). *Preventing school violence: Plenary papers of the 1999 conference on criminal justice research evaluation: Enhancing policy and practice through research, Volume 2* (NCJ Publication No. 180972). Washington, DC: U.S. Department of Justice.

Small, M., & Tetrick, K. D. (2001). School violence: An overview. *Juvenile Justice, 8,* 3-12.

U.S. Departments of Education and Justice. (2000). *2000 annual report on school safety.* Washington, DC: Government Printing Office.

U.S. Department of Health and Human Services. (1994, August 19). Occupational injury deaths of postal workers–United States, 1980-89. *Morbidity and Mortality Weekly Report, 43,* 587-595.

U.S. Department of Labor, Bureau of Statistics. (1995, April). Compensation and working conditions. *Violence in the Workplace, 47*(4), 1-8.

AGGRESSION, ABUSE, AND HARASSMENT IN THE WORKPLACE

A 10-Year Clinical Case Study to an Incident of Workplace Violence

Angelea Panos
Patrick Panos
Patty Dulle

SUMMARY. This study evaluated the effects of an incident of workplace violence on a group of employees over a 10-year period of time. Quantitative and qualitative methods were used to document the long-term effects of the trauma and the effectiveness of interventions provided. Results indicated that some employees suffered from long-term symptoms of Posttraumatic Stress Disorder. Many interventions were rated as helpful by employees; however, a small but significant subgroup of employees found debriefings and initial family support groups to be unhelpful. Other prolonged effects of the trauma included all pregnant employees suffering miscarriages, long-term loss of interest in sex-

Address correspondence to: Angelea Panos, PhD, Intermountain Health Care, 9649 South 700 East, Sandy, UT 84070 (E-mail: DrAngiePanos@yahoo.com).

[Haworth co-indexing entry note]: "A 10-Year Clinical Case Study to an Incident of Workplace Violence." Panos, Angelea, Patrick Panos, and Patty Dulle. Co-published simultaneously in *Journal of Emotional Abuse* (The Haworth Maltreatment & Trauma Press, an imprint of The Haworth Press, Inc.) Vol. 4, No. 3/4, 2004, pp. 23-47; and: *Aggression in Organizations: Violence, Abuse, and Harassment at Work and in Schools* (ed: Robert Geffner et al.) The Haworth Maltreatment & Trauma Press, an imprint of The Haworth Press, Inc., 2004, pp. 23-47. Single or multiple copies of this article are available for a fee from The Haworth Document Delivery Service [1-800-HAWORTH, 9:00 a.m. - 5:00 p.m. (EST). E-mail address: docdelivery@haworthpress.com].

ual intimacy, and long-term triggers or reactions to reminders of the trauma. *[Article copies available for a fee from The Haworth Document Delivery Service: 1-800-HAWORTH. E-mail address: <docdelivery@haworthpress.com> Website: <http://www.HaworthPress.com> © 2004 by The Haworth Press, Inc. All rights reserved.]*

KEYWORDS. Posttraumatic Stress Disorder, workplace violence, longitudinal research, treatment outcome

Workplace violence is increasingly becoming recognized as a significant danger faced by both employers and employees (Mossman, 1995). For instance, a relatively recent national survey conducted by Northwestern National Life Insurance Company (1993) found that during a one-year period, more than 2.2 million workers were physically assaulted while on duty and over 6 million were threatened with violence. In a second study, the National Institute for Occupational Safety and Health (1996) found that on average, 20 employees are murdered each week while working and approximately 18,000 individuals are assaulted on the job each week. Currently, homicide is the first leading cause of death for women and the second leading cause of death for men in the American workplace, exceeded only by traffic accidents (Jenkins, 1996; NIOSH, 1997).

As interest in this occupational and mental health topic has grown, numerous authors have noted the paucity of research that examines the consequences of workplace violence (Barling, 1996; Budd, Arvey, & Lawless, 1996; LeBlanc & Kelloway, 2002; Schat & Kelloway, 2000). It is known, however, that experiencing the abuse of workplace violence can have significant, immediate emotional effects on employees and their families. For instance, Flannery (2001) noted that victimized employees often exhibit anxiety, depression, increases in substance abuse, and have a higher likelihood of committing a subsequent violent act themselves. Depression, anxiety, and low job satisfaction were also found by Driscoll, Worthington, and Hurrell (1995). Budd et al. (1996) found that employees who are victims of violence also experience lower job satisfaction, greater job stress, increased considerations of job change, and an increased likelihood of bringing a weapon to work. Other sets of researchers (Barling, Rogers, & Kelloway, 2000; Rogers & Kelloway, 1997) also found that exposure to workplace violence led to an increased rate of "fear of future violence," which in turn led to negative psychological and somatic symptoms, as well as increase in intent to leave the organization. All of these studies only investigated the relative immediate consequences of workplace violence on the employee, and none examined the long-term consequences of workplace violence. Little or no longitudinal research data has been collected that would evaluate the long-term emotional effect of workplace violence.

The purpose of this study was to evaluate the emotional effects of an incident of workplace violence and abuse on a group of employees over a 10-year period. Quantitative and qualitative methods were used to understand the effects of the trauma, the effectiveness of the healing interventions offered, and the longitudinal outcomes.

BACKGROUND

The incident of workplace violence that this study focuses on was a homicide and hostage situation that took place in a 75-bed suburban Utah hospital. The event occurred September 20, 1991, around 11:40 p.m. The gunman, R.W., armed with a hand gun, a shot gun, and bombs, entered this small maternity hospital by breaking in a second story window and came into a patient's room. An emergency room employee was walking to her car and came face to face with R.W. as he was trying to break into the window. He pointed his gun at her, but for some reason he turned away. She walked back into the hospital and called 911. Meanwhile, the gunman became tangled for a moment in the window blinds in the patient's room and began shouting obscenities. This awoke the patient, and even though she was heavily sedated and paralyzed from the waist down, she was able to crawl out of her room. With the aid of a nurse, the patient escaped through a fire exit.

The gunman, R.W., was searching for a doctor (Dr. C.) that had, with written consent, performed a tubal ligation on R.W.'s wife two years prior. Even though he had at the time signed the consent, he had never come to terms with this limitation on his fatherhood. He contested the bill for the tubal ligation, and the hospital agreed to forgive the charges in exchange for his release to the hospital and doctor for liability. Even though he agreed and accepted the financial settlement, he still could not accept the situation. Thus, the perpetrator was determined to kill the doctor in revenge for his wife's sterilization. Yelling and brandishing a shotgun plus a .357 revolver, he cornered Nurse A. and demanded to see Dr. C. Another employee, Nurse B., tried to protect Nurse A., and the gunman marched them both down the hallway at gunpoint. A security guard confronted the trio, and R.W. aimed a gun at his head and ordered him to leave or he would kill them all. The security guard surrendered and backed away.

R.W. forced the nurses to each take a newborn baby from the nursery and push them toward delivery room 2310. The gunman again demanded that Dr. C. be summoned. He threatened to kill the babies and fired the first gunshots randomly into walls and furniture. R.W. kicked in the door to room 2310 where a woman was in labor. He forced the two nurses down the hall and down the stairs leading outside. Around 11:45 p.m., the police reached the hospital's parking lot. R.W. forced the nurses at gunpoint outside through the main entrance and then propped the doors open so he could reenter. As he continued shouting obscenities, he also made threats to the police that he would kill the nurses. Nurse A. attempted to grab the gun that he held in her side. When she failed to pull it from his grasp, she began to run away. After she took only two or three steps, R.W. cocked his gun and shot her in the back. She died at the scene minutes later. Using Nurse B. as a shield, R.W. proceeded to his car in the parking lot to get some explosives. He then took Nurse B. back into the hospital, went back to room 2310 with the explosives, and ordered its occupants, the laboring mother's sister, another employee, Nurse C., the expectant father, and the patient-in-labor to get down on the floor.

R.W. held his gun to the laboring patient's stomach and told her spouse to go outside and get the bombs (that were hidden in the bushes outside the hospital door) and return within two minutes or else he would kill the mother and unborn child. The expectant father had to fight the police to return into the building with the bombs and save his wife and expectant child. The gunman, having already murdered one nurse, was now holding a group of seven people hostage, which included two nurses, a female patient (in labor), her male partner and her sister, and two new-born babies that had been taken from the nursery. At 12:34 p.m., the gunman ordered the hostage group up the stairs to the offices on the top floor of the building. Because the laboring mother had been administered an epidural block, she was paralyzed from the waist down by the anesthesia. Thus, she had to be dragged on a sheet. This left the nurses without equipment, food, and medicine to care for the mother-in-labor and the hostage newborn babies.

Meanwhile, in other parts of the hospital, approximately 70 employees were trying to protect patients ($n = 27$) and visitors while waiting for the police to allow them to evacuate. The emergency room was the first to be evacuated, but the rest of the hospital proved to be more difficult. It would be three and a half to four hours later before the rest of the employees and patients would get out. During this time many of them were alone, not sure where others were, and hiding in rooms with the doors locked. Numerous shots were being fired, and there was yelling and confusion. Staff and patients quickly became aware that there was an angry gunman somewhere in the hospital and that a nurse had been killed. Word was also given that the gunman had bombs and had planted them in the hospital.

During the wait, the power was cut from much of the building and telephone communication was limited. The dark, chaotic atmosphere that this created was reported by the employees to be terror-inducing. Family members of the hostage patients, newborn babies, and employees heard through media reports that their loved ones were being held hostage and that bombs had been planted throughout the hospital.

The police had no idea exactly where the gunman was, how many hostages he had taken, or how many people he had killed. R.W. continued to tell hostages that he was going to kill everyone. The hostages asked if there was anything that they could do to get out alive. He told them, "No, definitely no!" The hostages became aware that his goal was not only to kill Dr. C., but probably to die himself.

The doctors' offices where they had moved to were well decorated with crystal figurines, mirrors, fine furniture, and artwork. R.W. destroyed everything, including patients' charts, computer screens, and even the carpet. Rounds of ammunition were shot through windows and computer screens. He then told the hostages that they had to decide who would be killed first.

About three- and one-half hours after the siege had begun, the hospital was finally evacuated except for the seven remaining hostages (the two nurses, two babies, one visitor, one expectant father, and one patient in labor). Around 3:23 a.m., the mother gave birth on the floor with assistance from the nurses. The eight hostages would be held for a total of 18 hours without food or bottles for the babies. Nurse C. was able to create a rapport with the gunman and influenced him to consider surrender. Finally, at 5:33 p.m. the following day, the negotiations with R.W. showed results and he surrendered.

As a result of this event, the employees of the hospital experienced different amounts of trauma and victimization. Some employees were actually held at gunpoint, threatened with death, and watched as their colleague was shot and killed. Other employees never saw the gunman, but heard him and were in constant fear of a possible confrontation as they evacuated patients. They also were never certain whether the bombs that were planted throughout the building would be set off. Finally, other employees had to cope with the violation of their place of employment, death of a co-worker, and the gruesome task of cleaning up the blood and damage at the scene.

METHOD

Immediately after the incident, the hospital administration attempted to respond to the needs of the employees who had been victimized by this incident of violence. Unfortunately, it quickly became apparent to the administration that they lacked critical information. For instance, there was no accurate information regarding how many employees were at the hospital at the time of siege, how many subsequently escaped, how many were stopped at the barriers, or how many stayed at home as a result of the news reports. After this initial information was gathered, the hospital administration agreed to conduct both quantitative and qualitative studies in order to gain better information about how many people were affected and how they had adjusted since the event for the purpose of providing more effective interventions and support. The design of this project was reviewed and approved by appropriate Institutional Review Boards (IRBs), and all participants signed informed consent forms to allow the publication of findings. Due to the fact that all participants were healthcare workers in a teaching and research facility, there was a high level of interest, cooperation, and consent. Only one person declined to give consent, and his/her information was not included in this study.

Quantitative assessments consisting of a demographic survey, as well as two clinical instruments (the Impact of Events Scale [IES] and the Symptom Checklist 90-Revised [SCL-90-R]) were given to affected employees 6 months and 5 years after the violent event. Qualitative assessments consisting of formal clinical interviews and focus group discussions were given to affected employees 6 months, 1 year, 2 years, 5 years, 7 years, and 10 years after the incident. During this time period, treatment and support was made available to employees and their families. This support included debriefings, individual counseling, initial support groups, a hospital reopening ceremony, follow-up education sessions, ongoing peer support groups, a chapel dedication, and a memorial service (offered on Memorial Day, 8 months after the event), a one-year anniversary support newsletter, as well as individual and group counseling, initial family debriefing, and initial family support groups. Employees were also encouraged to seek their own types of supportive interventions, which included journal writing, rituals, fitness classes, counseling, and therapeutic recreation, such as their own artistic or creative endeavors. For example, one victim found a type of needlework "cross-stitching" to be relaxing. She found healing phrases and then expressed them in her stitchery (Clark, 1996).

Participants

In an effort to determine the extent of trauma that was experienced by their employees, the hospital management supported the development and administration of both a general survey and a clinical survey and questionnaire, which were distributed with employee pay checks and included with a cover letter from the hospital administrator. As a result of an initial survey, it was determined that at the time of the hostage taking on September 20, 1991, of the 468 employees of the 70-bed community hospital, approximately 184 reported directly being exposed to the violent incident (e.g., taken hostage, involved in the hospital evacuation and patient care during the siege, or cleaning up of their co-workers' blood in the aftermath). All of the 184 employees were subsequently contacted and asked to participate in this study. Six months after the violent incident, a total of 166 employees completed the quantitative clinical questionnaire, resulting in a response rate of 90.2% (see Table 1). One hundred and forty-six (88.0%) of the respondents were female, and 20 (12.0%) were male. All were over 18 years of age and represented a wide range of socioeconomic classes and professions (e.g., housekeepers, nurses aides, nurses, and doctors). In addition to the clinical assessment, participants were also given a survey questionnaire, which sought both demographic and exposure information. Major results of this assessment were originally reported as part of an unpublished doctoral dissertation (Panos, 1994).

The same clinical assessment was again sent to the last known address of all 184 original participants 5 years after the violent incident occurred. It should be noted that the hospital is situated in a small community with a relatively stable workforce. Only 7% (13/184) of the participants had left the company's employment during this five-year period, which was statistically equivalent to the 8% turnover normally experienced by this hospital. Seventy-one of the employees or former employees responded; however, data from seven participants was excluded due to incomplete responses, resulting in 64 assessments for a final response rate of 34.8% (64/184) (see Table 1). Sixty of the respondents were female (93.7%) and four (6.3%) were male. Results of this assessment were originally reported as part of an unpublished Master's degree project (Dulle, 1996). In regard to the qualitative evaluation, it was found that the participants typically were the

TABLE 1. Number of Employees Assessed at Each Time Period

Time Period	Quantitative Assessment	Qualitative Assessment
6-months	166	172
1-year		141
2-years		99
5-years	64	68
7-years		65
10-years		61

same people that responded to the quantitative survey, with slightly more people being willing to respond to the qualitative assessments (see Table 1).

As mentioned previously, in addition to the clinical assessment instruments, demographic survey questions were included, which allowed participants to be classified into four categories:

1. High Physical Involvement/High Danger Group–This group included those who were taken hostage, those who saw and heard the gunman but hid, and those who were confined to other parts of the building and were unsure if they would meet the gunman. At six months, 21 (12.7% or 21/166) of the respondents were classified as having high involvement, while at 5 years only four respondents (6.3% or 4/64) were part of this group.
2. Medium Physical Involvement/Medium Danger Group–This group suffered from a moderate amount of danger from sniper fire or the possible explosion of bombs within the facility, although they were not in direct contact with the perpetrator. At six months, 37 (22.3% or 37/166) of the participants were members of this group, and at 5 years, 16 (25.0% or 16/64) were classified into this category.
3. Low Physical Involvement/Low Danger Group–Although this group was not in the hospital at the time of the siege, respondents in this group reported having the perception that their workplace space had been violated and identified with their colleagues and friends who had suffered directly from the attack. At six months, 103 (62.0% or 103/166) of the participants comprised this group, while at 5 years, 47 (73.4% or 47/64) of the respondents comprised this group.
4. No Response Group–Six months after the attack, five employees (3.0% or 5/166) declined to identify their level of involvement, while at 5 years, all participants willingly disclosed their level of involvement.

Clinical Assessment Instruments

In 1991, two assessment instruments, the Impact of Events Scale (IES) and the Symptom Checklist 90-Revised (SCL-90-R), were identified as being appropriate for this study for several reasons. First, they have shown a high degree of validity in assessing PTSD (Green, 1991; Kulka et al., 1991; Resnick, Kilpatrick, & Lipovsky, 1991). Second, they have been validated on populations other than Vietnam vets (Kilpatrick, Amick-McMullan, Lipovsky, & Resnick, 1988; Kilpatrick, Saunders, Amick-McMullan, Best, Veronen, & Resnick, 1989; Saunders, Mandoki, & Kilpatrick, 1990), which were the focus of most PTSD assessments at the time. Third, they were consistently cited in a large number of studies and appear to be highly accepted by PTSD researchers. The psychometric properties of the two assessment instruments used in this study are described below.

Impact of Events Scale (IES). The IES (Horowitz,Wilner, & Alvarez, 1979) is a 15-item self-report questionnaire that measures current subjective distress about a specific traumatic life event. This assessment examines two general categories of responses to stressful events: (1) "Intrusion," in which the person experiences intrusive and involuntary ideas, images, feelings, or bad dreams about the event, and (2) "Avoidance," in which the person consciously avoids certain ideas, feelings, or situations related to the event. These categories were designed to parallel the symptom categories that originally defined PTSD in the DSM-III-R (Horowitz, 1973; Horowitz, 1974). This assessment was originally shown to have a high general split-half reliability ($r = 0.86$) and high test-retest reliability (general scale = 0.87, intrusion subscale = 0.89, avoidance subscale = 0.79). Internal consistencies of the subscales were also high (intrusion = 0.78, avoidance = 0.82; Horowitz et al., 1979). Comparable results were found in subsequent cross-validation studies (Zilberg, Weiss, & Horowitz, 1982).

Symptom Checklist 90-R (SCL-90-R). The SCL-90-R (Derogatis, 1977) is a 90-item self-report symptom inventory in which subjects rate themselves on the degree they feel discomfort with different symptoms (e.g., "Headaches," "Feeling fearful"). The rating uses a 5-point scale ranging from 0 ("Not at all") to 4 ("Extremely"), which is used to calculate both global and individual scale (dimension) scores. For the nine different primary symptom dimensions of the SCL-90-R, Derogatis (1977) reported high degrees of test-retest reliability ranging from 0.78 to 0.90. Additionally, internal consistencies of the dimensions were also high, ranging from an 0.77 to 0.90. Comparable results were found in subsequent cross validation studies (Derogatis, Rickels, & Rock, 1976). Subsequent to the original development of the SCL-90-R, Saunders et al. (1990) developed a Crime-Related PTSD (CR-PTSD) scale by selecting 28 items that were initially judged to be PTSD related. Using analysis of variance, Saunders et al. (1990) demonstrated that the CR-PTSD scale was able to correctly classify 89.3% of patients who had been independently diagnosed as having PTSD. In a follow-up study, Green et al. (1990) reported the CR-PTSD showed an appropriate degree of specificity in diagnosing PTSD. According to Green (1991), the CR-PTSD scale does "indeed predict who has and does not have PTSD" (p. 541).

RESULTS

Diagnostic Findings

The number of employees who developed PTSD were identified through clinical interviews as part of the formal qualitative assessment process. Additionally, the number of employees who reported having symptoms of PTSD but who did not meet the criteria for the full diagnosis were also identified. The reliability of the clinical diagnostic interviews was verified by comparing the findings to the quantitative clinical results obtained using the IES and SCL-90-R. It was found that 23% of respondents suffered from PTSD six months after the event, with this number decreasing to 3% ten years after the incident (see Table 2 and Figure 1). The number of participants who experienced symptoms of PTSD ranged from 67% six months after the attack to 13% ten years after the attack. In both cases, the declines were gradual with a relatively constant slope, with a drop in those suffering from PTSD occurring more rapidly. At both the 6-month mark and the 5-year mark, there were no statistically significant differences in the rates of PTSD diagnoses and symptoms between the different Levels of Physical Involvement/Danger groups. In other words, relatively the same percentage of employees developed PTSD or some of its symptoms, regardless of their level of exposure to the actual violent incident.

Ratings of Interventions

It is known from the above-mentioned data that the mental health consequences to the event did improve in employees over time. Employees were asked to rate the extent to which they found the different interventions to be helpful in their recovery. These ratings were collected using both focus groups

TABLE 2. Clinical Reaction to the Event

Time Period	Quantitative Assessment Instruments		Diagnostic Interview	
	PTSD Diagnosis	PTSD Symptoms	PTSD Diagnosis	PTSD Symptoms
6-months	15.7% (26/166)	44.0% (73/166)	23.3% (40/172)	67.4% (116/172)
1-year			21.3% (30/141)	65.2% (92/141)
2-years			18.1% (18/99)	58.6% (58/99)
5-years	10.9% (7/64)	37.5% (24/64)	13.2% (9/68)	32.4% (22/68)
7-years			4.6% (3/65)	18.5% (12/65)
10-years			3.2% (1/61)	13.1% (8/61)

FIGURE 1. Clinical Reaction to the Event

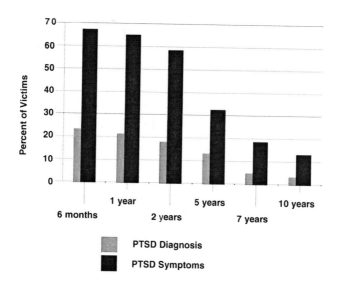

■ PTSD Diagnosis
■ PTSD Symptoms

and semi-structured clinical interviews. Ratings for the different rating periods are shown individually in Table 3 and as a 10-year average in Table 4. The ratings remained amazingly consistent over time. In other words, once developed, employees' perceptions regarding the helpfulness of an intervention did not change with time or in retrospection, and they appeared to know immediately whether an intervention was effective in dealing with their reactions. This finding is interesting to note because relative to additional interventions offered over time, the perceptions did not change regarding the earlier interventions. So not only does it mean that the opinion was consistently held, but it also means in comparison to interventions offered later and healing factors that they may have initiated individually, it did not change their perceptions. All of the interventions were seen as helpful by the majority of participants; however, significant minorities of individuals found the debriefings and the initial support group as being mildly or extremely unhelpful. Additionally, there were no significant differences in perceptions regarding the helpfulness of specific interventions and the level of physical involvement/danger experienced by the employee.

TABLE 3. Ratings of Interventions

Type of Intervention	6-Month Rating				
	Extremely Unhelpful	Mildly Unhelpful	Neutral	Somewhat Helpful	Extremely Helpful
Debriefing	8.8% (15/172)	5.2% (9/172)	1.2% (2/172)	27.9% (48/172)	57.0% (98/172)
Initial Support Group	0% (0/172)	0% (0/172)	6.3% (11/172)	39.0% (67/172)	54.7% (94/172)
Hospital Reopening Ceremony	0% (0/172)	0% (0/172)	0% (0/172)	30.8% (53/172)	69.2% (119/172)
2-Month Follow-up Educational Session	0% (0/172)	0% (0/172)	0% (0/172)	33.1% (57/172)	66.9% (115/172)
Peer Support Group	0% (0/172)	0% (0/172)	0% (0/172)	19.8% (34/172)	80.2% (138/172)
Memorial Service (8-Month)	0% (0/172)	0% (0/172)	0% (0/172)	22.7% (39/172)	77.3% (133/172)
One-Year Anniversary Support	0% (0/172)	0% (0/172)	0% (0/172)	45.9% (79/172)	54.1% (93/172)
One-on-One Counseling	0% (0/172)	0% (0/172)	0% (0/172)	47.1% (81/172)	52.9% (91/172)
Initial Family Debriefing	4.7% (8/172)	4.7% (8/172)	7.6% (13/172)	52.9% (91/172)	30.2% (52/172)
Initial Family Support Group	0% (0/172)	0% (0/172)	0% (0/172)	48.3% (83/172)	51.7% (89/172)

Type of Intervention	1-Year Rating				
	Extremely Unhelpful	Mildly Unhelpful	Neutral	Somewhat Helpful	Extremely Helpful
Debriefing	9.9% (14/141)	5.0% (7/141)	2.1% (3/141)	28.4% (40/141)	54.6% (77/141)
Initial Support Group	0% (0/141)	0% (0/141)	6.4% (9/141)	41.1% (58/141)	52.5% (74/141)
Hospital Reopening Ceremony	0% (0/141)	0% (0/141)	0% (0/141)	26.2% (37/141)	73.8% (104/141)
2-Month Follow-up Educational Session	0% (0/141)	0% (0/141)	0% (0/141)	33.3% (47/141)	66.7% (94/141)
Peer Support Group	0% (0/141)	0% (0/141)	0% (0/141)	17.7% (25/141)	82.3% (116/141)
Memorial Service (8-Month)	0% (0/141)	0% (0/141)	0% (0/141)	20.6% (29/141)	79.4% (112/141)
One-Year Anniversary Support	0% (0/141)	0% (0/141)	0% (0/141)	46.8% (66/141)	53.2% (75/141)
One-on-One Counseling	0% (0/141)	0% (0/141)	0% (0/141)	44.0% (62/141)	56.0% (79/141)
Initial Family Debriefing	5.0% (7/141)	5.0% (7/141)	7.1% (10/141)	53.9% (76/141)	29.1% (41/141)
Initial Family Support Group	0% (0/141)	0% (0/141)	0% (0/141)	48.2% (68/141)	51.8% (73/141)

TABLE 3 (continued)

Type of Intervention	2-Years Rating				
	Extremely Unhelpful	Mildly Unhelpful	Neutral	Somewhat Helpful	Extremely Helpful
Debriefing	10.1% (10/99)	5.0% (5/99)	2.0% (2/99)	27.3% (27/99)	55.6% (55/99)
Initial Support Group	0% (0/99)	0% (0/99)	6.1% (6/99)	39.4% (39/99)	54.5% (54/99)
Hospital Reopening Ceremony	0% (0/99)	0% (0/99)	0% (0/99)	34.3% (34/99)	65.7% (65/99)
2-Month Follow-up Educational Session	0% (0/99)	0% (0/99)	0% (0/99)	34.3% (34/99)	65.7% (65/99)
Peer Support Group	0% (0/99)	0% (0/99)	0% (0/99)	21.2% (21/99)	78.8% (78/99)
Memorial Service (8-Month)	0% (0/99)	0% (0/99)	0% (0/99)	26.3% (26/99)	73.7% (73/99)
One-Year Anniversary Support	0% (0/99)	0% (0/99)	0% (0/99)	50.5% (50/99)	49.5% (49/99)
One-on-One Counseling	0% (0/99)	0% (0/99)	0% (0/99)	47.5% (47/99)	52.5% (52/99)
Initial Family Debriefing	5.0% (5/99)	5.0% (5/99)	7.1% (7/99)	49.5% (49/99)	33.3% (33/99)
Initial Family Support Group	0% (0/99)	0% (0/99)	0% (0/99)	47.5% (47/99)	52.5% (52/99)

Type of Intervention	5-Years Rating				
	Extremely Unhelpful	Mildly Unhelpful	Neutral	Somewhat Helpful	Extremely Helpful
Debriefing	8.8% (6/68)	5.9% (4/68)	1.5% (1/68)	27.9% (19/68)	55.9% (38/68)
Initial Support Group	0% (0/68)	0% (0/68)	7.4% (5/68)	40.0% (26/68)	54.4% (37/68)
Hospital Reopening Ceremony	0% (0/68)	0% (0/68)	0% (0/68)	29.4% (20/68)	70.6% (48/68)
2-Month Follow-up Educational Session	0% (0/68)	0% (0/68)	0% (0/68)	33.8% (23/68)	66.2% (45/68)
Peer Support Group	0% (0/68)	0% (0/68)	0% (0/68)	19.1% (13/68)	80.9% (55/68)
Memorial Service (8-Month)	0% (0/68)	0% (0/68)	0% (0/68)	22.1% (15/68)	77.9% (53/68)
One-Year Anniversary Support	0% (0/68)	0% (0/68)	0% (0/68)	48.5% (33/68)	51.5% (35/68)
One-on-One Counseling	0% (0/68)	0% (0/68)	0% (0/68)	45.7% (31/68)	54.3% (37/68)
Initial Family Debriefing	4.4% (3/68)	4.4% (3/68)	7.4% (5/68)	52.9% (36/68)	30.9% (21/68)
Initial Family Support Group	0% (0/68)	0% (0/68)	0% (0/68)	51.5% (35/68)	48.5% (33/68)

TABLE 3 (continued)

Type of Intervention	7-Years Rating				
	Extremely Unhelpful	Mildly Unhelpful	Neutral	Somewhat Helpful	Extremely Helpful
Debriefing	9.2% (6/65)	4.6% (3/65)	1.5% (1/65)	27.7% (18/65)	56.9% (37/65)
Initial Support Group	0% (0/65)	0% (0/65)	7.7% (5/65)	40.0% (26/65)	52.3% (34/65)
Hospital Reopening Ceremony	0% (0/65)	0% (0/65)	0% (0/65)	30.8% (20/65)	69.2% (45/65)
2-Month Follow-up Educational Session	0% (0/65)	0% (0/65)	0% (0/65)	33.8% (22/65)	66.2% (43/65)
Peer Support Group	0% (0/65)	0% (0/65)	0% (0/65)	20.0% (13/65)	80.0% (52/65)
Memorial Service (8-Month)	0% (0/65)	0% (0/65)	0% (0/65)	23.1% (15/65)	76.9% (50/65)
One-Year Anniversary Support	0% (0/65)	0% (0/65)	0% (0/65)	47.7% (31/65)	52.3% (34/65)
One-on-One Counseling	0% (0/65)	0% (0/65)	0% (0/65)	46.2% (30/65)	53.8% (35/65)
Initial Family Debriefing	4.6% (3/65)	4.6% (3/65)	7.7% (5/65)	53.8% (35/65)	29.2% (19/65)
Initial Family Support Group	0% (0/65)	0% (0/65)	0% (0/65)	47.7% (31/65)	52.3% (34/65)

Type of Intervention	10-Years Rating				
	Extremely Unhelpful	Mildly Unhelpful	Neutral	Somewhat Helpful	Extremely Helpful
Debriefing	6.6% (4/61)	3.3% (2/61)	1.6% (1/61)	29.5% (18/61)	59.0% (36/61)
Initial Support Group	0% (0/61)	0% (0/61)	6.6% (4/61)	39.3% (24/61)	54.1% (33/61)
Hospital Reopening Ceremony	0% (0/61)	0% (0/61)	0% (0/61)	29.5% (18/61)	70.8% (43/61)
2-Month Follow-up Educational Session	0% (0/61)	0% (0/61)	0% (0/61)	36.1% (22/61)	63.9% (39/61)
Peer Support Group	0% (0/61)	0% (0/61)	0% (0/61)	16.4% (10/61)	83.6% (51/61)
Memorial Service (8-Month)	0% (0/61)	0% (0/61)	0% (0/61)	21.3% (13/61)	78.7% (48/61)
One-Year Anniversary Support	0% (0/61)	0% (0/61)	0% (0/61)	47.5% (29/61)	52.5% (32/61)
One-on-One Counseling	0% (0/61)	0% (0/61)	0% (0/61)	45.9% (28/61)	54.1% (33/61)
Initial Family Debriefing	4.9% (3/61)	4.9% (3/61)	9.8% (6/61)	52.5% (32/61)	27.9% (17/61)
Initial Family Support Group	0% (0/61)	0% (0/61)	0% (0/61)	47.5% (29/61)	52.5% (32/61)

TABLE 4. Average Ratings of Interventions

Type of Intervention	Average Ratings				
	Extremely Unhelpful	Mildly Unhelpful	Neutral	Somewhat Helpful	Extremely Helpful
Debriefing	9.1%	4.9%	1.7%	28.1%	56.3%
Initial Support Group	0%	0%	6.7%	39.6%	53.8%
Hospital Reopening Ceremony	0%	0%	0%	30.0%	70.0%
2-Month Follow-up Educational Session	0%	0%	0%	33.8%	66.2%
Peer Support Group	0%	0%	0%	19.1%	80.9%
Memorial Service (8-Month)	0%	0%	0%	22.6%	77.4%
One-Year Anniversary Support	0%	0%	0%	47.5%	52.5%
One-on-One Counseling	0%	0%	0%	46.0%	54.0%
Initial Family Debriefing	4.8%	4.8%	7.6%	52.6%	30.2%
Initial Family Support Group	0%	0%	0%	48.3%	51.7%

Qualitative Findings

In addition to the quantitative findings reported above, there were several important themes and issues that were identified during the focus groups and semi-structured clinical interviews, which were found to have clinical significance for the employees. Knowledge of these issues may prove beneficial to those providing support and treatment to victims of workplace violence and are therefore being reported.

Reproductive/sexual health. Five employees reported that they were pregnant at the time of the trauma, ranging in their pregnancies from 8 weeks to 26 weeks. In all five cases (100%), the women subsequently miscarried shortly after the event (compared to the normal 16% miscarriage rate in Utah; Alan Guttmacher Institute, 2002). This was despite the fact that, according to their own self-reports, their pregnancies previously appeared to be normal. In examining the research literature, however, there appears to be a paucity of information regarding the effects of experiencing violence or a traumatic event and its subsequent effect on pregnancy. Unfortunately, no conclusions can be drawn on the basis of this study due to the low number of employees who were pregnant ($n = 5$) at the time of the trauma. It is strongly recommended that this topic become a focus of future studies by researchers.

In addition to apparent effects on pregnancy, employees also reported experiencing significant disruptions in their ability to experience sexual intimacy with their partners.

In fact, the most common reported symptom on the SCL-90-R and in qualitative interviews was a decrease in their libido after the trauma. Specifically, 97.0% (161/166) of all participants reported a "loss of sexual interest or pleasure" during the 6-month assessment, and 23.4% (15/64) endorsed the same symptom during the 5-year assessment. In both cases, the loss of sexual interest or pleasure was the most frequently endorsed of all symptom items. During qualitative interviews, depression was continually a clinical issue, and this symptom appeared to have a strong association with this reaction. Once again, the effects on sexual intimacy do not appear to be mentioned in the research literature for non-sexual types of trauma and may prove to be an area of interest for future researchers.

Emotional triggers to reminders of the trauma. The participants reported a number of emotional triggers. One type of trigger reported was an "anniversary reaction," defined as an emotional response by an individual to the anniversary date (or time of year) associated with an original trauma (Gabriel, 1992; Musaph, 1990). Profound emotional triggers, some of which were related to anniversaries of the event, were experienced by significant numbers of the employees interviewed as part of this study. For instance, in late September, approximately one year after the violent event, on the same day of the week and on the same shift (graveyard), a noise was heard in a wastebasket at the hospital. Security was called, and they determined it could be a bomb. The entire hospital was evacuated and the bomb squad was brought in. The police bomb squad determined that a small battery-operated fan had been disposed of in the trash and had somehow been jolted on and was making the noise. It is unlikely that under different circumstances a noise from a wastebasket could have caused such alarm.

On another occasion in September, young boys throwing some rocks at a hospital window were mistaken for gunfire. Unfortunately, the media picked up police radio reports and reported a breaking news story that the hospital was once again under siege. Many patients were lying quietly in their beds when they heard the reports while they watched television. It took a couple of hours to inform all the patients, families, and employees that there was no significant event that occurred.

Finally, at the 9-year anniversary period, a young female employee who had only been working at the hospital for a few months but had heard stories of the siege was assisting a disgruntled husband of a patient with billing problems. She became alarmed when she heard him make reference to the perpetrator R.W. and comments that she felt were threatening. She called the police, and until the man was arrested and in custody, the hospital was partially closed down and evacuated. Again, it is unlikely that a similar circumstance would have warranted a similar response without the history or the emotional triggers to the trauma. The impact of the event on the history and culture of the workplace, and its relative ease in being transferred inadvertently to new staff members, is interesting to note. No information about the event is given during any formal training or orientation sessions for the hospital.

Posttraumatic Stress Disorder (PTSD). As reported previously, a small but significant number of employees met the criteria for PTSD 5- to 10-years after the event. These employees were subsequently interviewed to determine why they were still experiencing profound reactions to the event. In each case, the participants meeting criteria for PTSD after 5 years all had additional exposures to traumatic events in their personal lives which met the criteria defined by the DSM-IV (American Psychological Association, 1994) for being "outside the realm of usual human experience" (e.g., witnessing death of a toddler, witnessing suicide of co-worker, and gang violence). In each case, the effects of this additional trauma appeared to be the factor keeping the original trauma emotionally active. Research on the neurobiology of PTSD including both hormonal and autonomic nervous dimensions suggest processes such as "kindling" create a vulnerability to develop PTSD when subsequently exposed to additional trauma (van der Kolk, 1996; Adamec, 1997). However, results of overall PTSD reported in this study are lower than what is expected from general population epidemiological results. Specifically, The National Comorbidity Survey (NCS) found that the estimated lifetime prevalence of PTSD among adult Americans is 7.8% (Kessler, Sonnega, Bromet, Hughes, & Nelson, 1995). Therefore, there appears to be a dichotomous reaction in which exposure to trauma may build resiliency in some victims, while creating vulnerability in others. Future research looking at long-term effects on the exposure of traumatic stress needs to explore these findings further.

Effectiveness of interventions offered. The goal of this study was to evaluate the different types of support and interventions offered. As mentioned previously, all of the interventions were reported to be helpful by the majority of participants. This finding suggests that almost "any" intervention that demonstrates concern and support by the employer is appreciated and seen positively by employees. In other words, in judging the efficacy of interventions to deal with workplace violence, the possibility of a nonspecific ("placebo") effect in which the employee will perceive the intervention to be helpful should be considered. Additionally, PTSD symptoms are often reported to be resolved naturally, even with little or no intervention (Conlon, Fahy, & Conroy, 1999; Rauch, Hembree, & Foa, 2001). In light of this apparent natural inclination to see all interventions positively, it is surprising to find that approximately 15% of employees (see Table 4 and Figure 2) found the debriefings and initial family support groups, unlike other interven-

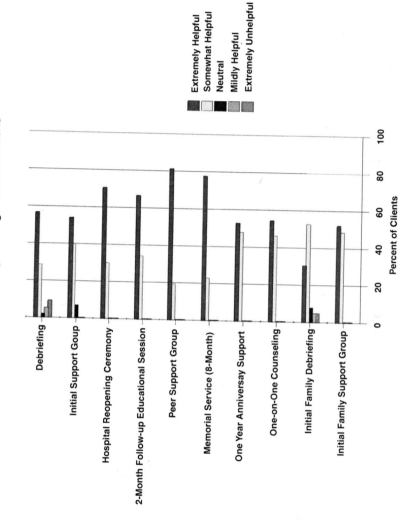

FIGURE 2. Average Ratings of Interventions

Type of Intervention

Percent of Clients

Extremely Helpful
Somewhat Helpful
Neutral
Mildly Helpful
Extremely Unhelpful

Debriefing
Initial Support Goup
Hospital Reopening Ceremony
2-Month Follow-up Educational Session
Peer Support Group
Memorial Service (8-Month)
One Year Anniversay Support
One-on-One Counseling
Initial Family Debriefing
Initial Family Support Group

tions, to be unhelpful. In other words, there was a small subset of recipients who had negative reaction to debriefings, which are one of the most common interventions given in response to workplace violence (Deahl, 2000). Clinical interviews were therefore given to determine the cause of these negative reactions. The most common negative response to the debriefings was the timing of interventions. Although immediate support appears to be intuitively appropriate, these individuals reported that they felt they were still in a state of shock when the debriefings were offered and that they were "not ready" to deal with the event. They further suggested that interventions held approximately two months after the event were less intrusive and more effective. Clearly, future research needs to examine if debriefings may be contraindicated for certain subsets of individuals who are experiencing high reactivity and hyperarousal.

DISCUSSION AND CONCLUSIONS

This study used both quantitative and qualitative methods to examine the long-term effects of a workplace violence event over a 10-year period. It found that 23% of respondents suffered from PTSD 6 months after the event, with this number decreasing to 3% ten years after the incident. The number of participants who experienced symptoms of PTSD ranged from 67% 6 months after the attack to 13% ten years after the attack. Surprisingly, the rate of PTSD was unrelated to level of physical involvement/danger during the traumatic event. Qualitative findings suggest that those who still suffered from PTSD or its symptoms ten years after the event had experienced additional trauma during the intervening time period.

All interventions provided were rated as being helpful by all employees, with the exception of the debriefings and initial family support groups. Qualitative findings suggest that these interventions were rated as unhelpful because they were unprepared to deal with the trauma when these interventions were offered.

Additionally, this study identified some prolonged effects of workplace violence which have previously been undocumented, including all pregnant employees suffering miscarriages, long-term loss of interest in sexual intimacy, and long-term emotional triggers to reminders of the traumatic event.

REFERENCES

Adamec, R. (1997). Transmitter systems involved in neural plasticity underlying increased anxiety and defense–Implications for understanding anxiety following traumatic stress. *Neuroscience & Biobehavioral Reviews, 21*(6), 755-765.

Alan Guttmacher Institute (2002). *Pregnancy outcomes in Utah*. Retrieved June 21, 2003 from http://www.guttmacher.org/pubs/state_data/states/utah.html.

American Psychological Association. (1994). *Diagnostic and statistical manual of mental disorders* (4th ed.). Washington, DC: Author.

Barling, J. (1996). The prediction, experience, and consequences of workplace violence. In G. R. VandenBos, & E. Q. Bulatao (Eds.), *Violence on the job: Identifying risks and developing solutions* (pp. 29-49). Washington, DC: American Psychological Association.

Barling, J., Rogers, A. G., & Kelloway, E. K. (2000). Behind closed doors: In-home workers' experience of sexual harassment and workplace violence. *Journal of Occupational Health Psychology, 6*(3), 255-269.

Budd, J. W., Arvey, R. D., & Lawless, P. (1996). Correlates and consequences of workplace violence. *Journal of Occupational Health Psychology, 1*(2), 197-210.

Clark, M. D. (1996). The anthropology of crisis: A case study of reactions to a hostage siege. *Dissertation Abstracts International, 56*(12), 4833.

Conlon, L., Fahy, T. J., & Conroy, R. (1999). PTSD in ambulant RTA victims: A randomized controlled trial of debriefing. *Journal of Psychosomatic Research, 46*(1), 37-44.

Deahl, M. (2000). Psychological debriefing: Controversy and challenge. *Australian & New Zealand Journal of Psychiatry, 34*(6), 929-939.

Derogatis, L. R. (1977). *SCL-90-R: Administration, scoring, and procedures manual-II for the revised version and other instruments of the psychopathology rating scale series.* Towson, MD: Clinical Psychometric Research.

Derogatis, L. R., Rickels, K., & Rock, A. F. (1976). The SCL-90 and the MMPI: A step in the validation of a new self-report scale. *British Journal of Psychiatry, 128*, 280-289.

Driscoll, R. J., Worthington, K. A., & Hurrell, J. J. (1995). Workplace assault an emerging job stressor. *Consulting and Psychology: Practice and Research, 47*(4), 205-212.

Dulle, P. (1996). *Long term effects following a hostage event.* Unpublished master's project, University of Utah, Salt Lake City, UT.

Flannery, R. B. (2001). The employee victim of violence: Recognizing the impact of untreated psychological trauma. *American Journal of Alzheimer's Disease, 16*(4), 230-233.

Gabriel, M. A. (1992). Anniversary reactions: Trauma revisited. *Clinical Social Work Journal, 20*(2), 179-192.

Green, B. L. (1991). Evaluating the effects of disasters. Psychological Assessment: *A Journal of Consulting & Clinical Psychology, 3*, 538-546.

Green, B. L., Lindy, J. D., Grace, M. C., Gleser, G. C., Leonard, A. C., Korol, J., & Winget, C. (1990). Buffalo Creek survivors in the second decade: Stability of stress symptoms. *American Journal of Orthopsychiatry, 3*, 43-50.

Horowitz, M. J. (1973). Phase oriented treatment of stress response syndromes. *American Journal of Psychotherapy, 27*, 506-515.

Horowitz, M. J. (1974). Stress response syndromes: Character style and brief psychotherapy. *American Journal of Psychotherapy, 31*, 768-781.

Horowitz, M. J., Wilner, N., & Alvarez, W. (1979). Impact of Event Scale: A measure of subjective stress. *Psychosomatic Medicine, 41*, 209-218.

Kessler, R. C., Sonnega, A., Bromet, E. J., Hughes, M., & Nelson, C. B. (1995). Post-traumatic stress disorder in the National Comorbidity Survey. *Archives of General Psychiatry, 52*(12), 1048-1060.

Kilpatrick, D. G., Amick-McMullan, A., Lipovsky, J., & Resnick, H. S. (1988, November). *Can self-report inventories discriminate cases of crime-related post-traumatic stress disorder?* Paper presented at the 22nd Annual Meeting of the Association for the Advancement of Behavior Therapy, New York.

Kilpatrick, B. G., Saunders, B. E., Amick-McMullin, A., Best, C. L., Veronen, L. J., & Resnick, H. S. (1989). Victim and crime factors associated with the development of crime-related post-traumatic stress disorder. *Behavior Therapy, 20,* 199-214.

Kulka, R. A., Schlenger, W. E., Fairbank, J. A., Jordan, B. K., Hough, R. L., Marmar, C. R., & Weiss, D. S. (1991). Assessment of post-traumatic stress disorder in the community: Prospects and pitfalls from recent studies of Vietnam veterans. *Psychological Assessment: A Journal of Consulting & Clinical Psychology, 3,* 547-560.

LeBlanc, M. M., & Kelloway, E. K. (2002). Predictors and outcomes of workplace violence and aggression. *Journal of Applied Psychology, 87*(3), 444-453.

Mossman, D. (1995). Violence prediction, workplace violence, and the mental health expert. *Consulting Psychology Journal: Practice and Research, 47*(4), 223-233.

Musaph, H. (1990). Anniversary reaction as a symptom of grief in traumatized persons. *Israel Journal of Psychiatry & Related Sciences, 27*(3), 175-179.

National Institute for Occupational Safety and Health [NIOSH]. (1996). *Violence in the workplace.* Retrieved January 5, 2003, from http://www.cdc.gov/niosh/violfs.htm

National Institute for Occupational Safety and Health [NIOSH]. (1997). *NIOSH facts: Violence in the workplace.* Retrieved January 5, 2003, from http://www.cdc.gov/niosh/violfs.html

Northwestern National Life Insurance Company. (1993). *Fear and violence in the workplace.* Minneapolis, MN: Author.

Panos, P. T. (1994). A hospital hostage situation: The identification of variables that best predicted the development of posttraumatic stress and victimization symptoms in victims. (Doctoral Dissertation, Brigham Young University, 1994). *Dissertation Abstracts International, 54*(10-B), 5400.

Rauch, S. A. M., Hembree, E. A., & Foa, E. B. (2001). Acute psychosocial preventive interventions for posttraumatic stress disorder. *Advances in Mind-Body Medicine, 17*(3), 187-190.

Resnick, H. S., Kilpatrick, D. G., & Lipovsky, J. (1991). Assessment of rape-related post-traumatic stress disorder: Stressor and symptom dimensions. *Psychological Assessment: A Journal of Consulting and Clinical Psychology, 3,* 561-572.

Rogers, K. A., & Kelloway, E. K. (1997). Violence at work: Personal and organizational outcomes. *Journal of Occupational Health Psychology, 2*(1), 63-71.

Saunders, B. E., Mandoki-Arata, K., & Kilpatrick, D. G. (1990). Development of a crime-related post-traumatic stress disorder scale within the Symptom Checklist-90-Revised. *Journal of Traumatic Stress, 3,* 439-448.

Schat, A. C. H., & Kelloway, E. K. (2000). Effects of perceived control on the outcomes of workplace aggression and violence. *Journal of Occupational Health Psychology, 5*(3), 386-402.

van der Kolk, B. (1996). The body keeps score: Approaches to the psychobiology of posttraumatic stress disorder. In B. A. van der Kolk, A. Bessel, & A. C. McFarlane (Eds.), *Traumatic stress: The effects of overwhelming experience on mind, body, and society* (pp. 214-241). New York: Guilford Press.

Zilberg, N. J., Weiss, D. S., & Horowitz, M. J. (1982). Impact of Event Scale: A cross-validation study and some empirical evidence supporting a conceptual model of stress response syndromes. *Journal of Consulting & Clinical Psychology, 50,* 407-414.

Factors Influencing Women's Perceptions of a Sexually Hostile Workplace

Nancy J. Amick
Richard C. Sorenson

SUMMARY. Factors influencing women's perceptions of a sexually hostile work environment including job type, gender mix of work contacts, level of resourcefulness, and perception of male work contacts' attitudes toward women were investigated to determine their relationship with perceptions of a sexually hostile work environment. One hundred seventy-seven working women participated in this investigation. Results suggest that a woman's job type and the gender mix of those with whom she works do not significantly influence her perception of a sexually hostile work environment. Rather, the more that women perceive their male work contacts as having traditional attitudes toward women and the less personally resourceful the women are, the more likely they are to perceive a sexually hostile work environment. *[Article copies available for a fee from The Haworth Document Delivery Service: 1-800-HAWORTH. E-mail address: <docdelivery@haworthpress.com> Website: <http://www. HaworthPress.com> © 2004 by The Haworth Press, Inc. All rights reserved.]*

Address correspondence to: Nancy J. Amick, PhD, P.O. Box 11628, Tempe, AZ 85284.

[Haworth co-indexing entry note]: "Factors Influencing Women's Perceptions of a Sexually Hostile Workplace." Amick, Nancy J., and Richard C. Sorenson. Co-published simultaneously in *Journal of Emotional Abuse* (The Haworth Maltreatment & Trauma Press, an imprint of The Haworth Press, Inc.) Vol. 4, No. 3/4, 2004, pp. 49-69; and: *Aggression in Organizations: Violence, Abuse, and Harassment at Work and in Schools* (ed: Robert Geffner et al.) The Haworth Maltreatment & Trauma Press, an imprint of The Haworth Press, Inc., 2004, pp. 49-69. Single or multiple copies of this article are available for a fee from The Haworth Document Delivery Service [1-800-HAWORTH, 9:00 a.m. - 5:00 p.m. (EST). E-mail address: docdelivery@ haworthpress.com].

49

KEYWORDS. Resourcefulness, sexual harassment, attitudes, hostile workplace

Sexual harassment, unwarranted and unwelcome sexual attention, is a serious social problem. Estimates suggest that approximately one-half of all women will be sexually harassed during the course of their academic or working lives, making sexual harassment more extensive than any other type of sexual victimization (Cochran, Frazier, & Olson, 1997; Fitzgerald, 1993; Fitzgerald & Shullman, 1993). Sexual harassment is ubiquitous–it occurs to women and men of all ages, occupations, and backgrounds. While research indicates that it is not gender exclusive, the majority of victims are women harassed by men (United States Merit Systems Protection Board, 1988). In 2003, 85% of the 13,566 sexual harassment charges filed with the federal Equal Employment Opportunity Commission or corresponding state agencies were filed by women (EEOC, 2004b). When compared to men, women are far more likely to quit or lose their job as a direct result of sexual harassment (Gutek, 1985). Hence, sexual harassment poses a considerable barrier to the career advancement and opportunities of working women.

Sexual harassment has negative consequences for both individuals and organizations. Victims experience deleterious effects on their health, psychological well being, and job satisfaction, while organizations suffer through financial loss, which is incurred via absenteeism, job turnover, and decreased work productivity (Jensen & Gutek, 1982). A large scale survey of over 8,500 Federally employed workers indicated that within a two-year period, sexual harassment cost the Federal Government approximately 267 million dollars (USMSPB, 1988).

Sexual harassment became illegal in 1980 when the United States Equal Employment Opportunity Commission (EEOC) deemed it a violation of Title VII of the Civil Rights Act, which prohibits discrimination based on gender (Fitzgerald, 1993; Gutek, 1993). Therefore, it was not until 1980 that a legal definition of sexual harassment was implemented. According to the EEOC, the current definition reads:

> Unwelcome sexual advances, requests for sexual favors, and other verbal or physical conduct of a sexual nature constitute sexual harassment when this conduct explicitly or implicitly affects an individual's employment, unreasonably interferes with an individual's work performance or creates an intimidating, hostile, or offensive working environment. (EEOC, 2004a)

The definition of sexual harassment underscores its subjectivity since behaviors deemed "unwelcome" and conduct creating an "intimidating, hostile, or offensive working environment" are dependent on the perception of the victim. As Hamada (1995, p. 163) notes, "Laws on sexual harassment focus primarily on the victim's perceptions rather than on the offender's intention. What is important is not the intent of the message being sent by the offender, but what emotions and reactions it stirs in the mind of the victim." Given the current definition of sexual harassment, an examination of the factors that influence women's perceptions of a sexually hostile work environment is imperative.

BACKGROUND

Perceptions of a sexually hostile work environment. A focused research approach on the perceptions of sexual harassment is in order since it is the perceptions of sexual harassment that may relate more directly to negative outcomes than the actual harassing behaviors themselves (Terpstra & Baker, 1986b). While researchers have found that the frequency of sexual harassment is related to consequences such as depression, anxiety, turnover, psychosomatic health complaints, and dissatisfaction with coworkers and supervisors for female victims (Barling, Dekker, Loughlin, Kelloway, Fullagar, & Johnson, 1996), Sorenson, Mangione-Lambie, and Luzio (1998) found that sexual harassment is also devastating to those who are bystanders. Specifically, in their study, both "bystanders" and "victims" reported an increase in negative affect, motivation loss, and assertive coping strategies as the severity of sexual harassment increased. Likewise, Hulin, Fitzgerald, and Drasgow (1996) suggested that employees who perceive no organizational consequences for sexual harassment might experience a stressful work environment regardless of whether or not they have been sexually harassed directly. They reported, "waiting for the sexual harassment shoe to drop, watching their colleagues be harassed with few or no sanctions for harassers, and wondering when or if it will happen to them are only a few of the experiences that may be nearly as stressful as being a direct target" (Hulin et al., 1996, p. 132).

Given the potential impact of sexual harassment not only on those who experience it directly, but also on those who are within its reach, this study examined variables that may influence individual perceptions of a sexually hostile work environment regardless of whether or not sexual harassment has yet been experienced directly. Since organizations seem to dictate which behaviors are appropriate or inappropriate based on the negative or positive consequences provided for any given action, employees in organizations that do not have negative consequences for harassing behaviors will likely regard the organization as tolerant of the dominance of certain groups over others. Therefore, to assess the organizational climate for any given behavior, one can examine employees' perceptions of whether or not the behavior results in organizational reinforcements (Hulin et al., 1996; Schneider & Reichers, 1983; Zohar, 1980). Specifically, in this study, women's perceptions of a sexually hostile work environment were investigated using a scale developed by Hulin et al. (1996) which examines individual perceptions of organizational tolerance for sexual harassment.

Theory. Although sexual harassment research has been underway for over two decades, there is not a predominant theory that has emerged in the literature. The difficulty with theoretical advancements may be directly related to the subjective nature of sexual harassment as evidenced by differing definitions, interpretations and reactions not only between men and women, but also among women themselves. Some theories that have emerged in the literature include the Sex Role Spillover Theory (Gutek, 1985; Gutek & Cohen, 1987; Gutek & Morasch, 1982; Konrad & Gutek, 1986), Demographic Composition Theories (Konrad, Winter, & Gutek, 1992), Person by Situation Interaction (Pryor, LaVite, & Stoller, 1993), the Organizational Model (Fitzgerald, Drasgow, Hulin, Gelfand, & Magley, 1997), the Natural/Biological Model and the Socio-Cultural Model (Tangri, Burt, & Johnson, 1982), and the Theory of Tokenism (Kanter, 1977a, 1977b, 1980).

Few theoretical models have been empirically tested, and few have considered a multifactor analysis encompassing the impact of several variables simultaneously on the perceptions of sexual harassment. In fact, with no clearly identified theory of sexual harassment, many studies (including the current study) are in the hypothesis-testing phase as a step towards the development of a sound theoretical model. Kanter's Theory of Tokenism suggests that the gender ratio of the work group can influence both the attitudes and behaviors of workers and impact how they interact with one another. In particular, Kanter refers to women who are a numerical minority in a work group of men as "tokens." Her theory states that token females in a work group of males encounter three particular difficulties. First, due to their obvious differences, token women are more visible in an organization. Consequently, because gender is their most salient characteristic, they tend to be perceived as members of the category "women" rather than as individuals with unique characteristics and contributions. Second, men may experience token women as a threat to their work environment. As a result, they may behave in ways that exaggerate their maleness in order to keep a clear boundary between them and those who are different. For instance, they may enunciate displays of potency and aggression by highlighting what they as men can do in contrast to women. They may also tell sexual jokes or discuss sexual adventures in order to test women to see how they respond to the male environment. Finally, Kanter states that in occupations where men are not used to working with women, men tend to draw on stereotypes and generalizations about women when interacting with the token few in their work group. According to Kanter, drawing upon familiar ways of relating to women decreases the uncertainty and ambiguity associated with being in the presence of one who is different. Consequently, men may induct women into stereotypical roles such as mother or sex object to preserve a familiar form of interaction (Kanter, 1977a, 1977b). When applied to sexual harassment, Kanter's theory would predict that environmental factors such as job type and gender mix of work contacts contribute to sex role stereotyping and sexual harassment.

Models such as those proposed by Terpstra and Baker (1986a), Fitzgerald and Shullman (1993), and Bill (1994) suggest the importance of an integrative model of sexual harassment, which includes organizational, individual, and environmental factors. Using Kanter's Theory of Tokenism as a foundation, the current study examined the influence of environmental, attitudinal, and individual factors on women's perceptions of a sexually hostile work environment.

ENVIRONMENTAL FACTORS

A comprehensive study of sexual harassment includes an examination of the environment within which it occurs–namely the job type (non-traditionally female, traditionally female, and integrated) and the gender mix of work contacts. Previous research indicates that job type can influence a woman's experience with sexual harassment. For instance, women employed in non-traditionally female occupations report a higher instance of sexual harassment than women in other job types (Gutek, 1985). Additionally, research on the gender mix of work contacts suggests that a skewed gender mix in favor of men also tends to increase a woman's probability of being sexually harassed (Baker, 1989; USMSPB, 1988). When applied to sexual harassment, the Theory of Tokenism suggests that non-traditionally employed women who work predominantly with men are more likely to be the recipients of sexual harassment as a result of their token status (Crocker & McGraw, 1984; Kanter, 1977a; Rosenberg, Perlstadt, & Phillips, 1993).

A study conducted by Baker (1989) highlights the importance of examining the gender mix of work contacts for traditionally employed women as well. Among traditionally employed women, Baker found that women in pink collar jobs (e.g., clerical) experienced greater levels of sexual harassment than women in blue-collar jobs (e.g., factory work). Therefore, there may be different degrees of being a token based upon the gender mix of one's work contacts. In other words, women in clerical positions may work predominantly with men, whereas women in factory positions may work predominantly with other women. The current study examined job type as well as the gender mix of work contacts as predictors of women's perceptions of a sexually hostile work environment.

ATTITUDINAL FACTORS

Few would dispute that traditionally a woman's role has been that of homemaker and a man's role that of breadwinner. With the entrance of many women into the workforce and into jobs that traditionally have been depicted as male, the nature of the interaction between men and women is changing. Due to these changes, there is considerable ambiguity as to what constitutes appropriate social sexual behavior at work (Gutek, 1985; Kanter, 1977a, 1980). As a result, gender roles, which are learned at a much earlier age than work roles, typically influence to some extent how men and women interact with one another (Gutek & Morasch, 1982; Kanter, 1977a, 1980; Konrad & Gutek, 1986). In occupations that have been traditionally dominated by men, men may bring gender-based expectations into the workplace, thereby resorting to familiar ways of relating to women (Kanter, 1977a, 1980). Therefore, occupations considered atypical for women are likely to be occupations where women are more apt to be the recipients of gender stereotyping, thereby creating an environment prime for sexual harassment to occur (Borgida, Rudman, & Manteufel, 1995; Kanter, 1977a, 1977b).

As our social conditions and sex role attitudes continue to be modified, updated research is needed on how such factors affect women at work (Stafford, 1984). The present study examined women's perceptions of their male work contacts' attitudes toward women. In particular, following the lines of Kanter's theory, it was expected that women employed in non-traditionally female occupations, and/or women who had predominantly male work contacts, were more likely to work in environments that were not only prime for sex role stereotyping but also for sexual harassment. Consequently, it was expected that women working in these environments would be more likely to perceive their male work contacts as having traditional (i.e., stereotypical) attitudes toward women, and therefore they would be more likely to perceive a sexually hostile work environment.

INDIVIDUAL FACTORS

Finally, the question arises, why do some women perceive certain behaviors as sexually harassing when others do not? Several studies have examined the role of individual disposition. For instance, sex role orientation (Powell, 1986), gender role socialization (Barr, 1993), erotophobia, sexual experience, attitudes towards women, defensive style, need for social approval, and rape myth acceptance (Barak, Fisher, & Houston, 1992), as well as introversion, self esteem, and religiosity (Terpstra & Baker, 1986b) appear to affect perceptions of sexual harassment. Although Kanter's Theory of Tokenism does not take into account any individual factors which may affect a woman's perception of sexual harassment, one would expect that some women have a personal disposition that contributes to their tendency to be resourceful in managing sexual overtures at work, thereby reducing their potential for perceiving sexual hostility in their working environment. The current study assessed one's ability to deal with noxious stimuli–also known as one's level of learned resourcefulness.

Learned resourcefulness refers to the skills and behaviors that aid a person in regulating his or her internal responses to stressful situations so the internal responses do not hinder his or her ability to respond effectively (Rosenbaum, 1990). According to Rosenbaum, learned resourcefulness is an enduring attribute that is learned over time and based on one's history and experience. He also states that high levels of resourcefulness are not expected to change one's perception of a stressful situation but are expected to influence how well one is able to manage his/her cognitions and affect in order to carry out the desired behavior. The cognitive/behavioral skills promoting resourcefulness include: (a) using cognitive self statements, (b) having a sense of self-efficacy, (c) delaying gratification, and (d) using problem solving techniques (Rosenbaum, 1980a). The current study examined learned resourcefulness as a moderator of the relationship between the perception of male contacts' attitudes toward women and perception of a sexually hostile work environment.

OBJECTIVES

The purpose of this study was to examine the factors influencing women's perceptions of a sexually hostile work environment while partially utilizing the Theory of Tokenism as proposed by Kanter (1977a, 1977b, 1980) and elaborated by Borgida et al. (1995). Past research examined various aspects of Tokenism (Baker, 1989; Crocker & McGraw, 1984; Rosenberg et al., 1993); however, most research has not focused on the integrated aspects of the theory. Unlike previous studies, this study not only assessed the job type and gender mix of work contacts, but also the stereotypical attitudes (or perceptions of them) which Kanter reports are likely to flourish in work environments where women are typically underrepresented. In addition, although Kanter's theory does not take into account individual factors which may influence how a woman experiences her work environment, this study attempted to elaborate on Kanter's theory by assessing the individual disposition of learned resourcefulness. The following hypotheses were formed:

H-1: Women's job type and work contacts and their interaction will predict the degree to which women will perceive their male work contacts as having traditional (i.e., stereotypical) attitudes toward women.

H-2: Women in more non-traditional occupations for females (job type) will perceive a sexually hostile work environment to a greater degree than women in more traditionally female occupations.

H-3: Women with more predominantly male work contacts (gender mix) will perceive a sexually hostile work environment to a greater degree than women with predominantly female work contacts.

H-4: The dispositional factor of learned resourcefulness will moderate the relationship between perception of male work contacts' attitudes toward women and perception of a sexually hostile work environment such that individuals who perceive male work contacts as traditional in their attitudes toward women will perceive their work environment as less sexually hostile if they have a high versus low level of learned resourcefulness.

H-5: The relationship of job type and gender mix of work contacts with perception of a sexually hostile work environment will be mediated by perception of male work contacts' attitudes toward women.

METHODS

Participants

Participants in this study were 177 female volunteers between the ages of 19 and 62 who were employed at least 30 hours per week in various job positions and work environments.

Procedures

The women involved in this study were for the most part recruited from a weekend-long community fair and business exposition where the researchers rented a booth for the purpose of data collection. After the fair, data were obtained from an additional nine women employed in non-traditional occupations. Participants were given an envelope containing a form to indicate their consent to participate and the following questionnaires in a randomly determined order: (a) a demographic questionnaire, (b) the Attitudes Toward Women Scale, (c) the Self Control Scale, and (d) the Organizational Tolerance for Sexual Harassment Scale. For all who participated in the study, two free movie tickets were offered.

Measurements

Demographic questionnaire. Demographic information was gathered by way of a self-report questionnaire. Participants were also asked if they had ever been sexually harassed and if they had ever filed a sexual harassment complaint.

Job type. Job type was assessed by comparing a participant's self reported job title with current published data provided by the United States Bureau of Labor Statistics (1994), which listed the percent of females typically represented in that occupation. Job type then was used as a continuous variable in the analyses–a high score indicating a traditional job for women.

Gender mix of work contacts. The gender mix of work contacts was addressed in the demographic questionnaire. Participants were asked the following two questions: (a) "Of all the people you interact with at work, are they predominantly men or women? Please include peers, supervisors, subordinates, employees, patients, customers, vendors . . ." and (b) "At your current place of employment, what percent of your time is spent interacting with men, and what percent of your time is spent interacting with women? In your calculation, please include peers, supervisors, subordinates, employees, patients, customers, vendors . . ." The total percent of time interacting with males at work was used as a continuous variable to assess gender mix of work contacts.

Attitudes Toward Women Scale-Short Form (AWS-Short Form). The AWS-short form was used as a measure of how women perceive the men in their work environment relative to liberal versus traditional attitudes toward women. The AWS-Short Form, developed by Spence, Helmreich, and Strapp (1973) was designed to assess attitudes toward women's rights and roles in contemporary society. The scale consists of 25 statements taken from the full length AWS to which participants respond on a four point scale ranging from "agree strongly" to "disagree strongly." Additionally, 12 items are reverse coded and the items are summed to yield a total score that falls between 25 and 100 (25 = extremely traditional and 100 = extremely liberal).

Items selected for inclusion in the AWS-Short Form were normed on a population of 241 female and male college students who were administered the full length AWS. Based on their scores, students were divided into quartiles and a separate item analysis was completed for each sex. The 25 items chosen for inclusion in the AWS-short form discriminated best among the quartiles for each sex and maintained the highest item-total correlations (Spence et al., 1973).

The internal consistency reliability for the AWS-Short Form was estimated by Stanley, Boots and Johnson (1975). Coefficient alpha was .81 for 99 girls ages 12 to 16; .82 for 72 women; and .89 for 62 female and 88 male college students.

Spence et al. (1973) assessed validity of the AWS-Short Form through correlations with the full length AWS. Correlations were .97 for 241 college women, .97 for 286 college men, .96 for 232 fathers of college students, and .97 for 292 mothers of college students.

Significant correlations were reported between scores on the AWS-Short Form and on the Personal Attributes Questionnaire, a measure of masculinity-femininity (Spence, Helmreich, & Strapp, 1975). Minnegerode (1976) also found a significant correlation between the AWS-Short Form and the BEM Sex Role Inventory.

In order to use this scale to assess how women perceive the men in their work environment relative to liberal versus traditional attitudes toward women, women were instructed to answer the questions the way they thought most men they interacted with at work would answer them. A high score indicates the strong perception that male coworkers have liberal, non-traditional attitudes toward women.

Self Control Scale (SCS). The SCS is a self-report instrument that was used to assess participants on the dispositional variable known as learned resourcefulness. The SCS, developed by Rosenbaum (1980b), was designed to measure one's ability and tendency to employ self-control techniques. It consists of 36 statements to which participants respond on a six-point scale ranging from "very characteristic of me, extremely descriptive" to "very uncharacteristic of me, extremely non-descriptive."

According to Rosenbaum and Ben-Ari (1985), the 36 statements that make up the SCS were chosen from a pool of 60 statements based on content validity as judged by two clinical psychologists. Following the item selection, the SCS was administered to six groups of subjects to establish reliability and normative data (Rosenbaum, 1980b). Test-retest reliability indicated that the SCS had high stability over a four-week period ($r = .86, p < .01$). The internal consistency reliability for the SCS ranged from .78 to .84 for the various norming groups. Kiefer, Rabin, and Sorenson (2002) studied a sample of 313 adult volunteers ranging in age from 18 to 75 and found the internal consistency reliability to be .73 and the stability over a six-week interval to also be .73. They further found that scores of males and females did not differ significantly, that the SCS scores did not correlate significantly with age nor with social desirability response bias, and that the SCS was significantly correlated with measures of healthy coping strategies ($r = .57, p < .01$) and emotional intelligence ($r = .40, p < .01$); thus, providing evidence for the construct validity of the measure of resourcefulness. A high score indicates more resourcefulness.

Organizational Tolerance for Sexual Harassment Scale (OTSH). The Organizational Tolerance for Sexual Harassment Scale (OTSH) was used as a measure of women's perception of a sexually hostile work environment. The OTSH scale, developed by Hulin et al. (1996) was designed to assess individual perceptions of organizational tolerance for sexual harassment.

The scale consists of six scenarios that combine two types of harassers (supervisor and co-worker) and three types of harassing behaviors (sexual coercion, unwanted sexual attention, and gender harassment). Each scenario is followed by three questions designed to assess: (a) perceptions of risk to a woman who makes a formal complaint (1 = extremely risky and 5 = no risk); (b) likelihood that she would be taken seriously (1 = no chance she would be taken seriously and 5 = very good chance she would be taken seriously); and (c) likelihood that something might be done to the harasser (1 = nothing and 5 = very serious consequences to the harasser). Each item is weighted equally and the item scores are added to yield a total score that falls between 18 and 90, with higher scores indicating perception that an organization does not tolerate sexual harassment, and thus a low value on sexually hostile workplace.

Internal consistency reliability for the OTSH scale was calculated by Hulin et al. (1996) on a sample of 418 female employees. Coefficient alphas for each of the three responses (perceived risk, taken seriously, and likelihood of sanctions) were .94, .94, and .93, respectively. A coefficient alpha of .96 was obtained for the overall OTSH. When compared to male employees, female employees perceived the organization as more tolerant of sexual harassment. Additionally, male and female employees perceived the organization to be less tolerant of sexual harassment by employees than by supervisors. These findings were in the direction expected, thereby providing evidence for the construct validity of the OTSH.

The OTSH was administered to 697 males and 459 females who were employed in a Public Utility Company who reported actual experiences with sexual harassment (as assessed by the Sexual Experiences Questionnaire). After correction for unreliability, correlations with the sexual harassment criteria were .51, .43, and .30 for the gender harassment, unwanted sexual attention, and quid pro quo subscales, respectively.

Hulin et al. (1996) further assessed construct related validity by correlating the OTSH scale with other scales. The OTSH positively correlated with measures of job life satisfaction, mental health, physical health conditions, and health satisfaction, and negatively with withdrawal and posttraumatic stress disorder.

RESULTS

Table 1 shows the intercorrelations among all of the primary research variables and the reliabilities of the scales. The reliabilities were all equal to or greater than .80 and very similar to those found for these variables in previous studies. The correlation between Job Type and Gender Mix was negative as expected indicating that as the job became more feminine the contacts became predominately female. The most interesting correlations demonstrated the relationship of perceived attitude of women's male work contacts and women's resiliency with perceptions of a sexually hostile work environment. Two separate hierarchical regression analyses were conducted to assess the five hypotheses. In the first analysis, Perception of Attitudes Toward Women served as the outcome. In Step 1, Job Type and Gender Mix served as the predictors, and in Step Two, the interaction of Job Type and Gender Mix was entered. The re-

TABLE 1. Pearson Correlations Among Predictor and Outcome Variable

	Job Type	Gender Mix	OTSH	AWS	SCS	Reliability
Job Type	—	−.31*a	−.07	−.07	−.03	--
Gender Mix		—	−.06	−.03	.13	--
OTSH			—	.42*b	.31*c	.96
AWS				—	.13	.92
SCS					—	.80

Note: OTSH = Organizational Tolerance for Sexual Harassment; AWS = Perception of Attitudes Toward Women; SCS = Self Control Scale.
a. As a job becomes more traditionally female, the percent of male work contacts decreases. The 90% confidence interval for the correlation is 2.19, 2.42.
b. The more that women perceive their male work contacts as liberal and non-traditional in their attitudes toward women, the less likely they are to perceive a sexually hostile work environment. The 90% confidence interval for the correlation is .31, .52.
c. Women higher in resourcefulness are less likely to perceive a sexually hostile work environment. The 90% confidence interval for the correlation is .19, .42.
*$p \leq .001$.

sulting regression weight of each predictor was used to evaluate the hypothe-sized relationship.

All three of these variables explained only a non-significant 1% of the vari-ance in Perception of Attitudes Toward Women. Therefore, neither Job Type, Gender Mix, nor their interaction significantly predicted Perception of Atti-tudes Toward Women, and no support was found for Hypothesis 1.

In the second analysis, Perception of a Sexually Hostile Workplace served as the outcome. In Step 1, Job Type and Gender Mix were entered. In Step 2, Perception of Attitudes Toward Women was entered. In Step 3, Learned Re-sourcefulness was entered, and in Step Four, the interaction of Learned Re-sourcefulness and Perception of Attitudes Toward Women was entered. The resulting beta weight for each predictor was used to evaluate the hypotheses. In the second analysis, Job Type and Gender Mix explained only a non-signif-icant 1% of the variance in Perception of a Sexually Hostile Workplace. Therefore, neither Job Type nor Gender Mix significantly predicted Percep-tion of a Sexually Hostile Workplace. However, Perception of Attitudes To-ward Women significantly predicted 17% of the variance in Perception of a Sexually Hostile Workplace scores beyond that which was accounted for by Job Type and Gender Mix. Learned Resourcefulness significantly predicted 9% of the variance in Perception of a Sexually Hostile Workplace. No interac-tion was found between Perceptions of Attitudes Toward Women and Learned Resourcefulness in predicting Perception of a Sexually Hostile Workplace. Therefore, although Hypotheses 2, 3, and 4 were not supported, the results do suggest that Perception of Attitudes Toward Women and Learned Resource-fulness had a direct influence on Perception of a Sexually Hostile Workplace as shown in the model in Figure 1. Since Job Type and Gender Mix were not related to the proposed mediator or to the dependent variable, we found no support for the mediation hypothesis, Hypothesis 5.

CONCLUSION

In this study, the traditionality of job type and the gender mix of work con-tacts did not significantly influence women's perceptions of their male work contacts' attitudes toward women or their perception of a sexually hostile work environment. However, women's perceptions of their male work con-tacts' attitude toward women and their own level of learned resourcefulness significantly influenced their perceptions of a sexually hostile work environ-ment. In particular, the more that women perceive their male work contacts as traditional in their attitudes toward women, the *more* likely the women are to perceive a sexually hostile work environment. Additionally, the higher women

FIGURE 1. Resulting Model with Path Coefficients

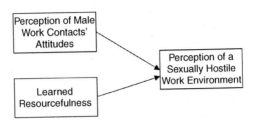

(Path coefficients are beta weights. Although learned resourcefulness did not moderate the relationship between perception of male work contacts' attitudes and perception of a sexually hostile work environment, there was a direct effect between learned resourcefulness and perception of a sexually hostile work environment.)

are in resourcefulness, the *less* likely they are to perceive a sexually hostile work environment.

DISCUSSION

Summary and Interpretation of the Findings

The purpose of this study was to examine the factors influencing women's perceptions of a sexually hostile work environment while partially utilizing the theory of Tokenism as proposed by Kanter (1977a, 1977b, 1980) and elaborated by Borgida et al. (1995). The results of this study provide both confirming and disconfirming support for the theoretical model suggested by Kanter's theory.

Based on Kanter's theory, it was hypothesized that women employed in non-traditional occupations for females, and women working predominantly with men, would be more likely than other women in the study to perceive a sexually hostile work environment due to their token status. These hypotheses were not supported. There are several possible reasons why this study failed to support these hypotheses. These findings may be due to the population of women studied. In the current sample, non-traditionally employed women were underrepresented, comprising only 12% of women studied. However, the failure to find support for the gender mix hypothesis is consistent with McKinney's (1990) finding that prevalence of sexual harassment failed to differ significantly for female respondents in male-dominated and female-dominated academic departments.

Based on Kanter's theory, it was hypothesized that women employed in non-traditionally female occupations, and women working predominantly with men, would be more likely to perceive their male work contacts as having traditional attitudes toward women. However, these hypotheses were not supported. Thus, if we assume women's perceptions are accurate, these findings failed to support Kanter's assumption that stereotypical attitudes are likely to flourish in occupations where women are typically under represented. Whereas this assumption may once have been correct, the results of this study suggest that it is no longer so.

Although the hypotheses regarding job type and gender mix were not supported, there was a significant direct effect between women's perception of their male work contacts as having traditional (i.e., stereotypical) attitudes toward women, and women's perceptions of their work environment as sexually hostile. These findings partially support the assumptions of Kanter's theory, which suggest that gender stereotyping may influence a sexually hostile work environment; although, her contention that these attitudes develop in environments where women are typically under represented was not supported. These findings are related, however, to those of Weiner, Hurt, Russell, Mannen, and Gasper (1997) who ". . . found that ambivalent sexist stereotypes play a decisive role in judgments of what constitutes hostile work environment harassment" (p. 90).

Some might argue that the direct effect between perception of attitudes and perception of a sexually hostile work environment may be bi-directional, such that a woman's experience of her work environment may influence the way she thinks about the men she works with. Although this correlational study cannot determine the actual direction of this effect, previous research suggests that it is likely that perception of attitudes predicts perception of a sexually hostile work environment versus the converse (Borgida et al., 1995; Kanter, 1977a, 1977b). Additionally, Mazer and Percival (1989) found that women who had experienced more sexual harassment were no different in their attitudes toward men and women from women who had less experience with sexual harassment, thereby suggesting women can separate their ideology from their experience. Further, some may argue that the relationships found in this research could have resulted from same source or method variance since the data were collected at the same time and with the same questionnaire. However, Spector (2001, p. 16) in commenting on the possibility of same source or mono-method variance states ". . . evidence that inflation generally occurs has not been found" and ". . . general mono-method bias normally does not occur."

We thought that women who perceived their male work contacts as traditional in their attitudes toward women would be less likely to perceive their work environment as sexually hostile if they had a high versus a low level of resourcefulness. It was expected that women high in resourcefulness would be more adept at carrying out the behaviors necessary to successfully manage sexual overtures at work. Although resourcefulness did not act as a moderator in this process, there was a direct effect between level of resourcefulness and perception of a sexually hostile work environment. In particular, as expected, women high in resourcefulness were less likely to perceive a sexually hostile work environment than women lower in resourcefulness.

Based on the assumptions underlying the Self Control Scale (i.e., learned resourcefulness), resourceful women may be more adept at managing their emotional reactions to sexual hostility, thereby permitting them to carry out the desired behaviors necessary for managing the situation. The more resourceful women may tend to make a more direct response (e.g., confronting or reporting the harasser), which is often the less frequent action taken, but the one leading to the greater satisfaction with the outcome (Cochran et al., 1997). This relationship may be analogous to the findings that high self-esteem is associated with low frequency of psychological abuse in dating relationships (Pipes & LeBov-Keeler, 1997), and with not having been raped as opposed to being date raped (Shapiro & Shwarz, 1997), and the ability to resist pressured sex (Zweig, Barber, & Eccles, 1997).

Implications for the Workplace

The findings from the current study have several important organizational implications. If what influences women's perceptions of a sexually hostile work environment is their perception that male co-workers hold stereotypical attitudes towards women, then interventions that focus on these attitudes may be effective in changing the degree to which women perceive their work environment as sexually hostile. For instance, organizations may benefit from training supervisors to identify sexist behaviors and to take action against such behaviors before they become a problem in the workplace. Organizations may also benefit from educating employees about the traditional attitudes that may be unintentionally offensive to women. Information could be demonstrated via a video presentation depicting different exchanges between men and women in order to clarify how certain attitudes and beliefs may appear to others.

Additionally, Hulin et al. (1996) noted that attitudes and behaviors of employees are likely reflective of what the organization tolerates or promotes. In other words, employees know what is and is not tolerated by the rewards or contingencies the organization administers for any given behavior. Therefore, given that women in this study who perceived their male work contacts as having stereotypical attitudes towards women perceived their work environment to be more sexually hostile, management may wish to examine their stance toward women employees and to regard themselves as examples of how to treat women at work. As Fiske and Glick (1995) note, management may wish to review their practices and procedures to see if they may be contributing to the continuance of stereotypical attitudes toward women. For example, do they give women traditional titles such as secretary? Do they ask women to perform stereotypical jobs such as making the coffee or ordering lunch? Do they provide information about the credentials of newly hired women? In other words, do they provide information to refute potential stereotypes?

Furthermore, an organization may wish to take action aimed at integrating men and women in a manner that reduces the barriers between them. For instance, Fiske and Glick (1995) suggest structuring the work environment such that men and women depend on each other for work-related outcomes. Relying on the expertise of others may help decrease stereotypes by providing ample evidence of what individuals can contribute uniquely to the organization.

The findings of the current investigation, which suggest resourceful women are less likely to perceive a sexually hostile work environment, have important implications. For instance, resourceful women may be better able to cope with instances that might otherwise contribute to a sexually hostile work environment, or they may directly or indirectly prevent such instances from occurring to them. Still, one can speculate that if resourceful women are better able to manage sexual hostility at work, then organizational training programs aimed at providing women with strategies for managing sexual harassment, thereby increasing their resourcefulness, may prove useful.

Limitations of the Study

Although the current study employed reliable and valid methodology and measures, there are some limitations that affect the interpretations of these findings. First, given that women are reticent to report sexual harassment for fear of job related consequences (Gutek, 1985; USMSPB, 1988), one might expect women to be less willing to accurately report their work experiences. However, participants in this study included women who attended a community fair and business exposition; thus, they were not recruited from their place of employment. In fact, they were not asked to disclose their place of employment, but rather were asked to list their job title. Thus, the environment selected for this study was intentionally aimed at reducing concerns about responding truthfully, which may not have occurred had the study been associated in any way with their employment sites.

Another potential limitation of this investigation concerns the generalizability of the sample of women studied. First, data were collected predominantly among women who attended a community fair and business exposition within a particular geographic region. However, it is important to note that participants in this study had a wide range of occupational titles, ages, and educational experience suggesting a reasonable degree of heterogeneity among participants. Furthermore, this study was an improvement over some studies of sexual harassment since it examined working women and did not rely solely upon the reports of student samples.

Directions for Future Research

Future studies should attempt to confirm the current findings that neither job type nor gender mix predicted perceptions of a sexually hostile work environment–particularly since these findings are contrary to popular research of a decade or two ago (Baker, 1989; Gutek, 1985; USMSPB, 1988). As Katz, Hannon, and Whitten (1996) point out, some of the relationships involving men and women at work are changing as men are becoming more aware of sexual harassment, its definition, and its consequences. Additionally, since this study demonstrated a relationship between women who are resourceful and women who are less likely to perceive a sexually hostile work environment, future studies should investigate this issue further to assess for any positive effects to being a working woman with a high degree of resourcefulness. In particular, an examination of resourceful women and how they manage sexual harassment may be one area of consideration.

REFERENCES

Baker, N. L. (1989). *Sexual harassment and job satisfaction in traditional and nontraditional industrial occupations.* Unpublished dissertation. California School of Professional Psychology, Los Angeles.

Barak, A., Fisher, W. A., & Houston, S. (1992). Individual difference correlates of the experience of sexual harassment among female university students. *Journal of Applied Social Psychology, 22*(1), 17-37.

Barling, J., Dekker, I., Loughlin, C. A., Kelloway, E. K., Fullagar, C., & Johnson, D. (1996). Prediction and replication of the organizational and personal consequences of workplace sexual harassment. *Journal of Managerial Psychology, 11*(5), 4-25.

Barr, P.A. (1993). Perceptions of sexual harassment. *Sociological Inquiry, 63*(4), 460-470.

Bill, J. B. (1994, August). *Sexual harassment as a work climate: Moving beyond the reasonable gender approach.* Paper presented at the Academy of Management annual conference, Dallas, TX.

Borgida, E., Rudman, L. A., & Manteufel, L. L. (1995). On the courtroom use and misuse of gender stereotyping research. *Journal of Social Issues, 51*(1), 181-192.

Cochran, C. C., Frazier, P. A., & Olson, A. M. (1997). Predictors of responses to unwanted sexual attention. *Psychology of Women Quarterly, 21,* 207-226.

Crocker, J., & McGraw, K. M. (1984). What's good for the goose is not good for the gander: Solo status as an obstacle to occupational achievement for males and females. *American Behavioral Scientist, 27*(3), 357-369.

Equal Employment Opportunity Commission. (2004a). Sexual harassment. Retrieved June 16, 2004, from http://www.eeoc.gov/types/sexual_harassment.html.

Equal Employment Opportunity Commission. (2004b). *Sexual harassment charges EEOC and FEPA combined: FY 1992-FY1993.* Retrieved June 16, 2004, from http://www.eeoc.gov/stats/harass.html.

Fiske, S. T., & Glick, P. (1995). Ambivalence and stereotypes cause sexual harassment: A theory with implications for organizational change. *Journal of Social Issues, 51*(1), 97-115.

Fitzgerald, L. F. (1993). Sexual harassment: Violence against women in the workplace. *American Psychologist, 48*(10), 1070-1076.

Fitzgerald, L. F., Drasgow, F., Hulin, C. L., Gelfand, M. J., & Magley, V. J. (1997). Antecedents and consequences of sexual harassment in organizations: A test of an integrated model. *Journal of Applied Psychology, 82*(4),578-589.

Fitzgerald, L. F., & Shullman, S. L. (1993). Sexual harassment: A research analysis and agenda for the 1990s. *Journal of Vocational Behavior, 42,* 5-27.

Gutek, B. A. (1985). *Sex and the workplace: Impact of sexual behavior and harassment on women, men, and organizations.* San Francisco: Jossey-Bass Inc.

Gutek, B. A. (1993). Sexual harassment: Rights and responsibilities. *Employee Responsibilities and Rights Journal, 6*(4), 325-340.

Gutek, B. A., & Cohen, A. G. (1987). Sex ratios, sex role spillover, and sex at work: A comparison of men's and women's experiences. *Human Relations, 40*(2), 97-115.

Gutek, B. A., & Morasch, B. (1982). Sex-ratios, sex-role spillover, and sexual harassment of women at work. *Journal of Social Issues, 38*(4), 55-74.

Hamada, T. (1995). Inventing cultural others in organizations: A case of anthropological reflexivity in a multinational firm. *Journal of Applied Behavioral Science, 31*(1), 162-185.

Hulin, C., Fitzgerald, L., & Drasgow, F. (1996). Organizational influences on sexual harassment. In M. S. Stockdale (Ed.), *Sexual Harassment in the workplace.* Thousand Oaks: Sage Publications, Inc.

Jensen, I. W., & Gutek, B. A. (1982). Attributions and assignment of responsibility in sexual harassment. *Journal of Social Issues, 38*(4), 121-136.

Kanter, R. M. (1977a). *Men and women of the corporation.* New York: Basic Books, Inc.

Kanter, R. M. (1977b). Some effects of proportions on group life: Skewed sex ratios and responses to token women. *American Journal of Sociology, 82*(5), 965-990.

Kanter, R. M. (1980). *A Tale of "O."* New York: Harper Row.

Katz, R. C., Hannon, R., & Whitten, L. (1996). Effects of gender and situation on the perception of sexual harassment. *Sex Roles, 34*(1/2), 35-42.

Kiefer, J., Rabin, A., & Sorenson, R. C. (2002, November). *Psychometric properties of the Self-Control Schedule and the Self-Control Questionnaire.* Paper presented at the convention of the Association for Advancement of Behavior Therapy, Reno, NV.

Konrad, A. M., & Gutek, B. A. (1986). Impact of work experiences on attitudes toward sexual harassment. *Administrative Science Quarterly, 31*, 422-438.

Konrad, A. M., Winter, S., & Gutek, B. A. (1992). Diversity in work group sex composition: Implications for majority and minority members. *Research in the Sociology of Organizations, 10*, 115-140.

Mazer, D. B., & Percival, E. F. (1989). Ideology or experience? The relationships among perceptions, attitudes, and experiences of sexual harassment in university students. *Sex Roles, 20*(3/4), 135-147.

McKinney, K. (1990). Sexual harassment of university faculty by colleagues and students. *Sex Roles, 23*, (7/8), 421-438.

Minnegerode, F. A. (1976). Attitudes toward women, sex role stereotyping, and locus of control. *Psychological Reports, 38*, 1301-1302.

Pipes, R. B., & LeBov-Keeler, K. (1997). Psychological abuse among college women in exclusive heterosexual dating relationships. *Sex Roles, 36*(9/10), 585-603.

Powell, G. N. (1986). Effects of sex role identity and sex on definitions of sexual harassment. *Sex Roles, 14*(1/2), 9-19.

Pryor, J. B., LaVite, C. M., & Stoller, L. M. (1993). A social psychological analysis of sexual harassment: The person/situation interaction. *Journal of Vocational Behavior, 42*, 68-93.

Rosenbaum, M. (1980a). Individual differences in self-control behaviors and tolerance of painful stimulation. *Journal of Abnormal Psychology, 89*(4), 581-590.

Rosenbaum, M. (1980b). A schedule for assessing self-control behaviors: Preliminary findings. *Behavior Therapy, 11*, 109-121.

Rosenbaum, M. (1990). The role of learned resourcefulness in the self-control of health behavior. In M. Rosenbaum (Ed.), *Learned resourcefulness: On coping skills, self-control, and adaptive behavior.* New York: Springer Publishing Company.

Rosenbaum, M., & Ben-Ari, K. (1985). Learned helplessness and learned resourcefulness: Effects of noncontingent success and failure on individuals differing in self control skills. *Journal of Personality and Social Psychology, 48*(1), 198-215.

Rosenberg, J., Perlstadt, H., & Phillips, W. R. F. (1993). Now that we are here: Discrimination, disparagement, and harassment at work and the experience of women lawyers. *Gender & Society, 7*(3), 415-433.

Schneider, B., & Reichers, A. E. (1983). On the etiology of climates. *Personnel Psychology, 36*, 19-39.

Shapiro, B.L., & Schwarz, J.C. (1997). Date rape: Its relationship to trauma symptoms and sexual self-esteem. *Journal of Interpersonal Violence, 12*, 3, 407-419.

Sorenson, R. C., Mangione-Lambie, M. G.,& Luzio, R. C (1998). Solving the chronic problem of sexual harassment in the workplace: An empirical study of factors affecting employee perceptions and consequences of sexual harassment. *California Western Law Review, 34,* 457-491.

Spector, P. E. (2001). Research methods in industrial and organizational psychology: Data collection and data analysis with special consideration to international issues. In N. Anderson, D. S. Ones, H. K. Sinangil, & C. Viswesvaran (Eds.), *Handbook of industrial and organizational psychology: Vol. 1. Personnel Psychology* (pp. 10- 26). Thousand Oaks, CA: Sage Publications.

Spence, J. T., Helmreich, R. L., & Strapp, J. (1973). A short version of the attitudes toward women scale (AWS). *Bulletin of the Psychonomic Society, 2,* 219-220.

Spence, J. T., Helmreich, R. L., & Strapp, J. (1975). Ratings of self and peers on sex role attributes and their relation to self-esteem and conceptions of masculinity and femininity. *Journal of Personality & Social Psychology, 32,* 29-39.

Stafford, I. P. (1984). Relation of attitudes toward women's roles and occupational behavior to women's self-esteem. *Journal of Counseling Psychology, 31*(3), 332-338.

Stanley, G., Boots, M., & Johnson, C. (1975). Some Australian data on a short version of the attitudes toward women scale (AWS). *Australian Psychologist, 10,* 319-323.

Tangri, S. S., Burt, M. R., & Johnson, L. B. (1982). Sexual harassment at work: Three explanatory models. *Journal of Social Issues, 38*(4), 33-54.

Terpstra, D. E., & Baker, D. D. (1986a). A framework for the study of sexual harassment. *Basic and Applied Social Psychology, 7*(1), 17-34.

Terpstra, D. E., & Baker, D. D. (1986b). Psychological and demographic correlates of perceptions of sexual harassment. *Genetic, Social, and General Psychology Monographs, 112*(4), 461-478.

U.S. Merit Systems Protection Board. (1988). *Sexual harassment in the federal government: An update.* Washington, DC: U.S. Government Printing Office.

U.S. Bureau of Labor Statistics. (1994). *Statistical abstract of the United States, 1994.* Washington, DC: Department of Commerce.

Weiner, R. L., Hurt, L., Russell, B., Mannen, K., & Gasper, C. (1997). Perceptions of sexual harassment: The effects of gender, legal standard, and ambivalent sexism. *Law and Human Behavior, 21*(1), 71-93.

Zohar, D. (1980). Safety climate in industrial organizations: Theoretical and applied implications. *Journal of Applied Psychology, 65*(1), 96-102

Zweig, J. M., Barber, B. L., & Eccles, J. S. (1997). Sexual coercion and well-being in young adulthood: Comparison by gender and college status. *Journal of Interpersonal Violence, 12*(2), 291-308.

The Emotionally Abusive Workplace

Michele Koonin

Thomas M. Green

SUMMARY. Workplace violence, in its many forms, constitutes a form of abuse that affects the mental health of victims by creating stress that ultimately becomes overwhelming. One of the most difficult and debilitating aspects of workplace abuse is that the victim is often seen as the problem and may take responsibility for the abuse. This paper examines two forms of workplace abuse, "bullying" and "mobbing," and offers suggestions for recognizing these forms of abuse. The paper concludes that organizations must have in place processes and procedures to address workplace abuse not only to protect its workers but also because it is in their financial self-interest to do so. *[Article copies available for a fee from The Haworth Document Delivery Service: 1-800-HAWORTH. E-mail address: <docdelivery@haworthpress.com> Website: <http://www.HaworthPress.com> © 2004 by The Haworth Press, Inc. All rights reserved.]*

KEYWORDS. Workplace violence, bullying, emotional abuse

Address correspondence to: Michele Koonin, LCSW, MBA, BCD, Director, American Continuing Education and Workplace Training Institute, LLC, 2725 Congress Street, Suite 2C, San Diego, CA 92110.

[Haworth co-indexing entry note]: "The Emotionally Abusive Workplace." Koonin, Michele, and Thomas M. Green. Co-published simultaneously in *Journal of Emotional Abuse* (The Haworth Maltreatment & Trauma Press, an imprint of The Haworth Press, Inc.) Vol. 4, No. 3/4, 2004, pp. 71-79; and: *Aggression in Organizations: Violence, Abuse, and Harassment at Work and in Schools* (ed: Robert Geffner et al.) The Haworth Maltreatment & Trauma Press, an imprint of The Haworth Press, Inc., 2004, pp. 71-79. Single or multiple copies of this article are available for a fee from The Haworth Document Delivery Service [1-800-HAWORTH, 9:00 a.m. - 5:00 p.m. (EST). E-mail address: docdelivery@haworthpress.com].

Digital Object Identifier: 10.1300/J135v04n03_05

Workplace violence is receiving attention on an ever-increasing basis. We are becoming more aware of the aspects of workplace violence, the forms of workplace violence, and the costs of workplace violence. But what about the long term emotional costs of workplace violence? What are those costs, how are they measured, and what can be done to recognize them, deal with them, and ultimately prevent them?

WORKPLACE ABUSE

Workplace abuse can be defined as a pattern of brutalizing and dehumanizing a person at work (DelBel, 2003; Einarsen & Skogstad, 1996; Hoel, Rayner, & Cooper, 1999; Olweus, 1999; Hoel & Cooper, 2000). Unfortunately, it is epidemic and most workplaces would be labeled as abusive in one form or another. Work abuse affects mental health by creating stress that ultimately becomes overwhelming. There are five levels of stress that can lead to debilitation (Wyatt, 2001). They are:

1. The abuse–in whatever form it appears
2. One's inability to protest it and protect from it
3. Being blamed and feeling guilty for reacting against it
4. Having to live in denial of the abuse happening
5. The sense of guilt for having a reaction, which disrupts one's functioning and decreases functioning.

One of the most difficult and disabling aspects of workplace abuse is that the victim is often seen as the problem, not the perpetrator, and that the victim goes along with this thinking and takes on the responsibility for the abusing. Workplace aggression comes in many forms. The 10 most common forms are:

1. Talking about someone behind his/her back
2. Interrupting others while they are speaking or working
3. Flaunting status or authority, acting in a condescending manner
4. Belittling someone's opinion to others
5. Failing to return phone calls or respond to memos
6. Giving others the silent treatment
7. Yelling, insults, and shouting
8. Verbal forms of sexual harassment
9. Staring, dirty looks, or other negative eye contact
10. Intentionally damning with faint praise (Neuman, 1998, cited in DeBare, 1998; see also Einarsen & Skogstad, 1996; Crick & Grotpeter, 1995; Björkqvist, Lagerspetz, & Kaukiainen, 1992)

Victims of workplace violence are more likely to be introverted, submissive, demonstrate little independence, and be highly conscientious, anxious, and neurotic (Coyne, Seigne, & Randall, 2000). Environment factors, such as organizational climate and working arrangements, also help to explain workplace victimization (LeBlanc & Kelloway, 2002; Smith & Shu, 2000; Eslea & Smith, 1998; Zapf, Knorz, & Kulla, 1996; Einarsen, Raknes, & Matthiesen, 1994). For more statistics and information on targets and perpetrators of workplace violence, see Gault (this volume).

Some effects of workplace aggression on the individual include: Fear reactions, depression, anxiety, sleep disturbances, gastrointestinal symptoms (Rogers & Kelloway, 1997; Schat & Kelloway, 2000), suicide (Namie, 2000), negative workplace attitude and job dissatisfaction (Budd, Arvey, & Lawless, 1996), job neglect (Barling, Rogers, & Kelloway, 2001; Schat & Kelloway, 2000), and decreased job performance (Barling et al., 2001; Budd et al., 1996). Costs to organizations include: Recruitment and training of replacement workers; overtime; reduced morale and productivity; health care expenses (medical and psychiatric); increased errors; legal fees, including those related to harassment, hostile work environment, disability, and workers compensation; administrative costs for investigating complaints, responding to staffing, etc.; and decreased public image and trust (Lybecker & Sofield, 2000).

BULLYING/MOBBING

There are new phrases for these kinds of behaviors. One is "workplace bullying," introduced by Gary and Ruth Namie (Tarrant, 2000). They describe workplace bullying as hurtful and repeated mistreatment of people by their bosses, co-workers, and/or subordinates. Another phrase that is gaining attention is "mobbing" (Davenport, Schwartz, & Elliot, 1999). Mobbing is a ganging up on someone using rumor, innuendo, discrediting, humiliation, isolation, and intimidation in a concentrated and direct manner. Mobbing is a non-sexual, non-racial form of workplace harassment that is subtle and subversive (Hubert & Veldhoven, 2001; Zapf et al., 1996).

The first investigations of mobbing occurred in the mid-1980s (Leymann & Gustavsson, 1984; Leymann, 1993) in Scandinavia; mobbing appears in the research literature in Western Europe and the United States only after 1992 (Groeblinghoff & Becker, 1996). Mobbing appears in all levels, from superior to subordinate, and subordinate to superior. Mobbing occurs repeatedly over the time span of weeks, months, or years (Hubert, 1997). In mobbing, the person who is being attacked is portrayed as the person at fault (Invernizzi, 2000). The goal is to force the target out of the workplace.

There are no good estimates of the frequency of mobbing in the United States. The most comprehensive study to date (Hogh & Dofradottir, 2001) involves a subset of a randomized sample of 4,000 Danish adult citizens. Hogh and Dofradottir (2001) found that 19% of those who had been employed within the previous three months had been subjected to gossip and slander during the previous year; 6.5% had been subjected to malicious teasing. Approximately 2% had been slandered and/or teased between two times a month and daily during the past year. In addition, approximately 2% of the respondents had been bullied–82.8% by colleagues, 48.6% by a superior, 25.7% by subordinates, and 42.8% by customers/clients/pupils.

Hubert and Veldhoven (2001) found that the prevalence of mobbing by colleagues ranged from 10.1% in financial institutions to 21.7% in industry. Aggression from one's boss was highest among industrial workers (12.1%), followed by the construction industry (11%), services (10.6%), education (10.4%), transport (10.1%), and public utilities (9.3%). The prevalence rate in financial institutions was 5.1%.

There are several factors associated with the onset and continuation of mobbing. They are:

1. The office politics and corporate culture
2. Unclear expectations
3. Dishonesty
4. Withheld information
5. Discouraging responses
6. Tolerance of poor performance
7. Being taken for granted (Davenport et al., 1999).

To add insult to injury, emotional abuse is often ignored or denied. The abuse is put back onto the victim with statements such as "Don't be so sensitive," "I have no idea of what you are talking about," and "You are misinterpreting what I said." In other words, the problem becomes the responsibility of the victim and is ignored by the perpetrator. One of the responsibilities of any organization is to help members understand and recognize emotional abuse when it happens. Some examples of this form of workplace abuse include, but are not limited to:

1. Feelings of the target are ignored or belittled
2. The target's group of origin is ridiculed and insulted
3. Approval, appreciation, and acceptance are withheld

4. There is a constant pattern of criticism, name calling, and subtle forms of verbal abuse
5. Personal spaces are invaded, "searched," or messed up on the pretense of "looking for something." The result of this kind of invasion is a feeling of being totally unsafe in all areas of the workplace
6. Friends and associates of the target are singled out for criticism and/or excessive attention/scrutiny
7. There is public and private humiliation
8. Attempts are made to keep the target from assigned tasks
9. Good work is described as second-rate or not good enough
10. Criticism is offered repeatedly without remedies for improvement
11. There is a refusal of sharing information or resources
12. Information or achievements of the target are "shared" or "given away"
13. The target is blamed for any problems (real or imagined)
14. Personal property of the target is discarded without permission. Excuses are given for the behavior instead of apologies
15. All of the above behavior is denied and used as signs of the target being "crazy" (Davenport et al., 1999).

A specific example of mobbing involves Mrs. F., a 49-year-old director of the construction authority who answered directly to the mayor. A newly elected mayor began the workplace assault subtly by giving orders without explanation, some of which could not be performed legally. She became isolated within the administration: Her requests went unanswered; she was excluded from meetings; her co-workers excluded her from social events to which she had been previously invited; and critical information for doing her job was withheld. The abuse peaked with criminal charges against her, which were later dropped, and a disciplinary tribunal to force her out of her position (Groeblinghoff & Becker, 1996).

Unfortunately, this kind of behavior is often ignored or excused by organizations. While measures are being taken to ensure that physical violence is immediately addressed and rectified in the workplace, verbal and emotional abuse are far too often ignored or excused by supervisors and the organization as a whole. Difficult situations are allowed to simmer, often until they boil over into the physical arena.

The consequences of this laizzez-faire behavior can be dramatic. Emotional and verbal abuse takes a toll on the recipient of the abuse. Because the behavior is not interrupted, this toll becomes cumulative until the recipient cannot take any more. As the abuse becomes more dramatic and cumulative, various consequences can occur.

In the example of Mrs. F., above, she became confused, depressed, and anxious. She had suicidal thoughts and suffered severe or moderately severe irritability, inner unrest, restless legs, hypersensitivity to coldness, lower back pain, nausea, weakness, and dizziness (Groeblinghoff & Becker, 1996).

This kind of abuse occurs in many patterns. It may be supervisor to supervisee; supervisee to supervisor; co-worker to co-worker; customer to employee (Lybecker & Sofield, 2000). Because it is a subtle kind of behavior, this kind of abuse is often hard to see or prove. It may happen "behind closed doors," and the victim may be afraid to say anything about what is going on. All too often, the victim takes on the responsibility for the bullying behavior and attempts to change himself or herself in an effort to "fix" things. This kind of reaction keeps the real aggressor from being identified and dealt with in a timely manner.

The reasons for this kind of behavior are varied and many. Some abusers are sociopathic and have no compassion for others. Some abusers may feel threatened in their positions and they bully the ones they feel may have "an edge" on them. Behavioral changes often precede workplace violence. These changes may include increased agitation, pacing, sudden unusual calmness, shouting, hostility, tearfulness, clenched fists, invasion of body space, or expression of paranoid thoughts (Brennan, 1996).

Many abusers may come from dysfunctional backgrounds and may have been the victims of abuse themselves, including bullying in school (Smith, Singer, Hoel, & Cooper, 2003). However, they will never get the help they need if their behavior is not identified and efforts made to change it.

CONCLUSIONS

Unfortunately, some of the recent trends in business to focus on excellence and quality have increased the pressure on workers, line managers, and supervisors, creating an environment ripe for bullying (Lewis, 1999). Institutionalized bullying results when an organization values compliance over individual identity, reinforced by threatening employment security (Liefooghe & Davey, 2001).

Organizations need to take inventory of their corporate cultures and make changes. Workplace abuse occurs because it is allowed to occur, and it continues because it is not stopped. There need to be policies and procedures in place for dealing with workplace abuse. Policies need to be instituted that declare zero tolerance for abuse of any form. Procedures need to be put into place for reporting and investigating incidents of workplace abuse. Finally, training of all employees needs to be given for the purpose of recognizing, dealing with, and preventing any and all forms of workplace abuse (for example, see Occupational Safety and Health Administration, 2004).

Organizations need to address mobbing and bullying beyond the interpersonal level as an organizational issue. Human resources departments need to understand the wider practices that contribute to workplace abuse and focus on employee well being.

The Occupational Safety and Health Administration (OSHA) has identified environmental conditions associated with workplace assaults and have implemented control strategies in some work settings. However, OSHA has yet to initiate rulemaking in this area (OSHA, 2004). Developing policies and procedures have fallen to the states and to individual employers. For example, the state of Minnesota has developed policy guidelines for addressing workplace violence that include implementing a reporting system, developing formal written policies, establishing assessment teams, and instituting training programs and emergency protocols (Minnesota Department of Labor and Industry, 2004).

Why should organizations do this? The answer is simple: Because it is cost effective. Workplace abuse costs money in the forms of lost revenues, lost productivity, absenteeism, employee turnover, and lawsuits (Porteous, 2002). Like any other problem, when workplace abuse is dealt with in early stages or through preventive steps, the cost is much less than when the problem has grown to gigantic proportions. Just as nastiness can beget nastiness, so can kindness beget kindness. Remember: Satisfied employees are more productive employees than unsatisfied employees.

REFERENCES

Barling, J., Rogers, A. G., & Kelloway, E. K. (2001). Behind closed doors: In-home workers' experience of sexual harassment and workplace violence. *Journal of Occupational Health Psychology, 6*, 255-269.

Björkqvist, K., Lagerspetz, K. M. J., & Kaukiainen, A. (1992). Do girls manipulate and boys fight? Developmental trends in regard to direct and indirect aggression. *Aggressive Behavior, 18*, 117-127.

Brennan, W. J. (1996). Coping with aggression and violence at work. *The Safety & Health Practitioner, 14*(8), 46-49.

Budd, J. W., Arvey, R. D., & Lawless, P. (1996). Correlates and consequences of workplace violence. *Journal of Occupational Health Psychology, 1*, 197-210.

Coyne, I., Seigne, E., & Randall, P. E. (2000). Personality traits as predictors of workplace bully-victim status. *Proceedings of the British Psychological Society Occupational Psychology Conference*, 193-198.

Crick, N. R., & Grotpeter, J. K. (1995). Relational aggression, gender, and social-psychological adjustment. *Child Development, 66*, 710-722.

Davenport, N., Schwartz, R. D., & Elliot, G. P. (1999). *Mobbing: Emotional abuse in the American workplace*. Ames, IA: Civil Society Publishing.

DeBare, I. (1998, October 19). Getting bullied at work: Two psychologists initiate campaign to tackle problem. *San Francisco Chronicle*. Retrieved January 20, 2004, from http://sfgate.com/cgi-bin/article.cgi?file=/chronicle/archive/1998/10/19/BU72746.DTL

DelBel, J. C. (2003). De-escalating workplace aggression. *Nursing Management, 34*(9), 31-34.

Einarsen, S., Raknes, B. I., & Matthiesen, S. B. (1994). Bullying and harassment at work and their relationships to work environment quality: An exploratory study. *European Journal of Work and Organizational Psychology, 4*, 381-401.

Einarsen, S., & Skogstad, A. (1996). Bullying at work: Epidemiological findings in public and private organizations. *European Journal of Work and Organizational Psychology, 5*, 185-201.

Eslea, M. J., & Smith, P. K. (1998). The long-term effectiveness of anti-bullying work in primary schools. *Educational Research, 40*, 203-218.

Gault, D. L. (2004). Creating respectful, violence-free, productive workplaces: A community-level response to workplace violence. *Journal of Emotional Abuse, 4*(3/4), 119-138.

Groeblinghoff, D., & Becker, M. (1996). A cast study of mobbing and the clinical treatment of mobbing victims. *European Journal of Work and Organizational Psychology, 5*(2), 277-294.

Hoel, H., & Cooper, C. L. (2000). Working with victims of workplace bullying. In H. Kemshall, & J. Pritchard (Eds.), *Good practice in working with victims of violence* (pp. 101-118). London: Kingsley.

Hoel, H., Rayner, C., & Cooper, C. L. (1999). Workplace bullying. *International Review of Industrial and Organizational Psychology, 14*, 195-230.

Hogh, A., & Dofradottir, A. (2001). Coping with bullying in the workplace. *European Journal of Work and Organizational Psychology, 10*(4), 485-496.

Hubert, A. B. (1997). *Mobbing: Systematic bullying at a mixed production-office organization–A study on prevalence, observation, causes, and consequences of mobbing*. Leiden, The Netherlands: Faculteit der Sociale Wetenschappen.

Hubert, A. B., & Veldhoven, M. V. (2001). Risk sectors for undesirable behaviours and mobbing. *European Journal of Work and Organizational Psychology, 10*(4), 415-425.

Invernizzi, G. (2000). New concepts on the workplace relationships: The so called "mobbing." *New Trends in Experimental & Clinical Psychiatry, 16*(1-4), 5-6.

LeBlanc, M. M., & Kelloway, E. K. (2002). Predictors and outcomes of workplace violence and aggression. *Journal of Applied Psychology, 87*(3), 444-453.

Lewis, D. (1999). *UK workplace bullying: HRM, friend or foe?* Paper presented at the Ninth European Congress on Work and Organizational Psychology, Helsinki, Finland.

Leymann, H. (1993). *Mobbing. Psychoterror at the workplace, and how one can defend oneself*. Reinbek bei Hamburg: Rowohlt.

Leymann, H., & Gustavsson, B. (1984). *Psychological violence in workplaces. Two explorative studies*. Stockholm: Arbetskyddsstyrelsen.

Liefooghe, A. P. D., & Davey, K. M. (2001). Accounts of workplace bullying: The role of the organization. *European Journal of Work and Organizational Psychology, 10*(4), 375-392.

Lybecker, C., & Sofield, L. (2000). Verbal abuse. *Surgical Services Management, 6*(6), 32-38.

Minnesota Department of Labor and Industry. (2004). *Workplace violence prevention: A comprehensive guide for employers and employees.* Retrieved March 21, 2004, from http://www.doli.state.mn.us/vguide2.html

Namie, G. (2000, September). *U.S. Hostile Workplace Survey 2000.* The Workplace Bullying & Trauma Institute. Retrieved July 18, 2003, from http://bullyinginstitute.org/home/twd/bb/res/bullyinst.pdf.

Occupational Safety and Health Administration. (2004). *Elements of a workplace violence prevention program.* U.S. Department of Labor. Retrieved January 19, 2004, from http://www.osha.gov/workplace_violence/wrkplaceViolence.PartII.html.

Olweus, D. (1999). Sweden. In P. K. Smith, Y. Morita, J. Junger-Tas, D. Olweus, R. Catalano, & P. Slee (Eds.), *The nature of school bullying: A cross-national perspective* (pp. 2-27). London: Routledge.

Porteous, J. (2002). Bullying at work: The legal position. *Managerial, 44*(4), 77-90.

Rogers, K., & Kelloway, E. K. (1997). Violence at work: Personal and organizational outcomes. *Journal of Occupational Health Psychology, 2,* 63-71.

Schat, A. C. H., & Kelloway, E. K. (2000). The effects of perceived control on the outcomes of workplace aggression and violence. *Journal of Occupational Health Psychology, 4,* 386-402.

Smith, P. K., & Shu, S. (2000). What good schools can do about bullying: Findings from a survey in English schools after a decade of research and action. *Childhood, 7,* 193-212.

Smith, P. K., Singer, M., Hoel, H., & Cooper, C. L. (2003). Victimization in the school and the workplace: Are there any links? *British Journal of Psychology, 94*(2), 175-188.

Tarrant, D. (2000, October 9). Bully bosses: Businesses are under pressure to curtail overbearing tyrants of the workplace. *San Diego Union Tribune,* p. C1.

Wyatt, J. (2001). Understanding work abuse: Violating human needs at work. Retrieved July 18, 2003, from http://pw1.netcom.com/~workfam1/unders1.htm.

Zapf, D., Knorz, C., & Kulla, M. (1996). On the relationship between mobbing factors, and job content, social work environment, and health outcomes. *European Journal of Work and Organizational Psychology, 5,* 215-237.

Identifying the Aggressive Personality

Shawn M. Bergman
Michael D. McIntyre
Lawrence R. James

SUMMARY. Acts of workplace aggression by coworkers take a tremendous toll on organizations and their employees. This paper explores the thought processes used by aggressive individuals to rationalize hostile behaviors and discusses various types of workplace aggression. This paper also presents a new personality test, the Conditional Reasoning Test of Aggression, which addresses some of the shortcomings of self-report personality tests that have traditionally been used to identify and screen out aggressive applicants. *[Article copies available for a fee from The Haworth Document Delivery Service: 1-800-HAWORTH. E-mail address: <docdelivery@haworthpress.com> Website: <http://www.HaworthPress.com> © 2004 by The Haworth Press, Inc. All rights reserved.]*

KEYWORDS. Conditional reasoning, employee selection, personality, workplace aggression

Address correspondence to: Michael D. McIntyre, PhD, The University of Tennessee, 408 Stokely Management Center, Knoxville, TN 37996-0545 (E-mail: mmcintyr @utk.edu).

The authors would like to thank the editors and reviewers for their comments and suggestions on earlier versions of this article.

[Haworth co-indexing entry note]: "Identifying the Aggressive Personality." Bergman, Shawn M., Michael D. McIntyre, and Lawrence R. James. Co-published simultaneously in *Journal of Emotional Abuse* (The Haworth Maltreatment & Trauma Press, an imprint of The Haworth Press, Inc.) Vol. 4, No. 3/4, 2004, pp. 81-93; and: *Aggression in Organizations: Violence, Abuse, and Harassment at Work and in Schools* (ed: Robert Geffner et al.) The Haworth Maltreatment & Trauma Press, an imprint of The Haworth Press, Inc., 2004, pp. 81-93. Single or multiple copies of this article are available for a fee from The Haworth Document Delivery Service [1-800-HAWORTH, 9:00 a.m. - 5:00 p.m. (EST). E-mail address: docdelivery@ haworthpress.com].

Workplace aggression, including workplace violence, is a problem for both employers and employees. Overt and covert acts of workplace aggression cost companies billions of dollars annually (Bennett & Robinson, 2000) and exact a tremendous toll on the emotional and physical health of employees (LeBlanc & Kelloway, 2002; Rogers & Kelloway, 1997; Schat & Kelloway, 2000). Hostile workplace acts have also been linked to numerous organizational outcomes, including job dissatisfaction, intentions to quit, and decreased productivity (Barling, Rogers, & Kelloway, 2001; Budd, Arvey, & Lawless, 1996; LeBlanc & Kelloway, 2002).

For the purposes of this paper, we differentiate between "aggression in the workplace" and "workplace aggression." Aggression in the workplace refers broadly to aggression committed *by anyone* (e.g., stranger, customer, client, or employee) in a place of work. In contrast, workplace aggression refers more narrowly to hostile acts committed by an individual employed by the organization. This paper focuses on the latter.

One way for organizations to address the problem of workplace aggression is to reduce the number of aggression-prone individuals that it brings into the organization. That is, organizations can try to identify and screen out aggression-prone individuals in the hiring process. The logic behind this strategy is that reducing the number of aggression-prone individuals will lower the probability of aggressive behavior.

There are numerous personality tests available to organizations for identifying aggression-prone individuals, including the California Personality Inventory (Gough, 1956), the Minnesota Multiphasic Personality Inventory-2 (Butcher, Dahlstrom, Graham, Tellegen, & Kaemmer, 1989), the Multidimensional Personality Questionnaire (Tellegen & Walker, 1994), the Revised NEO Personality Inventory (Costa & McCrae, 1992), and the State-Trait Anger Expression Inventory (Spielberger, 1996). The aforementioned tests are all direct or self-report tests composed of straightforward questions that alert respondents to what is being measured. The validity of these tests depends on the ability and willingness of respondents to describe themselves accurately. Illustrative items from these tests include "I have a violent temper," "I often get disgusted with people I have to deal with," "I often get angry at the way people treat me," and "At times, I feel like smashing things."

An obvious shortcoming of direct or self-report measures in a hiring context is that respondents may alter their answers, either consciously or unconsciously, in an effort to present themselves in a favorable light to prospective employers (Heneman, Heneman, & Judge, 1997; James & Mazerolle, 2002). This response distortion is likely to undermine the effectiveness of self-report tests at identifying aggression-prone individuals in the hiring process.

This paper presents a new, indirect personality instrument that offers an alternative to self-report tests for identifying aggression-prone individuals. Before introducing the Conditional Reasoning Test of Aggression, however, we will first discuss the personality trait of aggression and various forms of aggressive behavior in the workplace.

THE AGGRESSIVE PERSONALITY

While there are numerous causes of aggressive behavior, it is our contention that a primary cause of such behavior is the personality trait of aggression. Individuals with aggressive personalities are more likely to engage in hostile workplace acts than non-aggressive individuals (Douglas & Martinko, 2001; Frost, 2003; Glomb & Liao, 2003; James & Mazerolle, 2002; Jockin, Arvey, & McGue, 2001; Neuman & Baron, 1998). The following description of the aggressive personality illustrates how the trait of aggression operates to facilitate aggressive behavior.

The aggressive personality includes both a need component and a cognitive component. From a need perspective, the aggressive personality denotes a desire or motive to overcome opposition forcefully, to fight, to revenge an injury, to attack another with intent to injure or kill, and to oppose forcefully or punish another (Murray, 1938). Accompanying the need to aggress are both implicit and explicit cognitions that influence how aggressive individuals view and interact with the world (James & Mazerolle, 2002; Winter, John, Stewart, Klohnen, & Duncan, 1998). Contemporary views of the aggressive personality suggest that aggressive individuals: (a) often view some form of aggression as the most effective way to deal with frustrating situations and anger; (b) dislike the target of aggressive acts; (c) desire to inflict some type of harm on the target; and (d) lack strong control over their aggressive impulses (Bandura, 1973; Baron & Richardson, 1994; Baumeister, Smart, & Boden, 1996; Berkowitz, 1993; Crick & Dodge, 1994; Gay, 1993; Huesmann, 1988; Millon, 1990; O'Leary-Kelly, Griffin, & Glew, 1996).

Work by James and colleagues suggests that not only do aggressive individuals respond to evocative situations in a more hostile manner, they also use different analytic processes to make sense of the world than non-aggressive individuals (James, 1998; James & Mazerolle, 2002; James & McIntyre, 2000). For example, non-aggressive individuals' reasoning processes are bounded by cultural norms and values that define socially adaptive behavior in our society (James & Mazerolle, 2002; Wright & Mischel, 1987). These norms and values shape and guide the inferences that non-aggressive people make about what is reasonable behavior. Conclusions that non-aggressive individuals draw tend to be consistent with cultural norms and ideologies and are thus thought of as sensible and rational (Kuhn, 1991).

In contrast, the analytic processes used by aggressive individuals are typically bounded by a different set of values. Aggressive individuals tend to have an unrecognized bias to see malevolent intent as the most reasonable explanation for the actions of others (Anderson, 1994; Crick & Dodge, 1994; Dodge & Coie, 1987; Tedeschi & Nesler, 1993; Toch, 1993) and have a propensity to implicitly believe that they are victims of exploitation or oppression by powerful others. These beliefs guide a confirmatory search for evidence supporting the idea that they are being victimized, which is used to justify their acts of aggression as legitimate strikes against oppression (Averill, 1993; Finnegan, 1997; Tedeschi & Nesler, 1993; Toch, 1993). Aggressive individuals also have a tendency to characterize targets of their hostile acts as immoral or untrustworthy, making the targets more deserving of such treatment (Averill, 1993; Gay, 1993; Toch, 1993).

Additionally, aggressive individuals interpret interactions with others as contests to establish dominance (Anderson, 1994; Baron & Richardson, 1994; Crick & Dodge, 1994; Gay, 1993; Hogan & Hogan, 1989; Millon, 1990; Tedeschi & Nesler, 1993; Wright & Mischel, 1987). Thus, aggressive people may believe that behaving in a hostile manner is an act of strength or bravery that gains respect from others and that not acting aggressively shows weakness and invites others to take advantage of them. Furthermore, the thought processes of aggressive individuals focus on how to seek retribution and avenge the perceived disrespect that they have suffered at the hands of others (Baumeister et al., 1996). Aggression is judged to be reasonable and justified because it offers a means to restore respect and to exact restitution for these perceived wrongs (Bradbury & Fincham, 1990; Dodge, 1986; Laursen & Collins, 1994; Nisbett, 1993).

Having described the aggressive personality, we now turn our attention to workplace aggression. While violence gets the lion's share of media attention, workplace aggression takes many other more common, insidious forms.

FORMS OF WORKPLACE AGGRESSION

Workplace aggression includes any form of behavior by a current or former employee that is intended to harm coworkers or the organization (Folger & Baron, 1996). Clearly, the most dramatic kinds of workplace aggression are physical and verbal attacks. Thankfully, however, these types of workplace aggression have a relatively low rate of occurrence. Budd et al. (1996) found that less than three percent of workers were physically attacked and less than eight percent were verbally threatened in a single year. Thus, extreme acts of hostility do not adequately represent the full gamut of workplace aggression (Baron & Richardson, 1994; Borum, 1996; Folger & Baron, 1996; Neuman & Baron, 1998).

Researchers have recognized that less dramatic, indirect forms of workplace aggression are more common. In fact, it has been suggested that most delinquent and counterproductive behaviors are actually intended to harm an organization and/or its employees (Bennett & Robinson, 2000; Robinson & Bennett, 1995; Skarlicki & Folger, 1997). Indirect forms of workplace aggression include early and disruptive attrition, showing up late or skipping work, lying, stealing, asocial conduct, spreading rumors, unreliable job performance, sabotage of projects or machinery, vandalism, and failure to issue timely warnings of impending physical or financial danger (Baron & Richardson, 1994; Bennett & Robinson, 2000; Buss, 1961; Folger & Baron, 1996; Hogan & Hogan, 1989; Jockin et al., 2001; LeBlanc & Kelloway, 2002; Neuman & Baron, 1998; O'Leary-Kelly et al., 1996; Robinson & Bennett, 1995).

Aggressive individuals use these passive forms of workplace aggression to exact revenge for a perceived injustice (Greenberg, 1990; Skarlicki & Folger, 1997). Such behaviors are intended to impede productivity, undermine authority, disrupt work schedules, weaken morale, encourage rebellious behavior, and "get even" with a boss or coworkers (James, 1998; James & Mazerolle, 2002; Pearson, 1998; Rotundo & Sackett, 2002; Tepper, Duffy, & Shaw, 2001).

To avoid punishment, aggressive individuals seldom engage in outright violent or aggressive behaviors that are easily detectable. Rather, they focus on indirect, passive-aggressive behaviors such as coming to work late, stealing from those they see as guilty of injustices, or lying to authority figures. These behaviors are often not seen as aggressive because aggressive individuals can easily conceal their hostile intentions. Subsequently, what is truly an indirect form of workplace aggression is attributed to nonhostile motives (Neuman & Baron, 1998).

While there is no claim that aggression is the only latent construct underlying behaviors such as habitual absences, low performance, theft, early and disruptive attrition, lying, and poor conduct, these acts are often intended to harm coworkers, supervisors, and/or company departments (Baron & Richardson, 1994; Bennett & Robinson, 2000; Buss, 1961; Folger & Baron, 1996; Hogan & Hogan, 1989; Jockin et al., 2001; LeBlanc & Kelloway, 2002; Neuman & Baron, 1998; O'Leary-Kelly et al., 1996; Robinson & Bennett, 1995). When accompanied by harmful intent, it is reasonable to consider these types of counterproductive acts as behavioral indicators of workplace aggression.

Additionally, these passive and indirect types of aggression are thought to precede more intense and destructive forms of violence (see LeBlanc & Kelloway, 2002).

Regardless of the form it takes, workplace aggression exacts tremendous monetary and psychological costs on both employees and employers (Bennett & Robinson, 2000; LeBlanc & Kelloway, 2002; Rogers & Kelloway, 1997; Schat & Kelloway, 2000). Given the adverse effects of workplace hostility and aggression, it is in an organization's best interest to attempt to screen out aggressive employees in the hiring process. The following section introduces a methodology that can be used to identify those individuals who think and reason in an aggressive manner.

IDENTIFYING AGGRESSIVE INDIVIDUALS

The Conditional Reasoning Test of Aggression (CRTA) is based on evidence suggesting that aggressive individuals' thought processes are designed to justify actions that are intended to inflict harm or injury (Bandura, 1973; Baron & Richardson, 1994; Baumeister et al., 1996; Berkowitz, 1993; Crick & Dodge, 1994; Gay, 1993; Huesmann, 1988; Millon, 1990; O'Leary-Kelly et al., 1996). James (1998) suggested that aggressive people are generally unaware of these biases and offered the term "justification mechanisms" to identify the implicit cognitive structures that guide and shape aggressive individuals' reasoning. However, by virtue of being implicit and hidden from introspection, justification mechanisms (JMs) cannot be assessed by the popular method of self-report (Nisbett & Wilson, 1977; Schwarz, 1999; Winter et al., 1998). That is, people cannot describe or report mental processes of which they are unaware.

Therefore, James and colleagues developed a new personality measure, the CRTA, which assesses the extent to which JMs for aggression implicitly shape an individual's reasoning (James & McIntyre, 2000). This measurement system is based on a novel type of inductive reasoning problem, analogous to traditional inductive reasoning tasks, that asks respondents to determine which general conclusion follows most reasonably from a set of premises (e.g., Sternberg, 1982). Respondents believe that a multiple-choice CRTA problem is comprised of objectively true and false conclusions, when the choices are really comprised of a logical conclusion drawn from JMs that justify aggression, a logical conclusion drawn from the non-aggressive counterparts to JMs, and two illogical conclusions (see Appendix for a CRTA example problem). As respondents use their analytic skills to identify the most logical conclusion, their reasoning is guided by their implicit assumptions about what constitutes rational behavior. What respondents judge to be the most reasonable answers are conditional on whether or not underlying biases, JMs, implicitly shape their reasoning processes.

Unlike traditional, self-report personality tests, the CRTA is expected to be resistant to response distortion. The CRTA is presented as a true inductive reasoning test with respondents asked to find the most logical answer. Thus, respondents are focused on trying to find the right answers to a reasoning test rather than the socially desirable answers to a personality test (see James, 1998; James & McIntyre, 2000; James & Mazerolle, 2002).

The scoring of the 22-item CRTA is designed such that higher scores indicate that JMs for aggression are more instrumental in guiding and shaping a respondent's reasoning. Individuals with higher scores on the CRTA, indicating more aggressive personalities, are better prepared to rationalize aggression and thus are expected to have a significantly greater probability of engaging in aggressive acts in both work and non-work settings than individuals with lower CRTA scores (see James, 1998; James & Mazerolle, 2002; James & McIntyre, 2000, for a more in depth discussion of the development, psychometric properties, and scoring of the CRTA).

The CRTA has been shown to effectively identify aggressive individuals and significantly predict behavioral indicators of aggression inside and outside of the workplace (Frost, 2003; James & Mazerolle, 2002; James & McIntyre, 2000). Unlike most studies of aggression, these research initiatives used actual behavioral criteria for their dependent variables. For example, research in the workplace has demonstrated that both nuclear facility operators and shipping package handlers with higher CRTA scores were more likely to be absent from work, $r = .42$ and $r = .34$, respectively. Likewise, temporary workers with higher scores tended to refuse their work assignments or fail to report to their workplace assignments, $r = .43$. New restaurant employees with higher CRTA scores were more likely to quit within 30 days of being hired, $r = .32$ (see James & Mazerolle, 2002; James & McIntyre, 2000). Additionally, studies conducted outside of the workplace, but in conditions analogous to situations that occur on the job, have shown that participants who scored higher on the CRTA were more likely to steal office supplies from the laboratory after receiving negative feedback about their performance, $r = .64$, and were willing to lie about the number of points they earned for participating in out-of-class activities, $r = .49$ (see James & Mazerolle, 2002; James & McIntyre, 2000). Finally, individuals with more JMs in place to justify aggression had an increased likelihood of being involved in both physical, $r = .36$, and verbal, $r = .24$, altercations in intramural athletic competitions (Frost, 2003).

Together these research findings suggest that the CRTA offers a valid and efficient system for identifying individuals who are prone to commit both direct and indirect acts of aggression. These findings also support the notion that an aggressive personality underlies hostile and anti-social workplace behaviors. Accurately identifying aggressive individuals in the hiring process could reduce workplace aggression.

DISCUSSION

This paper explored the reasoning processes used by aggressive employees that lead them to engage in workplace aggression. For example, individuals who attack their coworkers often regard their violence as justifiable retaliation for having been victimized by their peers. The train of thought leading to this conclusion typically begins by framing interactions with coworkers as contests to establish dominance (Gay, 1993; James & Mazerolle, 2002; Tedeschi & Nesler, 1993). Submissive coworkers are regarded as easily intimidated and influenced, while assertive coworkers are viewed as potential bullies and tyrants. Aggressive individuals then reason that confronting potential intimidators is more rational than cooperating because cooperation shows weakness and invites harassment and mistreatment (Anderson, 1994; Baron & Richardson, 1994; Crick & Dodge, 1994).

To further justify the confrontation, aggressive individuals seek out evidence of the coworker's hostile intent. If a coworker offers assistance on a project, an aggressive individual may reason that the true intent of the offer is to gain access to his or her work and to sabotage it. If sabotage is not possible, then the aggressive individual may believe that the offer of assistance was just a way for the coworker to take or share in the credit for the work's success. Aggressive individuals also believe a coworker will attempt to undermine their credibility with the supervisor by blaming them whenever something goes wrong.

Aggressive individuals also progressively focus on how to get even for the wounded pride and disrespect that they have suffered due to perceived injustices. Thus, some form of aggression is judged to be reasonable and justified because it offers a means to restore respect and to exact restitution for these perceived wrongs (Bradbury & Fincham, 1990; Dodge, 1986; Laursen & Collins, 1994; Nisbett, 1993). Acts of retribution can take many forms, including verbal aggression (e.g., threats, character assassination, intimidation, spreading of malicious gossip), physical violence (e.g., shoving, fighting, attacks with weapons), or passive-aggressive acts (e.g., intentional nonattendance at team meetings, deliberate failure to return messages).

In fact, overtly hostile incidents constitute only a small percentage of workplace behaviors that are meant to harm others (Baron & Richardson, 1994;

Borum, 1996; Neuman & Baron, 1998). Subtler forms of aggression offer a safer means of getting even with coworkers or supervisors, because these passive or indirect acts of workplace aggression can be more easily concealed and attributed to non-aggressive motives.

One avenue for reducing the number of direct and indirect aggressive behaviors engaged in by employees is to screen out applicants who are prone to committing hostile workplace acts. While there are a number of self-report instruments designed to do just that (see Douglas & Martinko, 2001; Glomb & Liao, 2003; Jockin et al., 2001; Neuman & Baron, 1998; Skarlicki, Folger, & Tesluk, 1999), these measures are susceptible to response distortion. Using self-report instruments alone for hiring is likely to be problematic because applicants may alter their responses, which in turn can undermine the validity of these instruments (Barrick & Mount, 1996; Douglas, McDaniel, & Snell, 1996; Heneman et al., 1997; James & Mazerolle, 2002; Ones, Viswesvaran, & Reiss, 1996; Rosse, Stecher, Miller, & Levin, 1998). To address this issue, the CRTA was presented as a test to help identify aggressive individuals in the hiring process. The CRTA is expected to be resistant to response distortion by virtue of being presented as an inductive reasoning test, and it has been shown to significantly predict hostile and aggressive behavior (Frost, 2003; James & McIntyre, 2000; James & Mazerolle, 2002).

We encourage researchers to develop alternative methods to self-report tests as a way of improving the identification of aggression-prone individuals. We also encourage researchers to use objective rather than subjective indicators of aggressive behavior as criteria. Moreover, research using active, physical aggression needs to be conducted. While base rates for such behavior may be low in employee samples, other populations, such as athletes or prisoners, may offer a better opportunity for studying aggressive behavior.

REFERENCES

Anderson, E. (1994, May). The code of the streets. *The Atlantic Monthly*, 81-94.

Averill, J. R. (1993). Illusions of anger. In R. B. Felson, & J. T. Tedeschi (Eds.), *Aggression and violence: Social interactionist perspectives* (pp. 171-192). Washington, DC: American Psychological Association.

Bandura, A. (1973). *Aggression: A social learning analysis.* Englewood Cliffs, NJ: Prentice Hall.

Barling, J., Rogers, A. G., & Kelloway, E. K. (2001). Behind closed doors: In-home workers' experience of sexual harassment and workplace violence. *Journal of Occupational Health Psychology, 6*(3), 255-269.

Baron, R. A., & Richardson, D. R. (1994). *Human aggression* (2nd ed.). New York: Plenum.

Barrick, M. R., & Mount, M. K. (1996). Effects of impression management and self-deception on the predictive validity of personality constructs. *Journal of Applied Psychology, 81*(3), 261-272.

Baumeister, R. F., Smart, L., & Boden, J. M. (1996). Relation of threatened egotism to violence and aggression: The dark side of high self-esteem. *Psychological Review, 103*(1), 5-33.

Bennett, R. J., & Robinson, S. L. (2000). Development of a measure of workplace deviance. *Journal of Applied Psychology, 85*(3), 349-360.

Berkowitz, L. (1993). *Aggression: Its causes, consequences, and control.* New York: McGraw-Hill.

Borum, R. (1996). Improving the clinical practice of violence risk assessment: Technology, guidelines, and training. *American Psychologist, 51*(9), 945-956.

Bradbury, T. N., & Fincham, F. D. (1990). Attributions in marriage: Review and critique. *Psychological Bulletin, 107*(1), 3-33.

Budd, J. W., Arvey, R. D., & Lawless, P. (1996). Correlates and consequences of workplace violence. *Journal of Occupational Health Psychology, 1*(2), 197-210.

Buss, A. H. (1961). *The psychology of aggression.* New York: Wiley.

Butcher, J. N., Dahlstrom, W. G., Graham, J. R., Tellegen, A., & Kaemmer, B. (1989). Minnesota Multiphasic Personality Inventory-2: Manual for administration and scoring. Minneapolis, MN: University of Minnesota Press.

Costa, P. T., & McCrae, R. R. (1992). *Professional manual: Revised NEO Personality Inventory.* Odessa, FL: Psychological Assessment Resources, Inc.

Crick, N. R., & Dodge, K. A. (1994). A review and reformulation of social information-processing mechanisms in children's social adjustment. *Psychological Bulletin, 115*(1), 74-101.

Dodge, K. A. (1986). A social information processing model of social competence in children. In M. Perlmutter (Ed.), *The Minnesota symposium on child psychology* (pp. 77-125). Hillsdale, NJ: Erlbaum.

Dodge, K. A., & Coie, J. D. (1987). Social-information-processing factors in reactive and proactive aggression in children's peer groups. *Journal of Personality & Social Psychology, 53*(6), 1146-1158.

Douglas, S. C., & Martinko, M. J. (2001). Exploring the role of individual differences in the prediction of workplace aggression. *Journal of Applied Psychology, 86*(4), 547-559.

Douglas, E. F., McDaniel, M. A., & Snell, A. F. (1996, August). *The validity of non-cognitive measures decays when applicants fake.* Paper presented at the annual meeting of the Academy of Management, Cincinnati, OH.

Finnegan, W. (1997, December 1). The unwanted. *The New Yorker,* 61-78.

Folger, R., & Baron, R. A. (1996). Violence and hostility at work: A model of reactions to perceived injustice. In G. R. VandenBos, & E. Q. Bulatao (Eds.), *Violence on the job: Identifying risks and developing solutions* (pp. 51-85). Washington, DC: American Psychological Association.

Frost, B. C. (2003). *Implicit versus explicit aggression: Who's ready to rumble?* Unpublished manuscript, The University of Tennessee.

Gay, P. (1993). *The cultivation of hatred.* New York: W. W. Norton & Co.

Glomb, T. M., & Liao, H. (2003). Interpersonal aggression in work groups: Social influence, reciprocal, and individual effects. *Academy of Management Journal, 46*(4), 486-496.

Gough, H. G. (1956). *California Psychological Inventory.* Palo Alto, CA: Consulting Psychologists Press.

Greenberg, J. (1990). Employee theft as a reaction to underpayment inequity: The hidden cost of pay cuts. *Journal of Applied Psychology, 75*(6), 561-568.

Heneman, H. G., Heneman, R. L., & Judge, T. A. (1997). *Staffing organizations.* Madison, WI: Mendota House/Irwin.

Hogan, J., & Hogan, R. (1989). How to measure employee reliability. *Journal of Applied Psychology, 74*(2), 273-279.

Huesmann, L. R. (1988). An information processing model for the development of aggression. *Aggressive Behavior, 14*(1), 13-24.

James, L. R. (1998). Measurement of personality via conditional reasoning. *Organizational Research Methods, 1,* 131-163.

James, L. R., & Mazerolle, M. D. (2002). *Personality in work organizations.* Thousand Oaks, CA: Sage Publications.

James, L. R., & McIntyre, M. D. (2000). *Conditional Reasoning Test of Aggression test manual.* Knoxville, TN: Innovative Assessment Technology.

Jockin, V., Arvey, R. D., & McGue, M. (2001). Perceived victimization moderates self-reports of workplace aggression and conflict. *Journal of Applied Psychology, 86*(6), 1262-1269.

Kuhn, D. (1991). *The skills of argument.* New York: Cambridge University Press.

Laursen, B., & Collins, W. A. (1994). Interpersonal conflict during adolescence. *Psychological Bulletin, 115*(2), 197-209.

LeBlanc, M. M., & Kelloway, E. K. (2002). Predictors and outcomes of workplace violence and aggression. *Journal of Applied Psychology, 87*(3), 444-453.

Millon, T. (1990). The disorders of personality. In L. A. Pervin (Ed.), *Handbook of personality theory and research* (pp. 339-370). New York: Guilford Press.

Murray, H. A. (1938). *Explorations in personality.* New York: Oxford University Press.

Neuman, J. H., & Baron, R. A. (1998). Workplace violence and workplace aggression: Evidence concerning specific forms, potential causes, and preferred targets. *Journal of Management, 24*(3), 391-419.

Nisbett, R. E. (1993). Violence and U.S. regional culture. *American Psychologist, 48*(4), 441-449.

Nisbett, R. E., & Wilson, T. D. (1977). Telling more than we can know: Verbal reports on mental processes. *Psychological Review, 84*(3), 231-259.

O'Leary-Kelly, A. M., Griffin, R. W., & Glew, D. J. (1996). Organization-motivated aggression: A research framework. *Academy of Management Review, 21*(1), 225-253.

Ones, D. S., Viswesvaran, C., & Reiss, A. D. (1996). Role of social desirability in personality testing for personnel selection: The red herring. *Journal of Applied Psychology, 81*(6), 660-679.

Pearson, C. M. (1998). Organizations as targets and triggers of aggression and violence: Framing rational explanations for dramatic organizational deviance. In P. A. Bamberger & A. Peter (Eds.), *Research in the sociology of organizations* (Vol. 15, pp. 197-223). Stamford, CT: JAI Press, Inc.

Robinson, S., & Bennett, R. (1995). A typology of deviant workplace behaviors: A multi-dimensional scaling study. *Academy of Management Journal, 38*(2), 555-572.

Rogers, K. A., & Kelloway, K. E. (1997). Violence at work: Personal and organizational outcomes. *Journal of Occupational Health Psychology, 2*(1), 63-71.

Rosse, J. G., Stecher, M. D., Miller, J. L., & Levin, R. A. (1998). The impact of response distortion on preemployment personality testing and hiring decisions. *Journal of Applied Psychology, 83*(4), 634-644.

Rotundo, M., & Sackett, P. R. (2002). The relative importance of task, citizenship, and counterproductive performance to global ratings of job performance: A policy-capturing approach. *Journal of Applied Psychology, 87*(1), 66-80.

Schat, A. C. H., & Kelloway, E. K. (2000). The effects of perceived control on the outcomes of workplace aggression and violence. *Journal of Occupational Health Psychology,* 5(3), 386-402.

Schwarz, N. (1999). Self-reports: How the questions shape the answers. *American Psychologist, 54*(2), 93-105.

Skarlicki, D. P., & Folger, R. (1997). Retaliation in the workplace: The roles of distributive, procedural, and interaction justice. *Journal of Applied Psychology, 82*(2), 434-443.

Skarlicki, D. P., Folger, R., & Tesluk, P. (1999). Personality as a moderator in the relationship between fairness and retaliation. *Academy of Management Journal, 42*(1), 100-108.

Spielberger, C. D. (1996). *State-Trait Anger Expression Inventory, research edition: Professional manual.* Odessa, FL: Psychological Assessment Resources.

Sternberg, R. J. (1982). Reasoning, problem solving, and intelligence. In R. J. Sternberg (Ed.), *Handbook of human intelligence* (pp. 227-295). Cambridge: Cambridge University Press.

Tedeschi, J. T., & Nesler, M. S. (1993). Grievances: Development and reactions. In R. B. Felson & J. T. Tedeschi (Eds.), *Aggression and violence: Social interactionist perspectives* (pp. 13-46). Washington, DC: American Psychological Association.

Tellegen, A., & Walker, N. (1994). Exploring personality through test construction: Development of the Multidimensional Personality Questionnaire. In S. R. Briggs & J. M. Cheek (Eds.), *Personality measures: Development and evaluation* (Vol. 1, pp. 133-161). Greenwich, CT: JAI Press.

Tepper, B. J., Duffy, M. K., & Shaw, J. D. (2001). Personality moderators of the relationship between abusive supervision and subordinates' resistance. *Journal of Applied Psychology, 86*(5), 974-983.

Toch, H. (1993). Good violence and bad violence: Self-presentations of aggressors through accounts and war stories. In R. B. Felson, & J. T. Tedeschi (Eds.), *Aggression and violence: Social interactionist perspectives* (pp. 193-206). Washington, DC: American Psychological Association.

Winter, D. G., John, O. P., Stewart, A. J., Klohnen, E. C., & Duncan, L. E. (1998). Traits and motives: Toward an integration of two traditions in personality research. *Psychological Review, 105*(2), 230-250.

Wright, J. C., & Mischel, W. (1987). A conditional approach to dispositional constructs: The local predictability of social behavior. *Journal of Personality & Social Psychology, 53*(6), 1159-1177.

APPENDIX

A CRTA problem designed for entry-level jobs is as follows:

> The old saying, "an eye for an eye," means that if someone hurts you, then you should hurt that person back. If you are hit, then you should hit back. If someone burns your house, then you should burn that person's house.

> Which of the following is the biggest problem with the "eye for an eye" plan?

> a. It tells people to "turn the other cheek."
> b. It offers no way to settle a conflict in a friendly manner.
> c. It can only be used at certain times of the year.
> d. People have to wait until they are attacked before they can strike.

There are two logical solutions to this problem. Alternative D is the logical conclusion based on JMs that justify aggression. This conclusion intuitively appeals to aggressive individuals because it tacitly promotes retribution as being logically preferable to reconciliation and is grounded in the unstated assumption that powerful individuals will dominate the less powerful unless the less powerful strike first. Alternative B is the logical conclusion drawn from the non-aggressive counterpart to JMs. This conclusion will intuitively appeal to nonaggressive individuals' desire for a more prosocial alternative and counterbalances the cynicism and hostile tone of Alternative D.

To enhance the face validity of the task, and to protect the indirect nature of the measurement, alternatives A and C were included in the problem. These conclusions are meant to be clearly illogical and rejected by respondents, which they usually are.

Organizational Frustration
and Aggressive Behaviors

Nancy J. Heacox
Richard C. Sorenson

SUMMARY. This study, conducted in a large public agency and a large private transportation company in the U.S., found strong relationships between organizational characteristics and frustration. Role ambiguity, role conflict, work constraints, and warmth and support predicted the level of frustration experienced by employees. In turn, frustration predicted supervisor- and self-reported aggression. Frustration also predicted self-reported criterion behaviors such as withdrawal, aggression turned inward, and abandonment of goal. Frustration mediated the relationships between organizational characteristics and the criteria. In the study we developed two scales: (1) a self-report scale of behavioral reactions to frustration, and (2) the Workplace Aggressive Behaviors Scale, a guideline to increase supervisors' ability to judge the seriousness of aggressive behaviors in the work environment. *[Article copies available for a fee from The Haworth Document Delivery Service: 1-800-HAWORTH. E-mail address: <docdelivery@haworthpress.com> Website: <http://www. HaworthPress.com> © 2004 by The Haworth Press, Inc. All rights reserved.]*

Address correspondence to: Nancy J. Heacox, PhD, Pacific Science and Engineering Group, Incorporated, 9180 Brown Deer Road, San Diego, CA 92121 (E-mail: heacox@pacific-science.com).

[Haworth co-indexing entry note]: "Organizational Frustration and Aggressive Behaviors." Heacox, Nancy J., and Richard C. Sorenson. Co-published simultaneously in *Journal of Emotional Abuse* (The Haworth Maltreatment & Trauma Press, an imprint of The Haworth Press, Inc.) Vol. 4, No. 3/4, 2004, pp. 95-118; and: *Aggression in Organizations: Violence, Abuse, and Harassment at Work and in Schools* (ed: Robert Geffner et al.) The Haworth Maltreatment & Trauma Press, an imprint of The Haworth Press, Inc., 2004, pp. 95-118. Single or multiple copies of this article are available for a fee from The Haworth Document Delivery Service [1-800-HAWORTH, 9:00 a.m. - 5:00 p.m. (EST). E-mail address: docdelivery@ haworthpress.com].

KEYWORDS. Workplace violence, frustration, aggressive behavior, aggression

In the summer of 2003, CNN reported that Douglas Williams entered a factory where he was employed in Meridian, Mississippi, returned to a room where a short time previously he had been participating in a meeting dealing with business ethics, opened fire, and then proceeded through the plant shooting in an apparently arbitrary pattern. Five employees were killed, eight others wounded, and then Mr. Williams allegedly took his own life (CNN, 2003).

Events such as the Williams incident thankfully do not occur often; however, less dramatic and tragic examples of frustration, aggression, and violence do occur frequently in the United States. At a recent conference addressing this issue, it was reported that in the U.S. each week on the average 20 workers are murdered and 18,000 are assaulted. It was also reported that "the yearly cost of violence in the workplace in the United States amounts to $34.4 billion" (Di Martino, 2001, p. 9). In *Workplace Violence: A Report to the Nation* (2001), Loveless stated that ". . . homicide remains the third leading cause of fatal occupational injuries for all workers . . ." and in the U.S. annually ". . . an additional 2 million people are victims of non-fatal injuries due to violence while they are at work" (Loveless, 2001, p. 4). In a recent Canadian sample (Schat & Kelloway, 2003), two-thirds of those responding stated that during the previous year they had experienced some form of physical violence at work, while 89% reported being exposed to some form of aggression. A similar percentage of respondents reported exposure to vicarious violence. This vicarious, secondary, or bystander violence is important because it is likely that the effects on observers of vicarious violence and aggression in terms of fear, depression, and lowered motivation is similar to the effects on the actual victims, but of a lesser magnitude, as is the case with sexual harassment (Schat & Kelloway, 2000; Sorenson, Mangione-Lambie, & Luzio, 1998). Although many of these incidents of aggression and violence (a majority of the homicides) are related to robberies (Sygnatur & Toscano, 2000), a significant proportion (approximately 15-20% of the homicides) is related to workers, customers/clients, or people with whom employees are acquainted who become frustrated and aggressive (Duhart, 2001). Schat and Kelloway (2003) suggested that workplace aggression and resulting violence is also a major problem in Africa, Asia, Europe, and Latin America–in some areas a greater problem even than in North America.

BACKGROUND

The basic premise associated with the concept of organizational frustration is that there is a relationship between "sources of frustration in organizations, and effects on organizations through the reactions of individuals" (Spector, 1978, p. 818). Reactions include aggression against the organization or against individuals within the organization, as well as withdrawal, abandonment of goal, altered task performance, and taking alternative actions to achieve a goal. Sources of frustration include conditions of constraint, alienation, and injustice as perceived by employees. Frustration has been operationalized in much of the relevant research as a "negative affective reaction . . . to the perceived presence of inhibiting conditions" (Peters, O'Connor, & Rudolf, 1980, p. 84). Folger and Baron (1996) suggested "that frustration does often play an important role in many instances of human aggression . . . It also may play a key role in workplace violence and workplace aggression"[1] (p. 53). The following sections will more fully discuss components of our study, which tested a model of organizational frustration. We hypothesized that frustration would mediate the relationships between perceived workplace conditions of constraint or inhibition and aggressive actions. Information was gathered in the field from existing work groups.

ORGANIZATIONAL VARIABLES

Several situational variables hypothesized to have a relationship with aggressive behaviors of employees in organizations were studied.

Work constraints. In his model of organizational frustration, Spector (1978) noted categories of variables that might be perceived by an employee as interfering with goals and thus resulting in frustration. Among these are other persons in the work environment and the structure of the working environment, including procedures and rules. The key for Spector was *the perception of interference with task performance goals or personal goals.*

Researchers Peters, O'Connor, and their collaborators have sought to define, at a task-specific level, task resource variables that might be constraining to employees in their work performance. They identified the following eight dimensions and developed a scale to measure them: Job-related information, tools and equipment, materials and supplies, budgetary support, required services and help from others, task preparation, time availability, and physical work environment. In addition to finding support for hypothesized relationships between the task resource variables and work performance in field as well as laboratory studies, they also found relationships between the task resource variables and perceived frustration and dissatisfaction (O'Connor, Peters, Rudolf, & Pooyan, 1982; Peters et al., 1980).

Storms and Spector (1987) used a modification of the O'Connor et al. (1982) scale. They found "as hypothesized, the variable situational constraints . . . was positively related to perceived frustration . . . [and] perceived frustration was positively related to [counterproductive] behavioral reactions" (p. 231).

Keenan and Newton (1984) developed and employed a six-item scale of environmental characteristics related to self-reported frustration. In our study, "work constraints" was measured by their scale.

Role conflict and role ambiguity. Rizzo, House, and Lirtzman (1970) defined a role as "a set of expectations about behavior for a position in a social structure" (p. 155). They used the following working definition of role conflict for the development of their often-used questionnaire: "Role conflict is defined in terms of the dimensions of congruency-incongruency or compatibility-incompatibility in the requirements of the role, where congruency or compatibility is judged relative to a set of standards or conditions which impinge upon role performance" (Rizzo et al., 1970, p. 155).[2] In the same study, they defined role ambiguity "in terms of (1) the predictability of the outcome or responses to one's behavior . . . and (2) the existence or clarity of behavioral requirements . . . which would serve to guide behavior and provide knowledge that the behavior is appropriate" (Rizzo et al., 1970, pp. 155-156). Thus, both role conflict and role ambiguity are conceptualized as potential sources of constraint for employees.

Rizzo et al. (1970) found significant associations between high role conflict and low job satisfaction, high job pressure, and high general fatigue. They also found self reports of high role ambiguity to be significantly associated with low job satisfaction, high intentions to quit, and high level of general fatigue. Cook, Hepworth, Wall, and Warr (1981) noted that several other researchers who have studied relationships between job satisfaction and both role conflict and role ambiguity have obtained similar results. For example, Spector (1987) found significant positive correlations with the same measure of frustration (Peters et al., 1980) as we used. The Rizzo et al. (1970) role conflict and role ambiguity scales were used in our study.

Organizational warmth and support. Litwin and Stringer (1968) developed the Organizational Climate Questionnaire (OCQ) to measure dimensions of the organizational environment posited to influence employee behavior. Nine dimensions were identified; each dimension defines a subscale of the OCQ. Two subscales of the OCQ that have been suggested as having a relationship with levels of perceived work constraints were used in our study; namely, the warmth and support subscales (each five items). Warmth is defined as "the feeling of general good fellowship that prevails in the work group atmosphere; the emphasis on being well-liked; the prevalence of friendly and informal social groups" (Pfeiffer & Heslin, 1973, p. 253). Support is defined as "the perceived helpfulness of the managers and other employees in the group; emphasis on mutual support from above and below" (p. 254). Keenan and Newton (1984) employed the warmth and support subscales as their measure of organizational climate in their study of graduate engineers. They hypothesized that "frustration might be less in organizations where the general climate is warm and supportive, as the prevailing ethos would encourage mutual support in work tasks, rather than disruption of each other's endeavors" (p. 38).

Their predictions were confirmed-the level of warmth and support perceived was inversely related to the level of constraints reported. In fact, contrary to prediction, Keenan and Newton (1984) reported, "it seems that an atmosphere of warmth and support in the *organization as a whole* [italics added] is more important in relation to frustration levels than the support the individual receives from his immediate supervisor" (p. 64). In our study, the warmth and support variables were measured by the combined Litwin and Stringer (1968) subscales.

PERSON VARIABLES

Person variables were hypothesized to function as moderating variables in the relationship between organizational characteristics and frustration and in the relationship between frustration and aggressive behaviors by employees.

Locus of control. Locus of control refers to "a generalized expectancy that rewards, reinforcements or outcomes in life are controlled either by one's own actions (internality) or by other forces (externality)" (Spector, 1988, p. 335). According to Spector (1982), "those who ascribe control of events to themselves are said to have an internal locus of control ... People who attribute control to outside forces are said to have an external locus of control" (p. 482). Butterfield (1964) investigated, with college students, the relationship between locus of control and an inventory of reactions to frustration, wherein subjects assessed how well items reflected their most likely response to a frustrating situation. Frustration reactions became "less constructive as locus of control becomes more external" (p. 361). Brissett and Nowicki (1973) found similar results. Sadowski and Wenzel (1982) asked college students to complete a scale of locus of control with sub-scales of fatalism and social system control, and a hostility-aggression inventory. The total scale was significantly positively correlated with the hostility dimension, but only the fatalism sub-scale was significantly positively correlated with the aggression dimension. Allen and Greenberger (1980) suggested that behavior which is intentionally destructive enhances feelings of control for individuals who do not perceive themselves as able to secure mastery of their environment in constructive ways. Also, prior research (e.g., Butterfield, 1964) had suggested "a tendency for persons with low perceived control to respond counterproductively to frustrating conditions" (Storms & Spector, 1987, p. 229). In a longitudinal study (Perlow & Latham, 1993), newly hired direct-care employees in residential facilities for the mentally handicapped completed Rotter's (1990) locus of control scale, then "twenty-four months after the study commenced, data were collected to assess each subject's status as a client abuser" (p. 332). Client abuse encompassed various acts of physical aggression toward the residents. It was found that employees who behaved aggressively had obtained higher scores (had a more external locus of control orientation) than did employees who did not display aggressive behavior, confirming the researchers' hypothesis.

Most studies that investigate the effects of locus of control have used general measures, which include items applicable to many domains of an individual's life. However, Phares (1976) suggested, "more precise prediction will ultimately be achieved through subscale approaches that indicate the strength of an individual's locus of control beliefs in several different areas" (p. 175). Spector (1988) developed a domain-specific Work Locus of Control Scale (WLCS), in which each of the 16 items relate to employment issues. He found strongest relationships between the WLCS and job satisfaction, and he also found other significant relationships with organizational commitment, intention to quit, perceived influence, role conflict and role ambiguity, and initiating structure.

Storms and Spector (1987) used the WLCS in a study conducted in an organizational setting with self-report measures of reactions to frustration. Significant positive correlations were found with the group of subjects having an external orientation and overall counterproductive reactions, as well as subscales of aggression, sabotage, hostility, withdrawal, and intention to quit. They also found "some support for the hypothesis that locus of control played a significant role in the frustration-behavior reaction relationship" (p. 232). The WLCS (Spector, 1988) was used in our study to measure participant's locus of control in the work setting.

Gender. Main effects of gender upon aggression are commonly reported. For example, FBI crime reports for 1980 showed that males were arrested for crimes against persons (i.e., murder, manslaughter, robbery, aggravated assault) over nine times more frequently than females (Sarri, 1986). Palmer and Humphrey

(1990) wrote, "Those who commit violent crimes are from five to 10 times more likely to be male than female . . . Figures from 1987 show that in the United States, about 89 percent of arrestees for serious violent crimes were male and 11 percent female" (p. 95). Eighty-three percent of those arrested in the United States in 2001 for violent crimes were male (U.S. Department of Justice, 2002. p. 251). A recent report for 1993-1999 indicated that the gender of the offender in workplace violence was over six times as likely to be male as to be female (Duhart, 2001). In addition, research studies (e.g., Gladue, 1991; Rai & Gupta, 1988) have found a lower tolerance for frustration in male participants than in female participants.

However, research into psychological and sociological issues more often than not provides results laden with interactions. When Frodi, Macauley, and Thome (1977) reviewed studies of aggression that focused on gender differences, they found that angered men tend to respond with physical aggression more often than angered women do. They also discussed the importance of gender role norms and expectations upon the display of aggressive behavior. Biological (e.g., levels of testosterone, the Y chromosome) and sociopsychological (e.g., societal reinforcement for differential expressions of aggression) variables may interact to affect aggressive behavior.

Frustration. Bandura (1983) discussed a social learning model of aggression and wrote, "aversive stimulation produces a general state of emotional arousal that can facilitate any number of responses" (p. 12). He refers to "frustration or anger arousal" (p. 13) as facilitating aggressive behaviors. Our study posited that a negative affective reaction to conditions that constrain goal-directed activity would function as a mediator between the constraining conditions and aggressive behavioral reactions. In this study, the three-item scale of Peters et al. (1980) was used to measure frustration.

Behavioral reactions. Our research focused on aggressive behavior as a correlate of frustration. Research that has followed the classic Dollard, Miller, Doob, Mowrer, and Sears (1944) treatise on frustration-aggression has indicated that aggression is only one possible behavioral reaction that may follow frustration. Two years after the original publication, Neal E. Miller, one of Dollard's colleagues who co-authored the treatise, clarified that reactions to frustration other than aggression were possible (Berkowitz, 1989). Examples of other behaviors mentioned in the literature include rationalizing failures, making repeated unsuccessful attempts to attain a goal, repressing a frustrating incident, displaying childish behavior, or avoiding the situation by withdrawing from it (Wilkens & Haynes, 1974). In his model of organizational frustration, Spector (1978) included the behaviors of withdrawal and attempts at alternative courses of action, in addition to aggression. Spector (1978) wrote, "Unfortunately, little is known about the conditions which cause one reaction over another" (p. 821).

HYPOTHESES

In this study, we hypothesized that:

1. Perceived organizational characteristics of role conflict, role ambiguity, and work constraints would all be positively related to frustration, and warmth and support would be negatively related to frustration.
2. Perceived organizational characteristics of role conflict, role ambiguity, and work constraints would all be positively related to commission of aggressive acts, and warmth and support would be negatively related to the commission of aggressive acts. It was expected that these relationships would be mediated by frustration, and that the magnitude of relationship would be substantially reduced when the effect of frustration was statistically controlled.
3. Locus of control would act as a moderator variable in the organizational characteristics-frustration relationship. It was expected that the relationship between organizational characteristics and frustration would be stronger for those respondents with an external locus of control orientation.
4. Locus of control would act as a moderator variable in the frustration-aggression relationship. It was expected that the relationship between frustration and aggression would be stronger for those respondents with an external locus of control orientation.
5. Gender would act as a moderator variable in the organizational characteristics-frustration relationship. It was expected that the relationship between organizational characteristics and frustration would be stronger for males.
6. Gender would act as a moderator variable in the frustration-aggression relationship. It was expected that the relationship between frustration and aggression would be stronger for males.

PHASE I—WORKPLACE AGGRESSIVE BEHAVIORS SCALE

In order to study aggression in the workplace, we needed a scale for aggressive behavior. In order to develop such a scale, a number of vignettes depicting a range of aggressive behavior were developed from interviews with organizational members and review of the literature. The vignettes were short descriptors of overt behavior such as "The employee became agitated during a phone call, then slammed the receiver down, picked up the telephone and threw it against the wall." After the series of vignettes were piloted and revised, 16 resulting vignettes were administered to 29 experts—either law enforcement personnel or psychologists. Experts were instructed to rank the vignettes in terms of degree to which the behavior depicted in the vignette demonstrated aggressiveness. Two of the expert raters were outlier raters. These two raters were eliminated, leaving 27 raters. Because the purpose of the development of this scale was to provide a guideline for the use of individuals who are not necessarily schooled in the subject of human aggression, it was considered valuable to obtain rankings of non-experts to compare against the experts' rankings. A group of nine graduate students in a psychological measurement class ranked the behavioral vignettes. Then, the rankings were summed and averaged for each group (the 27 experts and the 9 graduate students), and a correlation of the two sets was calculated. The correlation coefficient between the average rankings of the group of nine graduate students and the average rankings of the group of 27 experts, considered over the 16 retained vignettes, was .94. This empirical demonstration was considered strong support of the veracity of Buss's proposal of an "implicit intensity hierarchy" (Buss, 1961, p. 6) of aggressive behaviors and indicated that further development of the scale would be a worthwhile endeavor.

To develop an interval scale from the rankings, paired comparison scaling based on Thurstone's law of comparative judgment (Nunnally & Bernstein, 1994; Thurstone, 1948) was used. This analysis resulted in the interval scale (provided in Table 1) of the 16 vignettes. This scale for aggressive behavior, including aggression against persons and aggression against the organization, was provided to supervisors in Phase II for guidance in rating aggressive behavior.

PHASE II–SUPERVISOR REPORTS OF AGGRESSION

Participants

Participants were non-supervisory employees of either of two organizations in the U.S.–a large public agency and a large private transportation company. The sample for Phase II consisted of 172 employees–78 (45%) from the public agency, and 94 (55%) from the private company. The participants were assured confidentiality and were told that their participation was strictly voluntary and that they could withdraw at any time. Participants were employees who volunteered following a description of the study. All participants agreed to participate in the study and for their responses to be used for research purposes by signing a participant informed consent agreement.

Procedures

Initially, a researcher met with supervisors to secure their agreement to provide data and to instruct them in procedures to be used for observation and

TABLE 1. Workplace Aggressive Behaviors Scale

---100---	During an argument, the employee used both hands to shove a co-worker backwards over a chair.
98---	A male employee pushed a female co-worker up against a wall and fondled her breast.
97---	When the building was unoccupied, the employee let himself in with a key, lit a fire using some flammable liquid stored in the stockroom, then quickly left the premises.
---- 90	
---- 80	
77---	During an argument with a co-worker, the employee picked up a pair of scissors and displayed them in a threatening manner
76---	The employee went to the parking lot and slashed the tires of the company truck.
72---	The employee walked into the crowded company cafeteria, picked up a saltshaker, and threw it in the direction of the cash register.
---70---	
67---	The employee wrote a note to his co-worker, "You will pay for what you did. I will even the score and you will be hurting."
66---	An employee said to co-workers, "The management around here is trying to get rid of me, I'll show them. I'm gonna take them down with me."
65---	The employee became agitated during a phone call, then slammed the receiver down, picked up the telephone and threw it against the wall.
---60---	
---50---	
---40---	
36--	The employee said to a co-worker, "You're just a stupid &@*#$@. I can't work with a #^%($*& worthless $%^(# like you."
32---	The employee waited until his co-worker left for the day, then he misfiled contracts which the co-worker had prepared for an early morning meeting.
---30---	
27---	After a discussion with his supervisor, the employee watched her walk away, then made an obscene gesture in her direction.
24---	When approached by his supervisor about failing to complete some work, the employee said, "I'm not doing it, and I don't care if you say it's part of my job."
23---	The employee responded to co-worker's requests for data with hostile remarks, then blamed others for the unavailability of the data.
--20---	
19---	The employee started a rumor that a supervisor and a co-worker were having an affair, which resulted in the co-worker receiving the best assignments.
--10---	The employee wasted company materials and resources that were available to him to complete his job duties.

The above actions have been rated as to their aggressiveness. The higher the number value assigned to each action, the more aggressive it is. Aggressive actions are intentional behaiors that are meant to hurt. They cause damage or have the potential to cause damage. The actions on this scale were chosen because they cover a wide range of aggressive actions that are costly to business.

reporting of data. Then, subordinate employees who agreed to participate completed a questionnaire of predictor variables. Questionnaires were collected directly by a researcher. During the ensuing three-month observation period, supervisors reported incidents of aggressive behavior to a researcher, using the Workplace Aggressive Behaviors Scale as a guideline to rate the degree of aggressiveness of the behaviors.

Methods

All participants in Phase II completed a self-report questionnaire of the following predictor variables: Work constraints (Keenan & Newton, 1984), organizational warmth and support (Litwin & Stringer, 1968), and role conflict and role ambiguity (Rizzo et al., 1970). Frustration at work (Peters et al., 1980) was also assessed. A five-point Likert response scale was used.

In Phase II, employee aggression was measured and reported by first-line supervisors of participants during the three-month observation period. Supervisors were provided with the Workplace Aggressive Behaviors Scale, developed in Phase I to use as a guideline to rate the aggressiveness of behavioral incidents perpetrated by their subordinates. To deter any potential observational bias, supervisors were instructed to report incidents of aggressive behavior demonstrated by any of their subordinates; supervisors were not informed as to which of their subordinates were participating in the study.

Results

Fourteen incidents were reported, involving 10 of 172 participants (6%). Eleven (79%) of the incidents involved verbal behaviors and three (21%) involved physical behaviors. Seven participants involved were employees of the private organization and three were employees of the public agency. Public agency employees were involved in five (36%) of the incidents; all of these were verbal. Private company employees were involved in nine (64%) of the incidents; of these, six (67%) were verbal and three (33%) were physical. A statistically significant relationship[3] was confirmed as hypothesized between the predictor variables and frustration. Frustration was related to aggressive behavior. However, the relationships between the predictor variables and aggression were not significant; so further tests of mediation were not done. Neither locus of control nor gender functioned as moderators with Phase II data.

PHASE III–SELF-REPORTS OF AGGRESSION

Participants

The sample for Phase III consisted of 66 additional employees–20 (30%) from the public agency, and 46 (70%) from the private company. The participants were assured anonymity and confidentiality and told that their participation was strictly voluntary. All participants agreed to participate in the study and for their responses to be used for research purposes by signing a participant informed consent agreement.

Procedures

Following the completion of Phase II, it was considered advisable to obtain data by an alternate method, either to corroborate or to contrast the supervisory reports. The alternate method chosen was self-report of behaviors under conditions of anonymity. In Spector's (1978) model of organizational frustration, he proposed that one factor deterring the manifestation of overt aggression is the threat of punishment. Following discussions with supervisors, employees and human resource professionals, the following was theorized: An overwhelming majority of employees have learned the proscriptions of their workplace against aggressive behaviors, and they have coping skills intact to the extent that they can respond to frustration in socially acceptable ways or at least contain their displays of aggression to victims or times that are safe (e.g., kick the dog, intimidate a co-worker when the supervisor is absent). In addition, Spector and associates (Chen & Spector, 1991; Spector, 1975; Storms & Spector, 1987) used the method of anonymous self report and found significant positive relationships between organizational frustration and several categories of behaviors, including aggressive and withdrawal behaviors. We developed a participant questionnaire that contained the same predictor variables as in Phase II, with additional items regarding frequency of overt and covert behaviors.

Methods

In Phase III, in another sample of employees from the same organizations, anonymous self-report of aggressive behaviors was used to compare with the Phase II supervisory reports. It was hypothesized that, due in part to controls within the workplace that inhibit aggression, many employees may react to frustrating working conditions in less socially proscribed ways. The measures of the organizational conditions, moderators, and frustration used in Phase III were the same as in Phase II. In addition, a 12-item self-report scale was developed and used. Five items described acts of overt aggression representing a wide range of aggressiveness from the Workplace Aggressive Behaviors Scale. Seven items described other behaviors that were proposed by the model to be reactions to frustration–withdrawal, abandonment of goal, alternative actions, altered task performance, and aggression turned inward. Subscales were formed for use as criterion variables for Phase III–an Overt Aggression subscale and an Other Behaviors subscale.

Participants were asked how often during the past three months at work (chosen to coincide with the observation period of Phase II) they had felt or acted the way described by the items. A five-point response scale was used, which was anchored by *never* to *almost all the time.* An item was considered to be endorsed if the respondent marked any response category other than "never." An item-by-item analysis of the 12-item self-report scale used with Phase III participants showed that the group of items describing aggressive behaviors had lower means and, correspondingly, was endorsed less than the group of items describing other behaviors. The modal response for items on the Overt Aggression subscale was 1 ("never"); modal responses for items on the Other Behaviors subscale ranged from 1 to 3 ("sometimes"). However, even the item with the lowest percentage of endorsement ("Physically hit or shoved someone") was endorsed by over 9% of the respondents. The range of endorsement for the Overt Aggression subscale was 9.4% to 51.6%. The range of endorsement for the Other Behaviors subscale was 64.1% to 98.4%. It is acknowledged that there is a question of social desirability of the items themselves. However, the fact that blatantly proscribed behaviors was admitted, and at a rate higher than that resulting from third-person observation, suggests that the item format was not prohibitively threatening.

Results

Tests of hypotheses. Multiple regression analyses were conducted to test hypotheses. There were no significant differences between Phase II and Phase III samples on any of the scale responses. See Table 2 for Phase III correlations between study variables.

Hypothesis 1 predicted that perceived organizational characteristics of role conflict, role ambiguity, and work constraints would all be positively related to frustration, and warmth/support would be negatively related to frustration. (In reporting these results and henceforth in this paper we will speak of *lack of warmth and support* so that the relationships with the situational or organiza-

TABLE 2. Phase III Correlations of Organizational Variables with Frustration and Criteria

	Role Ambiguity	Role Conflict	Work Constraints	Lack of Warmth and Support	Frustration
Total Scale	.23	.24*	.36**	.41**	.53**
Overt Aggression	.11	.23	.22	.33**	.32**
Attack	.07	.30*	.16	.29*	.31*
Belligerence	.12	.14	.22	.29*	.26*
Other Behavior	.27*	.22	.39**	.40**	.57**
Performance	.15	.16	.32**	.26*	.38**
Abandonment	.30*	.19	.29*	.40**	.56**
Frustration	.32**	.36**	.45**	.52**	--

$p < .05$. **$p < .01$.

tional characteristic variables will be in the same direction.) Hypothesis 1 was supported in Phase III as well as in Phase II.[5]

Hypothesis 2 predicted that the organizational characteristics would be positively related to the self report of Overt Aggression, but these relationships would be mediated by frustration. The first step of the three-step method for testing mediation (Baron & Kenny, 1986) was done in testing Hypothesis 1, and a relationship was established. The second step, regressing the criterion variable on the predictor variables, was done–the score from the Overt Aggression subscale of the self-report behaviors scale was regressed on the four organizational characteristics. For the Overt Aggression subscale, Hypothesis 2 was not supported.[6]

Hypothesis 2 was tested for the second dependent variable of Phase III, the subscale of Other Behaviors. It was predicted that the organizational characteristics would be related to self-reported Other Behaviors, but these relationships would be mediated by frustration. Beginning again with the second step of the Baron and Kenny (1986) method for testing mediation, which is to regress the criterion variable on the predictor variables, the score from the Other Behaviors subscale was regressed on the four organizational characteristics. The predicted relationship was established.[7]

An exploratory factor analysis was conducted to compare the conceptual dimensions of the self-report behaviors scale with empirical data from this current sample. It was recognized that sample size is at the minimum level required for reliable factor analysis: Five cases per item (Tabachnick & Fidell, 1989). Four factors with eigenvalues greater than 1 emerged and were rotated using the Varimax method. In total, the solution accounted for 65.4% of the variance in the data:

> 1st factor = items associated with abandonment of goal (*Abandonment;* e.g., seriously considered quitting job)

> 2nd factor = items associated with interpersonal attack (*Attack;* e.g., physically hit or shoved someone)

> 3rd factor = items associated with belligerence (*Belligerence;* e.g., hostility toward employee/customer)

> 4th factor = items associated with lowered work performance (*Performance;* e.g., felt work performance was low)

Thus, two factors–Attack and Belligerence–contained all the items of the Overt Aggression subscale, while the remaining two factors–Abandonment and Performance–were more internally oriented and contained all the items of the Other Behaviors subscale.

As Baron and Kenny (1986) point out, to conclude analyses of mediation hypotheses one should employ the Sobel (1982) test. We used the online, interactive calculation tool for mediation tests (Preacher & Leonardelli, 2003). Table 3 provides the results of the Sobel test using the Goodman II test equation, which we felt would be most appropriate given the conservative nature of the Sobel test for small samples (Shrout & Bolger, 2002). Frustration was the mediator of the relationship between the situational variables and the total

TABLE 3. Sobel Test Statistics for Frustration as a Mediator

	Role Ambiguity	Role Conflict	Work Constraints	Lack of Warmth and Support
Total Scale	2.37*	2.58**	2.84**	2.81**
Overt Aggression	1.92	1.82	1.88	1.44
Attack	1.92	1.67	2.00*	1.48
Belligerence	1.66	1.67	1.44	1.11
Other Behaviors	2.43*	2.68**	3.01**	3.12**
Performance	2.08*	2.21*	2.06*	2.18*
Abandonment	2.40*	2.68**	3.08**	3.05**

Note: Table entries are the Sobel statistic divided by its standard error.
$*p < .05.$ $**p < .01.$

self-report behaviors scale, the Other Behaviors subscale, and the Abandonment and Performance factors. We tested for mediation even though the IV-DV relationship was not significant at the $p < .05$ level, as we followed Shrout and Bolger (2002) who observed, "it seems unwise to defer considering mediation until the bivariate association between X and Y is established" (p. 429). We were not able to confirm that frustration is a mediator between the organizational variables and the more overtly aggressive actions except between work constraints and attack.

Neither locus of control nor gender were moderators. However, locus of control was significantly related to each of the organizational variables and to frustration, to the total self-report behaviors scale, the Other Behaviors subscale, and to the Abandonment factor.

CONCLUSION

The goal of this study was to increase our knowledge of variables that correlate with aggressive behavior by employees. A model, adapted from Spector's (1978) model of organizational frustration, proposed that employee aggression is one behavioral reaction that may result from frustration, which in turn results from the perception of a constraining and unsupportive work environment.

In Phase II, predictor variable data were gathered from employee self report of perceived organizational characteristics and frustration, as well as self report of locus of control and gender (proposed moderating variables). Data for the dependent variable, employee aggression, were gathered via supervisor report. Supervisors were provided a guideline, the Workplace Aggressive Behaviors Scale (developed in Phase I of our study), to assist them in assessing the magnitude of aggressive acts. Because of low frequency of the dependent variable that was reported by supervisors, self reports of employee behaviors was gathered in Phase III. This final phase explored not only the level of self-reported aggression, but also the level of other reactions that were proposed in Spector's (1978) original model of organizational frustration.

The Organizational Characteristics-Frustration Relationship

It was hypothesized that the organizational characteristics would be positively related to frustration. This hypothesis was supported in both Phases II and III. Each organizational characteristic separately predicted frustration, and relationships were as predicted.

Locus of control was expected to act as a moderator variable in the organizational characteristics-frustration relationship. This hypothesis was not supported in either Phase II or Phase III. It was discovered through post-hoc analysis that locus of control functioned as a predictor of frustration rather than as a moderator in the organizational characteristics-frustration relationship. High locus of control score (indicative of external locus of control orientation) was associated with a high frustration score.

Gender was expected to act as a moderator variable in the organizational characteristics-frustration relationship. This hypothesis was not supported in either Phase II or Phase III, although males had higher scores on the criterion variables.

The Frustration-Behavioral Reactions Relationships

It was hypothesized that the organizational characteristics would be positively related to commission of aggressive acts, but these relationships would be mediated by frustration. In Phase II, the occurrence of the dependent variable–incidents of aggressive behavior as reported by supervisors–was too low to proceed with statistical analysis.

In Phase III, the method of self-report was used to gather data to test the relationships between organizational characteristics and self-reported behavioral reactions with the proposed mediating variable. There were several criterion variables defined from Phase III scales.[8] As a set, organizational variables predicted self-reported Other Behaviors, and frustration functioned as hypothesized as a mediator variable in this relationship. Separately, each predictor had a positive relationship with the criterion. As a set, organizational characteristics did not predict self-reported Overt Aggression.

Separately, only lack of warmth and support independently predicted self-reported Overt Aggression. Frustration functioned as a mediator variable only for the Attack factor.

It was hypothesized that locus of control would act as a moderator variable in the frustration-aggression relationship. This hypothesis was not supported in either Phase II or Phase III. However, locus of control increased the predictive capability of frustration for all criteria and functioned as an independent predictor of self-reported Other Behaviors. It was also hypothesized that gender would act as a moderator variable in the frustration-aggression relationship. This hypothesis was not supported in either Phase II or Phase III.

The Model of Observed Relationships

The predicted relationship between the set of organizational characteristics and frustration was strongly and consistently supported. There were observations of significant relationships between various organizational characteristics and the behavioral criteria. Most significant relationships between organizational characteristics and behavioral criteria were mediated by frustration.

Interaction effects of locus of control and gender did not emerge as predicted. In all significant relationships, the effects of locus of control and gender were main effects. Locus of control independently predicted frustration (Phase II only) and each of the behavioral reactions. Gender independently predicted frustration (Phase II only).

On a consistent basis, frustration alone had nearly as much predictive capability with behavioral criteria as did sets that included frustration and other predictors. The model in Figure 1 shows the pattern of the strongest and most consistent relationships found in the study.

Supervisor-Reported Aggression (Phase II)

Although all participating supervisors agreed to mail reports of aggressive incidents to the researcher and periodic written communications were sent to the supervisors, 90% of the incident reports were not received until a researcher met face-to-face with the supervisors. A semi-structured format was used for these meetings; categories of aggressive behavior were discussed, and supportive documents (e.g., customer complaints, supervisors' logs) were checked. Two common responses of supervisors for not initiating the submission of incidents were, "I just didn't remember to submit it," and "I wasn't sure if it qualified." One supervisor who wanted such verification of an incident then remarked, "Now that I have labeled it *aggression*, I have to do something about it." Such denial is a prime target of trainers in the field of workplace aggression; the goal is to promote supervisor awareness while at the same time providing supervisors with tools to intervene. Following data collection, the researchers provided in-service training to supervisors at the participating agencies. Topics included recognition of warning signs of employee frustration and discussion of the cycle of aggression, as well as counseling strategies.

Supervisors reported to a researcher that the Workplace Aggressive Behaviors Scale was a valuable aid in promoting awareness of the hierarchy of aggression. Supervisors, when describing incidents of aggression, were able to quickly gain proficiency in using the Workplace Aggressive Behaviors Scale as a guideline to rate the incidents to their satisfaction. It was observed by the researchers that individual supervisors presented a consistent hierarchy of incidents when rating multiple incidents. However, there was much variation between supervisors at rating relatively similar incidents. In large part, this seemed to be reflective of contextual components of the incident that had questionable relevance to the actual aggressiveness of the incident. For example, there was a tendency to

FIGURE 1. Model of Observed Relationships

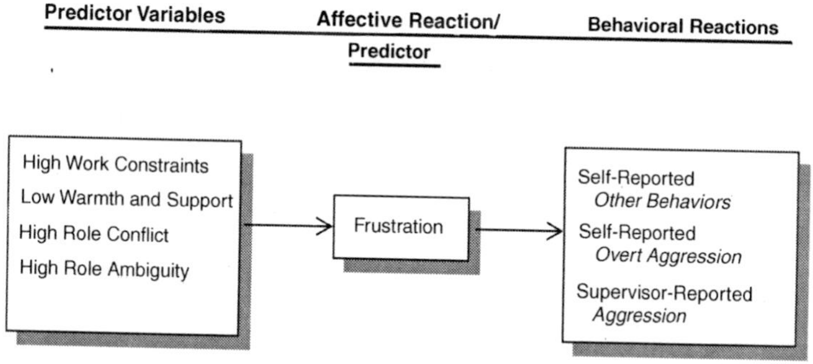

Predictor Variables	Affective Reaction/ Predictor	Behavioral Reactions
High Work Constraints Low Warmth and Support High Role Conflict High Role Ambiguity	Frustration	Self-Reported *Other Behaviors* Self-Reported *Overt Aggression* Supervisor-Reported *Aggression*

rate incidents with a high score if they were a direct threat to supervisor's authority. Also, the "bigger picture" was considered; if a favored employee was involved in an aggressive incident, there was a tendency to downplay the aggressiveness of the act. In addition, supervisors considered contextual components that relate to specific organizational culture, e.g., certain behaviors may be taboo in one setting (and thus given a higher aggression rating) and tolerated in another. Finally, there are components of the work setting that affect whether aggressive behaviors are observed, e.g., the amount of supervisor presence and the type of work being done.

Nearly two-thirds of the employees involved in aggressive incidents that were reported were non-participants. As a check for bias due to self-selection and/or demand characteristics, the number of involved employees was divided by the total number of employees per group, to yield the following rates of employees who were reported as acting aggressively: 7.8% of total employees, 9.8% of non-participants, and 5.8% of participants. These rates are not statistically significant different. The per-month participant incident rate in this study was 2.7%. In two studies conducted by Latham and Perlow (1993), a 1% per-month incident rate was found. However, it was expected that the current study would produce an even higher incident rate, due to a theoretically-expanded range of targeted behaviors; that is, a range which included low level aggression.

Self-Reported Aggression and Other Behaviors (Phase III)

An item-by-item analysis of the 12-item self-report scale used with Phase III participants showed that the group of items describing aggressive behaviors had lower means and, correspondingly, was endorsed less than the group of items describing other behaviors. The modal response for items on the Overt Aggression subscale was 1 ("never"); modal responses for items on the Other Behaviors subscale ranged from 1 to 3 ("sometimes"). However, even the item with the lowest percentage of endorsement ("Physically hit or shoved someone") was endorsed by over 9% of the respondents. The range of endorsement for the Overt Aggression subscale was 9.4% to 51.6%. The range of endorsement for the Other Behaviors subscale was 64.1% to 98.4%. It is acknowledged that there is a question of social desirability of the items themselves. However, the fact that blatantly proscribed behaviors were admitted, and at a rate higher than that resulting from third-person observation, suggests that the item format was not prohibitively threatening.

In our study, frustration predicted both self-reported Overt Aggression and self-reported Other Behaviors. The pattern of response frequencies suggests that, in the workplace at least, behavioral reactions other than overt aggression are favored. This may be due to social controls that function to discourage aggressive behavior, and/or social learning, which sends the message that certain coping styles will be more readily accepted than others will. The pattern of response frequencies is also suggestive of a greater prevalence of aggressive behaviors than was reported by supervisors.

DISCUSSION

This study confirmed the importance of the effect of frustration on consequential aggressive behaviors. Employees who perceive a high level of constraints or role conflict or ambiguity and/or a low level of warmth and support in their work environment are more likely to exhibit counterproductive behaviors. These behaviors may include overt aggression. They may also include withdrawal or other "leaving the field" behaviors, lowered performance, or aggression turned inward.

A comprehensive intervention could entail an organizational evaluation to identify aspects of the work environment that are perceived as obstructive or unsupportive. A multi-method approach is suggested—one that includes observation of work processes, confidential interviews (individual or focus groups) of supervisory and non-supervisory employees, and confidential, anonymous survey of the work environment. For maximum value, a survey could be constructed of standardized sub-scales such as used in this study (e.g., lack of warmth and support, frustration) and customized sub-scales applicable to the specific workplace, to identify areas of perceived constraints. The areas identified by Peters, O'Connor, and their colleagues (e.g., required services and help from others, tools and equipment; O'Connor et al., 1982; Peters et al., 1980) would be excellent candidates for inclusion in such a survey. Of course, paramount to an effort of this type is support of management for data collection *and* follow-up. This cannot be over-emphasized. Organizational evaluations create expectations that meaningful changes will ensue. If these expectations are thwarted, the effort put forth by employees to provide sensitive information will be viewed as trust misplaced and will be catalogued as another example of constraint within the workplace.

Other possible interventions could include:

- Training employees–both supervisory and non-supervisory–in the cycle of aggression and warning signs of employee frustration.
- Establishing a non-punitive environment where employees have outlets for problem solving.
- Establishing a climate that does not tolerate bullying behavior.
- Careful screening of applicants for supervisory and non-supervisory positions to identify previous counterproductive behaviors, especially in similar environments.

NOTES

1. Cox and Leather (1994) noted, "the terms aggression and violence are often used interchangeably" (p. 216), although "the term violence has a greater common currency in the workplace than that of aggression" (p. 218). Berkowitz (1974) noted, "aggression is usually defined as the intentional injury of another" (p. 165). Many researchers (e.g., Hales, Seligman, Newman, & Timbrook, 1988; Kurland, 1993; Thomas, 1992) use the term *violence* to specifically define parameters of behavior.

2. They explained that role conflict could occur due to; (a) a mismatch between internal values and role demands (e.g., an individual believes that aspects of the role requirements are unethical or immoral), (b) a mismatch between capabilities and role demands, (c) demands of multiple roles, including non-employment roles, or (d) incompatible demands from multiple sources within an organization.

3. $R = .68$; $F_{(4,165)} = 36.22$, $p < .001$. Reliabilities (Cronbach's $\pm$) of predictor and frustration scales were .74 or higher (range = .74 to .94).

4. ($r = .24$; $p = .001$)

5. The multiple correlation in the regression equation was .54. A significant $F_{(4,61)} = 6.32, p = .001$ allowed for rejection of the null hypothesis. Relationships of the organizational characteristics to frustration were in the direction predicted ($R^2 = .29$).

6. The multiple correlation was .38; $F_{(4,59)} = 2.45$, $p > .05$, so the null hypothesis could not be rejected.

7. The multiple correlation was .51; $F_{(4,59)} = 5.20, p < .001$, so the null hypothesis was rejected.

8. Self-reported Overt Aggression, self-reported Other Behaviors, the total self-report behavior scale, and four factors from the exploratory factor analysis–*Abandonment, Attack, Belligerence,* and *Performance.*

REFERENCES

Allen, V. L., & Greenberger, D. B. (1980). Destruction and perceived control. In A. Baum, & J. E. Singer (Eds.), *Advances in environmental psychology: Vol. 2. Applications of personal control* (pp. 85-109). Hillsdale, NJ: Lawrence Erlbaum Associates.

Bandura, A. (1983). Psychological mechanisms of aggression. In R. G. Geen, & E. I. Donnerstein (Eds.), *Aggression: Theoretical and empirial reviews: Vol. 1. Theoretical and methodological issues* (pp. 1-40). New York: Academic Press.

Baron, R. M., & Kenny, D. A. (1986). The moderator-mediator variable distinction in social psychological research: Conceptual, strategic, and statistical considerations. *Journal of Personality and Social Psychology, 51*(6), 1173-1182.

Berkowitz, L. (1974). Some determinants of impulsive aggression: Role of mediated associations with reinforcements for aggression. *Psychological Review, 81*(2), 165-176.

Berkowitz, L. (1989). Frustration-aggression hypothesis: Examination and reformulation. *Psychological Bulletin, 106*(1), 59-73.

Brissett, M., & Nowicki, S., Jr. (1973). Internal versus external control of reinforcement and reaction to frustration. *Journal of Personality and Social Psychology, 25*(1), 35-44.

Buss, A. H. (1961). *The psychology of aggression.* New York: Wiley.

Butterfield, E. C. (1964). Locus of control, test anxiety, reactions to frustration, and achievement attitudes. *Journal of Personality, 32,* 355-370.

Chen, P. Y., & Spector, P. E. (1991). Negative affectivity as the underlying cause of correlations between stressors and strains. *Journal of Applied Psychology, 76*(3), 398-407.

CNN. (2003). *Workplace shooter described as 'angry' man.* Retrieved July 29, 2003, from http://www.cnn.com/2003/US/South/07/08/plant.shoot/index.html.

Cook, J. D., Hepworth, S. J., Wall, T. D., & Warr, P. B. (1981). *The experience of work: A compendium and review of 249 measures and their use.* Orlando, FL: Academic Press.

Cox, T., & Leather, P. (1994). The prevention of violence at work: Application of a cognitive behavioural theory. In C. L. Cooper, & I. T. Robertson (Eds.), *International review of industrial and organizational psychology 1994: Vol. 9* (pp. 213-246). Chichester, England: John Wiley & Sons.

Di Martino, V. D. (2001, November). *Introduction to the issue of violence as a workplace risk.* Presentation at the Tri-National Conference on Violence as a Workplace Risk. Retrieved July 29, 2003, from http://www.dol.gov/ILAB/media/reports/nao/violenceworkrisk.htm.

Dollard, J., Miller, N. E., Doob, L. W., Mowrer, O. H., & Sears, R. T. (1944). *Frustration and aggression.* New Haven, CT: Yale University Press.

Duhart, D. T. (2001, December). Violence in the workplace, 1993-99. *Bureau of Justice Statistics Special Report (NCJ 190076).* Retrieved September 24, 2003, from http:// www.ojp.usdoj.gov/bjs/

Folger, R., & Baron, R. A. (1996). Violence and hostility at work: A model of reactions to perceived injustice. In G. R. VanderBos, & E.Q. Bulatao (Eds.), *Violence on the job: Identifying risks and developing solutions* (pp. 51-85). Washington, DC: American Psychological Association.

Frodi, A., Macauley, J., & Thome, P. R. (1977). Are women always less aggressive than men? A review of the experimental literature. *Psychological Bulletin, 84*(4), 634-660.

Gladue, B. A. (1991). Aggressive behavioral characteristics, hormones, and sexual orientation in men and women. *Aggressive Behavior, 17*(6), 313-326.

Hales, T., Seligman, P. J., Newman, S. C., & Timbrook, C. L. (1988). Occupational injuries due to violence. *Journal of Occupational Medicine, 30*(6), 483-487.

Keenan, A., & Newton, T. J. (1984). Frustration in organizations: Relationships to role stress, climate, and psychological strain. *Journal of Occupational Psychology, 57*, 57-65.

Kurland, O. M. (1993). Workplace violence. *Risk Management, 40*(6), 76-77.

Latham, L. L., & Perlow, R. (1993). The role of self-control, planning ability, and gender in organizational tenure and aggressive work behavior. Paper presented at the Fifty-Third Meeting of the Academy of Management, Atlanta, Georgia.

Litwin, G. H., & Stringer, R. A., Jr. (1968). *Motivation and organizational climate.* Harvard University Press: Boston.

Loveless, L. (Ed.) (2001, February). *Workplace violence: A report to the nation.* Iowa City, IA: The University of Iowa Injury Prevention Research Center.

Nunnally, J. C., & Bernstein, I. H. (1994). *Psychometric theory* (3rd ed.). New York: McGraw-Hill.

O'Connor, E. J., Peters, L. H., Rudolf, C. J., & Pooyan, A. (1982). Situational constraints and employee affective reactions: A partial field replication. *Group & Organization Studies, 7*(4), 418-428.

Palmer, S., & Humphrey, J. A. (1990). *Deviant behavior: Patterns, sources, and control.* New York: Plenum Press.

Perlow, R., & Latham, L. L. (1993). Relationship of client abuse with locus of control and gender: A longitudinal study in mental retardation facilities. *Journal of Applied Psychology, 78*(5), 831-834.

Peters, L. H., O'Connor, E. J., & Rudolf, C. J. (1980). The behavioral and affective consequences of performance-relevant situational variables. *Organizational Behavior and Human Performance, 25*, 79-96.

Pfeiffer, J. W., & Heslin, R. (1973). *Instrumentation in human relations training: A guide to 75 instruments with wide application to the behavioral sciences.* Iowa City, IA: University Associates.

Phares, E. J. (1976). *Locus of control in personality.* Morristown, NJ: General Learning Press.

Preacher, K. J., & Leonardelli, G. J. (2003). *Calculation for the Sobel test: An interactive calculation tool for mediation tests.* Retrieved October 23, 2003, from http://www.unc. edu/~preacher/sobel/sobel.htm.

Rai, S. N., & Gupta, M. D. (1988, October). Frustration tolerance in Machiavellians. *Indian Journal of Current Psychological Research, 3*(2), 115-119.

Rizzo, J. R., House, R. J., & Lirtzman, S. I. (1970). Role conflict and ambiguity in complex organizations. *Administrative Science Quarterly, 15*, 150-163.

Rotter, J. B. (1990). Internal versus external control of reinforcement: A case history of a variable. *American Psychologist, 45*, 489-493.

Sadowski, C. J., & Wenzel, D. M. (1982). The relationship of locus of control dimensions to reported hostility and aggression. *The Journal of Psychology*, *112*, 227-230.

Sarri, R. C. (1986). Gender and race differences in criminal justice processing. *Women's Studies International Forum*, *9*(1), 89-99.

Schat, A. H., & Kelloway, E. K. (2000). Effects of perceived control on the outcomes of workplace aggression and violence. *Journal of Occupational Health Psychology*, *5*, 386-402.

Schat, A. H., & Kelloway, E. K. (2003). Reducing the adverse consequences of workplace aggression and violence: The buffering effects of organizational support. *Journal of Occupational Health Psychology*, *2*, 110-122.

Shrout, P. E., & Bolger, N. (2002). Mediation in experimental and nonexperimental studies: New procedures and recommendations. *Psychological Methods*, *7*(4), 422-445.

Sobel, M. E. (1982). Asymptotic confidence intervals for indirect effects in structural models. In S. Leinhardt (Ed.), *Sociological methodology* (pp. 290-312). San Francisco: Jossey-Bass.

Sorenson, R. C., Mangione-Lambie, M. G., & Luzio, R. C. (1998). Solving the chronic problem of sexual harassment in the workplace: An empirical study of factors affecting employer perceptions and consequences of sexual harassment. *California Western Law Review*, *34*, 457-491.

Spector, P. E. (1975). Relationships of organizational frustration with reported behavioral reactions of employees. *Journal of Applied Psychology*, *60*(5), 635-637.

Spector, P. E. (1978). Organizational frustration: A model and review of the literature. *Personnel Psychology*, *31*, 815-829.

Spector, P. E. (1982). Behavior in organizations as a function of employee's locus of control. *Psychological Bulletin*, *91*(3), 482-497.

Spector, P. E. (1987). Interactive effects of perceived control and job stressors on affective reactions and health outcomes for clerical workers. *Work and Stress*, *1*(2), 155-162.

Spector, P. E. (1988). Development of the work locus of control scale. *Journal of Occupational Psychology*, *61*, 335-340.

Storms, P. L., & Spector, P. E. (1987). Relationships of organizational frustration with reported behavioural reactions: The moderating effect of locus of control. *Journal of Occupational Psychology*, *60*, 227-234.

Sygnatur, E. F., & Toscano, G. A. (2000, Spring). Work-related homicides: The facts. *Compensation and Working Conditions*, 3-8.

Tabachnick, B. G., & Fidell, L. S. (1989). *Using multivariate statistics* (2nd ed.). New York: Harper Collins Publishers, Inc.

Thurstone, L. L. (1948). Psychophysical Methods. In T. G. Andrews (Ed.), *Methods of Psychology* (pp. 124-157). New York: John Wiley and Sons, Inc.

U. S. Department of Justice, Federal Bureau of Investigation. (2002). Crime in the United States, 2001. Washington, DC: USGPO.

Wilkens, P. A., & Haynes, J. G. (1974). Understanding frustration-instigated behavior. *Personnel Journal*, *53*(10), 770-774.

Creating Respectful, Violence-Free, Productive Workplaces: A Community-Level Response to Workplace Violence

Donald L. Gault

SUMMARY. Workplaces throughout the United States are struggling to understand and address the issue of workplace violence. The Workplace Action Team of The Initiatives for Violence-Free Families and Communities in Ramsey and Hennepin Counties, Minnesota, is a group of Minneapolis-St. Paul professionals who have worked together since 1990 to create and implement tools that work, having built them around a comprehensive strategy of developing violence-free, respectful work environments. The purpose of this article is to describe the community-wide partnership that the Workplace Action Team represents, outline the principles the team has developed that underscore respectful, violence-free work environments, and demonstrate the tools and strate-

Address correspondence to: Donald L. Gault, MA, St. Paul-Ramsey County Department of Public Health, 50 West Kellogg Boulevard, Suite 930, Saint Paul, MN 55102 (E-mail: donald.gault@co.ramsey.mn.us).

[Haworth co-indexing entry note]: "Creating Respectful, Violence-Free, Productive Workplaces: A Community-Level Response to Workplace Violence." Gault, Donald L. Co-published simultaneously in *Journal of Emotional Abuse* (The Haworth Maltreatment & Trauma Press, an imprint of The Haworth Press, Inc.) Vol. 4, No. 3/4, 2004, pp. 119-138; and: *Aggression in Organizations: Violence, Abuse, and Harassment at Work and in Schools* (ed: Robert Geffner et al.) The Haworth Maltreatment & Trauma Press, an imprint of The Haworth Press, Inc., 2004, pp. 119-138. Single or multiple copies of this article are available for a fee from The Haworth Document Delivery Service [1-800-HAWORTH, 9:00 a.m. - 5:00 p.m. (EST). E-mail address: docdelivery@haworthpress.com].

gies that are beginning to make a difference in workplaces in the Minneapolis-St. Paul metropolitan area. *[Article copies available for a fee from The Haworth Document Delivery Service: 1-800-HAWORTH. E-mail address: <docdelivery@haworthpress.com> Website: <http://www.HaworthPress.com>*

KEYWORDS. Workplace violence, respect, employee productivity and morale, comprehensive approach

FORMATION AND PRINCIPLES
OF THE WORKPLACE ACTION TEAM

During the mid-1980s, Ramsey County (Minnesota) convened a series of "Abuse Councils" whose charge was to examine and improve county intervention services and programs that respond to family violence (child abuse, elder abuse, and domestic violence). Intervention services were improved and better connected, and elected officials and county leadership became much more aware of the financial and human costs of family violence in the Ramsey County community. However, in the late 1980s, a 5-year-old boy was kicked to death by his mother's boyfriend in St. Paul while the family's case was open to both county and community intervention and support services. This incident, in conjunction with the work of the Abuse Councils, led the Board of Ramsey County Commissioners to make a commitment to explore whether family violence could be prevented.

In April 1990, the League of Women Voters of Minneapolis published *Breaking the Cycle of Violence: A Focus on Primary Prevention Efforts*. The report identified primary prevention[1] as a central component to breaking the cycle of violence (see Appendix A for a discussion of the three levels of prevention):

> Primary prevention efforts encourage the development of healthy human beings and families . . . which in turn eliminates many of the causes of violent behaviors. Most efforts in social services, legal and educational fields . . . focus on intervention, that is programs that treat violent behavior after it has occurred. (p. 1)

The report also provided the rationale for a sustained, community-wide approach:

> Breaking the cycle of violence requires the cooperation of educational, business, religious, legal, medical, media, recreational, and

community organizations. The cooperative effort must focus on developing an understanding of how to prevent violent behavior, while at the same time moving forward with . . . public education programs that promote nonviolent behavior and support healthy, nurturing families. (p. 21)

While acknowledging and respecting the need to maintain and continually work to improve intervention approaches to family, workplace, and community violence, The Initiative for Violence-Free Families and Communities in Ramsey County (hereafter referred to simply as The Initiative) is based on a primary prevention model. Efforts have been built on the premise of providing messages and tools to entire populations in order to change the context and messages received by people in communities, schools, and/or workplaces, and to prevent acts of violence from occurring in the first place.

One of the eight original Initiative Action Teams formed in 1990 was the Workplace Action Team (WAT). The WAT is comprised of professionals from private, government, and non-profit workplaces in the Minneapolis-St. Paul area who join together to create tools and resources to prevent and address violence at work. WAT is a joint effort of the Ramsey and Hennepin County Violence Prevention Initiatives, with principal staffing coming from the St. Paul-Ramsey County Department of Public Health.

While its initial charge was to develop strategies to prevent family violence through workplace initiatives, WAT members quickly determined that it would be most effective by developing practical tools to address everyday issues of concern in business and public employment settings. By creating violence-free, respectful work environments, it is the belief of the WAT that incidents of violence both at home and in the workplace can be reduced.

The goal of the WAT is to create resources and encouragement for workplaces in the Minneapolis-St. Paul area and beyond to implement sustained efforts assuring respectful, violence-free workplaces. The action team encourages workplaces to simultaneously address workplace violence on four levels: Conflict between employees, conflict between employees and supervisors/managers, conflict between employees and customers/clients, and conflict within an employee's family that impacts the workplace. Resources created by the team are designed to facilitate discussion, awareness, policy development, and system change in organizations to prevent the full spectrum of workplace violence, which ranges from its most common form, verbal harassment and bullying, to severe acts of physical violence. Table 1 summarizes resources created by the WAT.

TABLE 1. WAT Resources and Strategies

- The *Violence in the Workplace* workbook and video set
- Three theatre-based trainings, *"Unless There's Blood," "From the Ground Up,"* and *"None of Your Business,"* commissioned by the WAT and developed/performed by Theatre at Work of St. Paul
- *"What Do Great Supervisors Look Like?"* booklets, sign to designate violence-free, respectful workplaces, and *"Take Action for a Violence-Free Workplace"* brochures
- One-on-one consultation with Action Team members

DEFINITIONS, PHILOSOPHICAL APPROACH, AND APPLICATION

The work and products of the WAT have been deeply impacted by the learning and process of the overall Initiative, as well as the practical application of these ideas and tools in workplace settings across the Minneapolis-St. Paul area. The basic assumptions behind The Initiative are summarized below, followed by definitions of violence and beliefs about root causes and fundamental prevention strategies that guide the work of all Initiative Action Teams.

The assumption/hypothesis guiding the work of The Initiative is that attitudes and behaviors in populations and individuals are shaped by complex and often random interactions of intentional and unintentional messages and incentives, delivered from community systems/institutions and key influential individuals. Initiative efforts and approaches to preventing violence are heavily influenced by principles and wisdom taken from the work of a number of individuals exploring the root causes of violence and prevention strategies and from definitions of violence.

The Initiative's definitions of violence identify that violence is a continuum of behaviors (see Table 2). They recognize the impacts of words (as well as silence), and that people must recognize and claim their power so that they are able to choose to use it wisely. Finally, these definitions identify that there is often a difference between the intentions and the impacts of one's actions and words.[2]

Table 3 illustrates principles and wisdom that are central to the work of The Initiative and the WAT. Ghandi points to the fact that we cannot end violence by focusing efforts on "them"; we must look within ourselves and our institutions and begin the change process there (QuoteDB.com, 2004). In order to prevent acts of violence, we must understand *why* individuals and groups choose to be violent. May's work suggests that part of the answer is to understand the impact of powerlessness and shame on human behavior (May, 1969); Kanter "translates" the powerlessness theme to the workplace. The challenge is to learn

TABLE 2. Initiative Definitions of Violence

- Violence is words and actions that hurt people
- Violence is the misuse of power and authority
- Violence is any words or actions where the intention *or* impact is to cause pain, fear, or hurt

TABLE 3. Guiding Principles/Wisdom

"You must be the change that you wish to see in the world."–*Ghandi*

"Deeds of violence in our society are performed largely by those trying to establish their self-esteem, to defend their self-image, and to demonstrate that they, too, are significant. Violence arises not out of superfluity of power but out of powerlessness."–*May (1969)*

"In organizations, it is powerlessness that "corrupts," not power. When people feel powerless, they behave in petty, territorial ways. They become rules-minded, and they are over-controlling, because they're trying to grab hold of some piece of the world that they do control and then over-manage it to death."–*Moss Kanter (1993)*

"All people have three fundamental needs: Stability, security, and affirmation."–*Garbarino (1998)*

how and why so many people in our culture and workplaces are feeling powerless and "overwhelmed by shame and humiliation." Garbarino provides a clear and powerful strategy for countering the sense of powerlessness and hopelessness that so often leads to acts of violence in communities and workplaces (Garbarino, 1998).

PROMOTING RESPECTFUL, NON-VIOLENT WORK ENVIRONMENTS: DATA AND INFORMATION ON INCIDENCE OF VIOLENCE IN THE WORKPLACE

In October 1993, the Northwestern National Life (NWNL) Insurance Company in Minneapolis published a research study titled *Fear and Violence in the Workplace: A Survey Documenting the Experience of American Workers.* This study, conducted by Peggy Lawless, NWNL Research Project Director, was and continues to be highly influential to the work of the WAT. Key findings of this study are summarized in Table 4. While this study is now almost a decade old, its theme and findings have been confirmed by more recent research, including the following University of North Carolina study (Pearson, 1999). Major findings of this study are summarized in Table 5. The NWNL and North Carolina study findings have been confirmed in interviews and discussions by the WAT with hundreds of employees and managers in Minneapolis-St. Paul workplaces during the course of consultation and training programs. In more than 30 consultations over

TABLE 4. Key Findings of the Fear and Violence in the Workplace Study (North-western National Life Insurance Company, 1993)

1. Violence and harassment in the workplace are pervasive.
2. Violence and harassment affect the health and productivity of victims and other workers.
3. There is a strong relationship between job stress and workplace harassment and violence.
4. American workers believe social issues–especially substance abuse, layoffs, and poverty–are major causes of workplace violence.
5. Harassers are usually co-workers or bosses, while attackers are more likely to be customers.
6. Improved interpersonal relations and effective preventive programs can result in lower levels of violence and harassment.

TABLE 5. Findings from Workplace Incivility, The Target's Eye View Study (Pearson, 1999)

78%	of U.S. workers say incivility has gotten worse in the past 10 years
12%	had to quit a job to avoid a rude co-worker
52%	had lost work time worrying about how they had been treated
22%	reported deliberately slowing down their work in response to rude or insensitive behavior

the past five years with hospitals and clinics, banks, manufacturing and high technology firms, and nonprofit and government agencies, when employees and managers are asked a simple, open-ended question, "What issues and concerns do you have about your workplace?" responses invariably mirror the findings found in Tables 4 and 5–and these responses are elicited *before* sharing the study findings or any other data or information. Responses also typically reflect May's (1969) and Kanter's (1993) themes of powerlessness and its impacts on people.

Based on the findings of the NWNL and University of North Carolina studies and the concurring firsthand statements of issues and concerns in Minneapolis-St. Paul workplaces, WAT members have developed a series of resources, training sessions, and interventions designed to help people begin to recognize and change underlying, dysfunctional patterns of communication and behavior in the workplace. What follows is a discussion of the application of WAT materials and strategies in dozens of workplaces throughout the Minneapolis-St. Paul metropolitan area (WAT materials can be viewed on the Ramsey County website under "Violence Prevention" at www.co.ramsey.mn.us).

TRAINING AND EDUCATIONAL FORUMS

Likely the most powerful "tool" developed and utilized by the WAT has been the collaborative creation of three theatre-based trainings with Theatre at Work, Inc. of St. Paul. Marysue Moses and Alfred Harrison of Theatre at Work have developed three live pieces that have been utilized in conferences and training sessions sponsored by the WAT and organizations throughout the Minneapolis-St. Paul metropolitan area and a variety of venues in cities across the nation. The Action Team has offered 11 major community forums built around these powerful theatre pieces that have provided information and training to over 1,500 people and have been hosted by a number of major Minneapolis-St. Paul employers and institutions, including Honeywell, Land O' Lakes, 3M, St. Paul Companies, University of St. Thomas, Dakota County, Metro State University, Medtronic, The University of Minnesota, and Ramsey County. In addition to Action Team-sponsored events, Theatre at Work has done over 70 performances of the three theatre pieces for employers and communities throughout Minnesota and in numerous cities across the U.S.

One outcome of WAT-sponsored conferences has been making connections with worksites interested in doing follow-up work to improve communication and overall working environments. Between 1998-2002, Action Team members have provided consultations and on-site trainings for over 30 Minneapolis-St. Paul employers, including hospitals, clinics and health care systems, non-profit social service agencies, media agencies, and manufacturing and private office settings. What follows is a description of education and development approaches used by the WAT in individual workplaces, followed by three case studies of one-on-one work with local workplaces.

WAT EDUCATION
AND PREVENTION/INTERVENTION STRATEGIES

WAT members have worked with over 30 Minneapolis-St. Paul employers on developing and implementing tools to assure violence-free, respectful work environments. Some of these encounters have consisted of one-time awareness training sessions, while in other cases WAT members have continued to work on developing and offering resources to employers over a number of years. Initial contact is often made in the form of a non-specific request for "training on workplace violence," while WAT-sponsored public forums and specific issues and events (usually negative) have also precipitated requests to the Team.

WAT services (with the exception of onsite performances by Theatre at Work) are offered free of charge, with the understanding that in-depth skill training and intervention (e.g., conflict resolution, mediation, etc.) would need to be provided separately by qualified professionals. Typically, a community WAT member pairs with staff from Saint Paul-Ramsey County Public Health to work with interested companies and organizations and offer workplaces any or all of the following options:

   1. *Assessing issues and concerns and strengths of the workplace.* WAT consultations begin with discussions with employees and managers to help WAT members evaluate the workplace so education and tools offered in later sessions with workgroups fit and resonate with the organization. These discussions typically result in a list of issues remarkably similar to those cited in the NWNL and University of North Carolina studies: Poor communication exacerbated by unclear standards of behavior and overlapping/confusing job assignments and responsibilities; verbal harassment and harsh language between staff as well as from customers and clients; underlying fears and concerns regarding physical safety; and encounters with family violence issues spilling over into the workplace.

   2. *"Thresholds of Violence" exercise.* This self-assessment tool, created by the WAT, is used to help co-workers and managers understand that we each come into the workplace with very different beliefs about and "thresholds" of violence (see Appendix B). People are reminded that the workplace is a highly unnatural setting; we typically spend more time with people we work with than we do with our families and friends, yet we rarely have honest and clear conversations with co-workers about things that might bother or offend us.

   Participants are asked to rate on a 1-10 scale how violent they perceive each item listed and then compare their responses in small group conversations. A large group discussion is then facilitated exploring why there are so many differences and what they mean in terms of creating respectful, violence-free work environments. Invariably, the thresholds exercise elicits significant differences in responses and beliefs. Two items that always generate important discussion are those concerning gossip and going into a private room and kicking the wall. Generally, most responders will give a low "violence rating" to gossiping about another co-worker's love life, although people who have experienced this in previous workplaces will speak strongly about its potentially devastating impacts. The example of kicking the wall will usually split responders down the middle, with half arguing that it can be a necessary and cathartic release of tension, while others will see such actions as either precursors to violence or in fact see the act of kicking walls as a violent behavior in and of itself. During these discussions, WAT facilitators clarify that there are no right or wrong answers in the thresholds exercise; rather, it is emphasized that we must all understand that we come into work settings with different attitudes and beliefs, and we must be open to learning about and respecting these differences. For a more comprehensive description on scales of workplace aggression, see Sorenson and Heacox (this volume).

Completing the "Thresholds of Violence" exercise and discussion is often a somewhat disorienting experience for participants, partly because they learn how differently colleagues see these common, everyday occurrences and partly because most employees and managers do not have clear, common agreements and understandings about what the term "workplace violence" means. Further, while many workplaces have in place clear standards and systems for addressing "obvious" forms of violence, such as sexual harassment and direct threats of physical violence, most are at a loss when determining if and how to address more subtle and common manifestations of workplace violence and/or inappropriate behaviors along the lines of those covered in the threshold exercise.

There is usually agreement that the behaviors listed in the threshold exercise are unpleasant and perhaps inappropriate, but there is often significant disagreement as to whether they connote "violence," in large part because the word violence implies negative intent and "perpetrators" who are "bad." If a workplace agrees that behaviors as common as gossip and kicking walls in frustration fall under the category of violence, its agreed upon standards of behavior would need to be reflective of this conviction.

3. Data on incidence, forms, and impacts of violence and disrespect in the workplace. Participants are typically led through a presentation of Initiative definitions of violence (words and actions that hurt people; misuse of power and authority; any words or actions where the intention *or* impact causes pain, fear, or hurt). Each workplace is encouraged to undertake their own process to define violence as well as to agree upon appropriate and inappropriate behaviors in their work setting. It is the contention of the WAT that organizations and individual workgroups must develop clear, common understandings and agreements of appropriate and inappropriate behaviors and then own and act on them. For example, one local hospital has a "kicking box" in its emergency room for the use of relieving tension. Whether or not one would agree that this is a healthy way to release tension, the designation of the box as an approved form of venting at least takes away the element of surprise and confusion in the event that a co-worker "uses" the box.

Following the presentation of Initiative violence definitions, participants are provided with data and explanations/perspectives on workplace violence (see Figure 1). "What is Workplace Violence?" data are presented to demonstrate that many preconceived notions about the incidence and face of violence in the workplace are inaccurate. When the subject is raised, two images come up for many: "Disgruntled employees" and "going postal." In fact, the vast majority of incidents of workplace violence involve non-physical violence, characterized in the NWNL study as "verbal harassment and bullying" and in the University of North Carolina study as "workplace incivility" (NWNL, 1993; Pearson, 1999).

A deeper exploration into the incidence of homicide in the American workplace reveals that the vast majority of this manifestation has nothing to do with "disgruntled employees;" indeed, 75% of U.S. workplace homicides are due to robberies (see Figure 2). Further analysis of these data show that the three greatest risk factors for an employee to be killed at work are: (a) working alone, (b) handling money, and (c) working evening and night shifts. So, rather than disgruntled employees or postal service workers, individuals most at risk for being killed at work are in fact cab drivers, pizza delivery people, and convenience store workers. We also see that domestic violence homicides in the workplace, labeled "personal," are roughly as prevalent as killings committed by "disgruntled" co-workers.

FIGURE 1. What Is Workplace Violence?

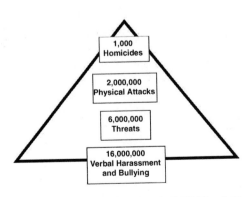

Annual Incidents in United States (out of 100,000,000 workers)

Sources: U.S. Bureau of Labor Statistics (1994-99), Northwestern National Life Insurance Co. (1993)

WAT presentations also clarify that the U.S. Postal Service actually exhibits very low rates of workplace violence, and that it has a very proactive system in place for both primary prevention and intervention (Larson, 2000). Three possibilities are offered for the popular and highly inaccurate notion of "going postal": (a) the U.S. Postal Service has historically been the first or second largest employer in the country, employing roughly one million people (or one percent of the total U.S. workforce); (b) media will typically flash reports of any violent incident involving post office employees across the nation, while the more common incidents of attacks on cab drivers, convenience store clerks, and related workers are highly unlikely to garner national attention; and (c) perhaps most important, by defining workplace violence as "them" (post office and/or disgruntled employees), we are able to distance the problem from "us."

Figure 3, titled "Workplace Harassment Perpetrators," is based on data from the 1993 NWNL study. The point of this graphic, corroborated by scores of conversations with employees and managers at various Minneapolis-St. Paul workplaces, is to show that the most common form of violence in American workplaces is verbal harassment and bullying (or "workplace incivility" in the more recent language of the 1999 Pearson study) between peer employees, closely followed by the same behaviors between employees and their supervisors. (For more information on bullying in the workplace, see Koonin & Green, this volume). This finding has strongly influenced the primary prevention tools and approaches developed and advocated by the WAT: To work with employees and managers to understand their power to both harm

FIGURE 2. U.S. Job Related Homicides

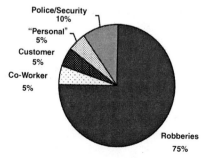

Source: U.S. Bureau of Labor Statistics (1994-99)

FIGURE 3. Workplace Harassment Perpetrators

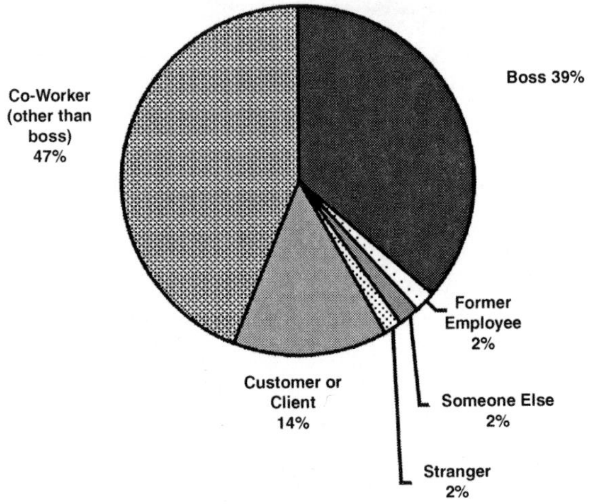

Source: Northwestern National Life Insurance Company (1993)

one another with words or actions, as well as their power to create and sustain a violence-free, respectful workplace culture.

4. *Specialized sessions, approaches, and tools.* Each encounter between WAT members and individuals and groups in a workplace begins by assessing issues, concerns, and strengths within the work environment. Following the process of identifying specific issues in workplaces outlined above, participants typically engage in one or more specialized experiences. These may include:

a. Experiential training using *What Do Great Supervisors Look Like* booklets (Workplace Action Team, 1995). Groups of managers and supervisors may be given the booklets and asked to portray/teach some or all of the key points provided in the booklet. For example:
    Point 10. *"Relationship is an action, not a feeling."* Okay, so think about putting your feelings into action here: support and respect the employee, and act responsibly on her behalf. Responsibility in relationships means being ready to do something to meet the needs of another human being.
    Point 11. *"Be a leader."* Every worker deserves to be encouraged. Every worker deserves to look forward to a good day. Every worker deserves adequate control over his or her own work. That's all. You can do that.

b. Training and development of tools to address issues specific to the workplace, such as reducing tensions for families and the incidence of children being mistreated in public (see WIC case study below).
c. Overviews on developing and implementing violence-free, respectful workplace policies.
d. Creation of tools for employees to use to form agreements of respectful conduct among each other (see hospitals case study below).
e. Training and sharing of resources to promote family-friendly workplaces, using tools created through other Initiative Action Teams. (See www.co.ramsey.mn.us under Violence Prevention/Peaceful Parenting for examples of tools.)

What follows are three case studies describing approaches and outcomes using the strategies and resources outlined above.

CASE STUDY 1:
INTERVENING IN A NOT-FOR-PROFIT
HUMAN SERVICES AGENCY

Background/issue. A local non-profit agency with a history of conflict among staff and between staff and management reached a crisis situation when several people in key leadership positions were placed on administrative leave and ultimately terminated over allegations of discrimination and other internal management problems. Direct service staff began to allege discrimination and harassment on the part of direct supervisors and refused to perform many basic job functions, and threats were made to take allegations and concerns to local news media.

Communication within and between departments became strained and was characterized by hostility and fear. Management and many staff recognized that escalation of hostilities would increase the likelihood of losing more key employees and continue affecting morale and productivity and, if unchecked, the agency might be in danger of losing public grant funds and support.

WAT solution/approach. Two WAT members met with a middle management support team to develop a course of action. After reviewing WAT materials and gaining perspective from data and experiences with other workplaces, it was determined that the best initial approach would be to separate long-term issues from immediate threats to the organization's short- and long-term viability. A decision was made to create a "Cease Fire Agreement" to attempt to end immediate, high-level hostilities (see Appendix C for text of agreement). This agreement was presented to and embraced by the agency's Senior Management Team and was presented to all staff. In addition, WAT "Respect" pins were distributed to all staff, and WAT "I can do my best work here, because we all . . ." signs[3] were posted throughout all agency offices and facilities.

Results/impact. Staff and management on all levels agreed that the "Cease Fire" and accompanying materials and discussion diffused immediate tension levels and improved short-term communication and relationship issues. The agency is in the process of sorting through long-term issues and needed changes.

CASE STUDY 2:
ENDING VERBAL AND PHYSICAL ABUSE
OF CHILDREN IN WIC CLINICS

Background/issue. In 1998, staff and management at nine WIC (Women, Infants, and Children federal nutrition program) clinics in St. Paul-Ramsey County identified concerns over harsh treatment of children, including verbal and physical abuse at clinic sites. Staff were unsure about when and how to intervene and were apprehensive about the likelihood that any intervention might exacerbate the situation, resulting in confrontations with parents at the clinic and/or increased physical punishment at home.

WAT solution/approach.[4] WAT and Peaceful Parenting Team members worked with WIC staff to assess underlying causes of the situation and develop prevention and intervention strategies. Two major areas were explored and addressed: Powerlessness (May, 1969) and financial strain. With regard to powerlessness, discussion with staff underscored the fact that in a culture such as the United States, where status and prestige are largely measured by material wealth, by definition many if not all of the people served by the WIC program may be feeling some degree of powerlessness. In addition, fiscal strain was also identified as a potential contributor to the violence seen in the clinics. In Ramsey County, as in many WIC programs in Minnesota, there is not enough grant money to pay rent for WIC clinic sites. This has led to local WIC clinics being located largely in donated spaces not originally designed to be clinics. Little or no resources were historically available for anything beyond the fundamental service priorities of the program.

Given these factors, it became evident that the behaviors being witnessed (children running around, parents feeling stressed and too often using harsh words and physical punishment to discipline their children in the clinics) were in fact predictable and perhaps preventable. Staff identified as a goal to promote peaceful parenting and create safe, non-violent clinic spaces. A three-step approach was developed and implemented in early 1998:

1. *Environment.* In order to promote the peaceful treatment of children in St. Paul-Ramsey County WIC clinics, the first step was changing environments. To create a more inviting environment for children, families, and staff, the following items were purchased and made available in each clinic site: Children's tables and chairs, play area rugs, paper and crayons, washable, durable toys, and soothing music tapes. Staff noticed that the simple availability of these items had an immediate, positive impact on children, parents, and clinic staff. By adding these simple resources into the physical environment, behaviors and the overall feel of the clinics changed in a profound and lasting manner.

2. *Messages and resources.* Beginning in late 1997, WIC staff started distributing refrigerator magnets and displaying posters promoting peaceful parenting.5 Staff were also trained and encouraged to genuinely greet all families with positive reinforcement and assurance. For example, "It's great to see you here today," and "It's OK for you/your child to be scared–many parents and children are" (the latter statement refers to the blood samples obtained via a finger stick to test for iron levels at some WIC visits).

3. *Responses/Intervention.* All WIC staff received training in late 1997 using the University of Minnesota's *Positive Parenting* curriculum, giving them core knowledge on discipline strategies based on alternatives to physical punishment ad some of the negative impacts that can result from harsh parenting and extreme physical punishment. Staff were then trained in three core techniques for responding to increasing tension and harsh treatment of children in the clinic: distraction, redirection, and enforcement (see Table 6).

Results/Impact. The environmental changes in St. Paul-Ramsey County WIC clinics had an immediate and profound effect on behaviors and the overall feel of the clinics. Previously observed behaviors of parents sometimes struggling and threatening/punishing their children in WIC clinics have essentially vanished. "Children's Corners" have been institutionalized in the clinics and both staff and families served by the WIC program have commented verbally and in satisfaction surveys that these efforts have significantly improved the environment and services provided at local WIC clinics. Six years into the effort, the placement of simple children's toys and amenities combined with the intentional, respectful, and caring greeting of parents who may be walking into the clinic under stress continue to have a clear, positive impact on families and the WIC staff who serve them.

TABLE 6. Response Techniques Taught in WIC Clinics

Distraction

The initial intervention to be used when staff first notice tension, which can include handing out food and toys, sharing common experiences and praising children and parents, and showing children and/or parents how scales, height measures, etc., are used in the clinic.

Redirection

Used when tensions have escalated further, using language such as "It looks like you're having a hard time–is there something I can do to help?"

Enforcement

Used when staff observe harsh words, physical punishment, and/or threats. Each clinic identified "interveners" who expressed willingness to be called on in these situations; interveners were provided with specific language to utilize in these extreme situations: "I have to ask you to not talk/act like that in our clinic" or "This is a safe place for children and families–please do not treat/speak to your child that way in our clinic." Enforcement statements are always followed with redirection (e.g., showing understanding to the parents and offering them community resources).

CASE STUDY 3:
ASSESSING AND ADDRESSING CONFLICT IN MINNEAPOLIS-ST. PAUL HOSPITALS

Background/issue. WAT members have worked directly with staff in several Minneapolis-St. Paul hospitals in assessing communication problems and abusive treatment of co-workers in emergency rooms, operating rooms, and maternity care floors. Conflicts and hurtful behaviors were occurring between physicians and nursing staff, among nursing staff, and between medical/nursing and support staff. Manifestations ranged from yelling and throwing objects (charts and equipment) at one another, to swearing in front of patients and their families, and to bickering and gossip.

WAT solution/approach. Each WAT hospital encounter started with meetings with hospital management, physicians, nurse managers, and various levels of staff. Following these initial meetings, WAT members worked with hospital staff to identify root causes of identified behaviors. In each case, major issues/causes revolved around lack of clarity about roles and functions within and across professional groups, minimal or no mechanisms to diffuse and deal with the stress inherent in working in the hospital setting, and long-standing patterns of harsh and often abusive communication which came to be seen as normal. In an interview with one nurse manager, concerns were raised about the impact of contemporary television shows in hospital settings depicting physicians and hospital employees yelling and abusing one another–the very behaviors this manager has seen in physicians and her own staff.

In each case, physicians and hospital staff developed tools to diffuse and prevent abusive and hurtful behaviors. These have included posters designed to set a caring tone for all people coming into one Maternity Care Center that read: "We care for you, for your baby, for your family, for each other," as well as reminder cards for emergency room physicians and staff with agreed upon language such as "I am concerned" to use to get one another's attention in stressful situations, rather than yelling at one another to be sure to get the attention of colleagues.

Results/impact. Early results of these efforts indicate that in those cases where there is consistent acceptance and usage from all levels of staff and management, the tools created by physicians and staff in conjunction with the educational information brought in by WAT members have been effective in lowering the incidence of overt negative behaviors. In the long run it will also be necessary to clarify ongoing concerns regarding roles among and across various professional disciplines as well as to develop and implement effective strategies for handling the stress and pain that can accompany work in today's health care environment.

CONCLUSION

Since 1990, the WAT has been working with public, private, and not-for-profit workplaces throughout the Minneapolis-St. Paul metropolitan area to help develop and promote violence-free, respectful workplaces. The term "workplace violence" often connotes images, fed by sensational media stories, of fictional "disgruntled employees." The WAT's experience has shown that understanding and preventing workplace violence often begins by asking a question from a quite different perspective: "How do we learn to truly listen to one another and treat each other with dignity and respect?"

We all have the choice and power to develop workplaces and businesses that at their core are built upon embracing and respecting the humanity of the people that both work at and use or purchase their products and services. The comprehensive approach advocated by the WAT, which is simultaneously complicated and remarkably simple, can enhance morale and productivity in the workplace.

NOTES

1. Primary prevention refers to reaching the entire population with tools and resources designed to prevent violence before it occurs.
2. The Initiative does not claim ownership of these definitions of violence. They are based on the work of many people involved for the past three decades in intervening in

domestic/family violence cases, as well as understandings brought by Action Team members gained previous to as well as a part of working on Initiative Action Teams.

3. See Ramsey County website for full text and graphics of this sign.

4. The clinics described in this case study are part of the St. Paul-Ramsey County Department of Public Health; the actions outlined were a collaborative effort of the WAT, the Initiative Peaceful Parenting Action Team, and staff of WIC and Public Health.

5. See Violence Prevention/Peaceful Parenting at www.co.ramsey.mn.us.

REFERENCES

Garbarino, J. (1998, September 29). *Ecological approaches to violence prevention.* Keynote Address, Community Approaches to Violence Prevention Conference, Grand Rapids, MI.

Heacox, N. J. & Sorenson, R. C., (2004). Organizational frustration and aggressive behaviors. *Journal of Emotional Abuse, 4*(3/4), pp. 95-118.

Kanter, R. M. (1993). *Men and women of the corporation.* New York: Basic Books.

Koonin, M., & Green, T. M. (2004). The emotionally abusive workplace. *Journal of Emotional Abuse, 4*(3/4), pp. 71-80.

Larson, L. (2000, October). *Navigating stormy waters.* Presentation at the National Union of Letter Carriers, Branch 9, St. Paul, MN.

League of Women Voters of Minneapolis. (1990, April). *Breaking the cycle of violence: A focus on primary prevention efforts.* Minneapolis, MN: League of Women Voters.

May, R. (1969). *Love and will.* New York: Delacourte Press.

Northwestern National Life Insurance Company. (1993, October). *Fear and violence in the workplace.* Minneapolis, MN: Author.

Pearson, C. (1999). *Workplace incivility: The target's eye view.* Chapel Hill, NC: University of North Carolina, Chapel Hill.

QuoteDB.com. (2004). Mahatma Ghandi. Retrieved July 13, 2004, from http://www.quotedb.com/quotes/2050.

U.S. Department of Labor, Bureau of Labor Statistics. (2004). *Census of fatal occupational injuries (averaged 1994-99).* Retrieved July 13, 2004, from www.bls.gov.

Workplace Action Team (1995) *What do great supervisors look like?* Minneapolis-St. Paul, MN: Author.

APPENDIX A

Three Levels of Prevention

In public health there is a differentiation between the primary, secondary, and tertiary prevention. In primary prevention, no group nor individual is designated "high risk;" instead, approaches are designed to bring a message or skill set to an entire population in order to prevent those individuals from ever beginning a risky behavior or practice. In secondary prevention, prevention messages and tools are targeted to individuals and groups who are already engaged in potentially damaging behaviors, but are not yet showing any ill effects as a result. In tertiary prevention, or intervention, strategies are geared toward people who are both engaged in risky behaviors *and* who are in need of treatment to address ill effects caused by these behaviors.

Cigarette smoking provides a simple analogy to illustrate the three levels of prevention. Primary prevention efforts are designed to provide populations with information and incentives in order to convince people to not start smoking in the first place; secondary prevention campaigns target people who are smokers, but have not yet developed any smoking-related illnesses, with messages and tools to quit smoking before they become ill; while tertiary intervention efforts must convince and assist smokers to break their habit while simultaneously providing treatment for emphysema, lung cancer, and other smoking-related diseases.

This analogy points to the difficulty and often seemingly poor results inherent in traditional approaches to intervening in cases of family violence (as well as other manifestations of violence in the workplace, community, schools, etc.). Intervention systems by definition must wait until serious, documented harm has occurred in a family/school/workplace setting and then come in to both break the cycle of violence, attempt to heal or undo the effects of violence to individuals, and provide consequences to "perpetrators" (while generally ignoring the effects on other people and community systems around them).

APPENDIX B

Thresholds of Violence Exercise

An important part of understanding violence in our homes, workplaces, and communities is to acknowledge that we each have different thresholds. Take a look at the following situations and rate them relative to your opinion concerning the level of violence they represent.

1 (non violent)---------------5 (moderately violent)--------------10 (very violent)

Situation   *Your violence rating (1-10)*

You gossip with a co-worker about another colleague's love life.   ----------

Your co-worker has a bad temper, so everyone tiptoes around her.   ----------

You get angry, go into a private room, and kick the wall.   ----------

You complete a phone call with an angry client, slam the phone
down, and call him a rude name.   ----------

Your supervisor tells one of your co-workers she is incompetent.   ----------

You are standing within hearing range and the supervisor knows it.   ----------

APPENDIX C

"Cease Fire Agreement" for Human Services Agency

In the spirit of kindness and respect, we acknowledge that in our current work environment, it is difficult for many of us to do our jobs well and feel supported by co-workers and the agency.

We are concerned about damage to individual and group relationships, as well as the reputation of (the agency) in the greater community, and our ability to best serve our clients and families.

There are deep and complicated issues that need to be addressed in the long term, and lasting solutions will require each of us to commit to healing and change.

In the short run, let us all commit to:

- Expressing concerns in a constructive, non-hurtful manner
- Talking about what can be done to promote a respectful environment
- Communicating positively about our co-workers and agency

Emotional Abuse in the Classroom: A Cultural Dilemma?

Almon Shumba

SUMMARY. Current research shows that emotional abuse has been under researched within the classroom and yet it is now considered to be the most devastating form of child abuse. The main objectives of the present study are to determine who the perpetrators of emotional abuse are, and why some teachers emotionally abuse pupils in Zimbabwean primary schools. The Teacher Trainees and Pupil Questionnaires were administered to randomly selected samples of teachers and teacher train-

Address correspondence to: Almon Shumba, PhD, Department of Educational Psychology, University of the North, Private Bag X1106, Sovenga 0727, South Africa (E-mail: almonshumba@yahoo.com).

The author would like to thank the Ministry of Education, Sport, and Culture, and the Ministry of Higher Education for granting him the permission to carry out this study in their schools and colleges, respectively. The author's thanks also go to all the teachers, teacher trainees, and pupils who participated in this study.

[Haworth co-indexing entry note]: "Emotional Abuse in the Classroom: A Cultural Dilemma?" Shumba, Almon. Co-published simultaneously in *Journal of Emotional Abuse* (The Haworth Maltreatment & Trauma Press, an imprint of The Haworth Press, Inc.) Vol. 4, No. 3/4, 2004, pp. 139-149; and: *Aggression in Organizations: Violence, Abuse, and Harassment at Work and in Schools* (ed: Robert Geffner et al.) The Haworth Maltreatment & Trauma Press, an imprint of The Haworth Press, Inc., 2004, pp. 139-149. Single or multiple copies of this article are available for a fee from The Haworth Document Delivery Service [1-800-HAWORTH, 9:00 a.m. - 5:00 p.m. (EST). E-mail address: docdelivery@haworthpress.com].

Digital Object Identifier: 10.1300/J135v04n03_09

ees, and Form One pupils, respectively. This was a retrospective study because teacher trainees were required to recall their experiences about why some teachers emotionally abuse their pupils in schools. Results clearly show that emotional abuse of pupils by teachers is a now reality in Zimbabwean primary schools. *[Article copies available for a fee from The Haworth Document Delivery Service: 1-800-HAWORTH. E-mail address: <docdelivery@haworthpress.com> Website: <http://www.HaworthPress.com> © 2004 by The Haworth Press, Inc. All rights reserved.]*

KEYWORDS. Emotional abuse, teachers, teacher trainees, pupils, causes, culture, schools

Although emotional abuse is now known to cause devastating damage to children in the same way as sexual and physical abuse, there is very little classroom research that has examined teachers' and pupils' perceptions of this form of child abuse (Doyle, 1997; Krugman & Krugman, 1984). Most studies have concentrated on defining emotional abuse and speculating at some of its main causes (Corson & Davidson, cited in Melton & Corson, 1987; Krugman & Krugman, 1984; Melton & Corson, 1987). For example, Corson and Davidson (cited in Melton & Corson, 1987) found that nine states in the United States include the term 'mental injury' in their definitions of emotional abuse under their laws. Trowell (1983) views emotional abuse as involving "parental indifference, lack of emotional warmth, love, protection, support, and discipline" (pg. 252). This definition implies that there is rejection of the child by parents involving verbal threats and abuse, scapegoating, constant criticism, and humiliation of the child (O'Brian & Lau, 1995).

Other studies suggest that emotional abuse is considered in some cultures as part of the child-rearing practices (Amdi, 1990; Garbarino, 1978; Korbin, 1980; O'Brian & Lau, 1995). In her study of child neglect in Nigeria, Amdi (1990) found that parents lack knowledge of what emotional abuse is and its consequences on child development. Under such a scenario, emotional abuse seems to be viewed as part of the child-rearing practices. Similarly, O'Brian and Lau (1995) in their study of child abuse among the Chinese in Hong Kong found that children are verbally abused and humiliated publicly by parents as part of the child-rearing practices. Despite the fact that such acts on children are considered to be a molding tool for the child's personality, it is also meant to scare the "would-be-culprits" from any form of misbehavior (Doyle, 1997; O'Brian & Lau, 1995; Rohner & Rohner, 1980; Shumba, 2002). It is also possible to speculate that one of the reasons why some teachers are not able to recognize emotional abuse as a form of child abuse is because some parents practice it on their children publicly and at home (O'Brian & Lau, 1995; Shumba, 2002). Other studies claim that emotional abuse is now viewed as the most devastating form of child abuse (Rohner & Rohner, 1980; Shumba, 2002). In this study, emotional abuse shall be considered as verbal aggression, humiliation, harassment, belittling, shouting, scolding, labeling, use of vulgar language, threatening, degrading, and terrorizing of pupils by teachers in schools.

EMOTIONAL ABUSE IN SCHOOLS

In their comprehensive study of emotional abuse in the classroom, Krugman and Krugman (1984) observed 17 elementary pupils who were abused by their teacher. The victims reported the following behaviors by their teacher: Harassment, verbal put-downs, labeling (e.g., "stupid," or "dummy"), screaming at children until they cried, inappropriate threats to try to control the class, allowing some children to harass and belittle others, use of homework as punishment, throwing homework at children, and physical punishment. In this study, abused pupils were found to exhibit the following symptoms: Excessive worry about school performance (88%), change from positive to negative self-perception (76%), changes in school performance from previous years (76%), verbalized fear that the teacher would hurt children (71%), excessive crying about school (35%), headaches (35%), stomach aches (29%), decreased functioning in social situations outside class (29%), nightmares or sleep disturbances (24%), school avoidance or refusal (24%), and withdrawal behavior or depression (18%). It is clear from these symptoms that emotional abuse has a devastating effect on the development of children and their performance in class. Therefore, there is a need to investigate emotional abuse in the classroom so that teachers, pupils, and parents can become aware of its effects on pupils in schools.

Similarly, in a recent study of emotional abuse in the classroom, Shumba (2002) found that the majority of teacher trainees (84.7%) and teachers (80.7%) believe that shouting, scolding, use of vulgar language, humiliation, and negatively labeling pupils as stupid, ugly, or foolish is mainly perpetrated by female teachers in schools. The study also found that teachers perpetrate the following forms of emotional abuse on their pupils: Shouting at pupils, scolding pupils for mistakes, use of vulgar language, humiliating pupils publicly, and negatively labeling pupils as stupid, ugly, or foolish. In the same study of emotional abuse in the classroom, Shumba (2002) found that during the period of January 1, 1990 through December 31, 1997 only one case was reported to the Public Service Commission by the school head through the Ministry of Education, Sport, and Culture. In this case, the perpetrator verbally abused and threatened to impregnate all 25 female pupils in his class. Given the emotionally abusive behaviors that teachers themselves reported engaging in, it appears that there is a distinct underreporting by teachers and pupils in schools.

In a similar vein, Hart, Germain, and Brassard (1983) found that emotional abuse can damage the behavioral, cognitive, affective, social, and physiological functioning of the child. McLean Hospital Researchers (Bolshakov, Carlezon, Kandel, & Teicher, 2000) found four types of brain abnormalities that are caused by child abuse and neglect, of which one form is linked to emotional abuse that is linked to permanent damage of the brain. The four types of brain abnormalities that they found are limbic irritability, arrested development of the left hemisphere, deficient integration between the left and right hemispheres, and increased verbal activity. The researchers also found that stress and neglect experienced early in life are linked to the development of fear, anxiety, and stress in children. These findings are very important to teachers, pupils, and parents because they impact the physical, cognitive, emotional, and social development of a child, as well as the child's performance within the classroom.

Unlike sexual and physical abuse, emotional abuse is considered to be the most difficult form of abuse to defend under the law because it is intangible (Hart, 1987; Hart & Brassard, 1991). The damage that emotional abuse causes to a child is difficult to measure because it is internal and affects the child's self-concept and emotions (Dean, 1979; Doyle, 1997). Emotional abuse is different from sexual abuse and physical abuse in that the perpetrator may not know that he or she is abusing someone and the victim may not realize that he or she is being abused (Krugman & Krugman, 1984; Melton & Corson, 1987). In most cases, the victim is on the receiving end because of a power differential (Jones, 1994). Since there are no consistent or clear legal criteria for determining emotional abuse globally (Ney, 1987), it implies that the child is vulnerable to this form of abuse. It appears from the available literature that most parents are ignorant of what emotional abuse is and the subsequent consequences it has on child development.

The present study seeks to determine who the perpetrators of emotional abuse are, and why some teachers emotionally abuse pupils in Zimbabwean primary schools. The study also examines possible African cultural practices that could influence teachers to abuse pupils emotionally within the classroom.

METHOD

Participants

The study used a randomly selected sample of 300 primary school teachers, 150 primary teacher trainees, and 200 Form One pupils in the Masvingo province of Zimbabwe. Form one pupils are first year secondary or high school pupils who are typically between 11 to 13-years-old. All the schools used in this study were public schools and each class had about 40 pupils. Teachers were randomly selected from 25 primary public schools; Form One pupils were randomly selected from five secondary schools; and teacher trainees were randomly selected from three primary teachers' colleges in three districts in Masvingo province.

Teachers themselves were used in this study because most studies on emotional abuse have never considered their perceptions of this form of child abuse in schools (Krugman & Krugman, 1984; Shumba, 2002). Form One pupils were used to reflect on their experiences when they were in primary school because the perpetrators are no longer present and they can freely verbalize their views.

Teacher trainees used in this study were in their final year of training, and had just completed a year of teaching practice in which they shadowed more experienced teachers to learn from them. Teacher trainees were used in this study because they observed how experienced teachers treated their pupils during their lessons. An equal number of both male and female primary teacher trainees were randomly selected in this study. The study assumes that these teacher trainees observed how experienced teachers treated their pupils in schools and why some of them emotionally abuse their pupils. It must be pointed out that this study is a part of a larger study that examined the epidemiology and aetiology of child abuse, including sexual abuse, physical abuse, and the "hidden curriculum of abuse," by teachers in schools. The "hidden curriculum of abuse" is a form of child abuse whereby pupils are sent to teachers' houses during school hours to do domestic chores, such as washing plates and pots, sweeping the teacher's house, making the teacher's bed, washing the teacher's clothes, or fetching water and firewood for the teacher, etc. (Shumba, 2000). This form of child abuse has been found to be prevalent in Zimbabwean rural primary schools (Shumba, 2000).

Permission to administer the questionnaires to Form one pupils was sought from the Ministry of Education, Sport, and Culture. To administer questionnaires to teacher trainees in primary teachers' colleges, permission was granted by the Ministry of Higher Education. In this study, emotional abuse refers to constant belittling of a pupil, the absence of a positive emotional atmosphere, verbal aggression, harassment, scolding, labeling, verbal abuse, and the humiliating and terrorizing of pupils by teachers in schools. Most research on this form of child abuse shows that it has profound effects on the self-concept and self-esteem of the child during development (Bolshakov et al., 2000; Krugman & Krugman, 1984; Shumba, 2002).

Materials

Data used to determine perpetrators of emotional abuse and why some teachers emotionally abuse pupils in Zimbabwean primary schools was collected using the Teacher Questionnaire (TQ; Shumba, 2000), Teacher Trainees Questionnaire (TTQ; Shumba, 2000), and the Pupil Questionnaire (PQ; Shumba, 2000). Each of these questionnaires contains a mixture of both closed and open-ended questions.

Design and Procedure

This was a retrospective study for the Form One pupils because they were required to recall how and why some teachers emotionally abused them during their primary education. Teacher trainees were also required to recall their observations of how and why some of their mentors emotionally abused pupils in schools during their teaching practice. All the subjects used in this study were also asked to give reasons why some teachers emotionally abuse pupils in schools.

RESULTS

Table 1 shows that the majority of pupils (69.5%) reported that male teachers engaged in verbal abuse such as labeling and name-calling, 56.5% reported that female teachers had engaged in verbal aggression such as shouting, and 59.5% reported that teachers had used aggressive and derogatory language toward students; in addition, 56.5% reported that they or other students had experienced negative emotional states following such abuse.

Table 2 shows that the majority of the respondents (75.5%) believe that teachers shout at pupils to discipline them, 66.5% believe that it is a means of controlling them, 61.5% believe that it is an expression of anger; and 50.5% believe that they deserve to be shouted at. Many of the respondents (42.3%) think that some teachers shout at them "to humiliate them," 35.2% "for refusing to have sex with them," (15.3%) "for refusing to fall in love with the teacher," and (9.2%) "to discipline them."

TABLE 1. Emotional Abuse Perpetrated on Their Pupils by the Perpetrator's Gender (*N* = 200)

	Perpetrator Gender	
Type of Abuse	Male	Female
a) shouting at me or others	87 (43.5%)	113 (56.5%)
b) using bad language on me or other pupils	119 (59.5%)	81 (40.5%)
c) deliberately making me or other pupils feel bad	113 (56.5%)	87 (43.5%)
d) calling me or other pupils names	139 (69.5%)	61 (30.5%)

TABLE 2. Reasons Why Teachers Shout at Pupils in School (*N* = 200)

Reason	True	False
a) they think it is the way to discipline pupils	151 (75.5%)	49 (24.5%)
c) they want to control pupils who do wrong things	133 (66.5%)	67 (33.5%)
b) they want to show their anger	123 (61.5%)	77 (38.5%)
d) they think pupils deserve it	101 (50.5%)	99 (49.5%)

Table 3 shows that the majority of teacher trainees (92.7%) and teachers (82.3%) believe that teachers emotionally abuse their pupils because "they want to control pupils who misbehave." On the contrary, the majority of teacher trainees (88.7%) and teachers (82.3%) believe that "it is a way to discipline pupils."

In this study, teacher trainees believe that teachers emotionally abuse their pupils in schools so that they can mould and shape their behavior; work harder and succeed in school; discourage other pupils from misbehaving; because they lack alternatives on how to deal with such pupils; to maintain discipline; it is habitual for some teachers to scold pupils; because they are short tempered; to build moral and upright pupils; because some teachers feel under-rated and powerless; and because some female teachers often use verbal punishment due to the fact that they are not bold enough to give corporal punishment, especially to big boys.

On the other hand, teachers emotionally abuse their pupils in schools because they are too emotional, harsh, hostile, or short-tempered; to maintain discipline; because some pupils are stubborn; they think that it is better than hitting pupils;

TABLE 3. Reasons Why Teachers Emotionally Abuse Their Pupils in School ($N = 300$)

Reason	Teacher Trainees		Teachers	
	True	False	True	False
a) they want to control pupils who misbehave	39 (92.7%)	11 (7.3%)	247 (82.3%)	53 (17.7%)
b) they think that it is a way to discipline pupils	133 (88.7%)	17 (11.3%)	247 (82.3%)	53 (17.7%)
c) they will be venting their anger and because of pressure of work	64 (42.7%)	86 (57.3%)	123 (41.0%)	177 (59.0%)
d) they feel that pupils deserve it	58 (38.7%)	92 (61.3%)	104 (34.7%)	196 (65.3%)

they believe that it educates the pupil; because of frustrations at home; because they are harsh; to control pupils' unruly behaviors; they do not want to be labeled as weak; and they lack knowledge on alternatives.

DISCUSSION

It is clear from the findings that most male teachers were engaged in verbal abuse such as labeling and name-calling while most female teachers were engaged in verbal aggression such as shouting at pupils in schools. As such, most pupils think that teachers do it as a way to discipline them; to control pupils who do wrong things; to show their anger; and they also believe that pupils deserve it. It is clear from the pupils' responses that some teachers appear to view shouting as a way of disciplining pupils within the school and not as abuse. While in some cultures this is viewed as child abuse, emotional abuse appears to be viewed as a way to discipline pupils within the Zimbabwean context. Similarly, both teacher trainees and teachers seem to agree with pupils' perceptions that what researchers have operationalized as emotional abuse is a way to discipline pupils in schools and is not abusive.

In contrast to students' beliefs, less than one-half of teacher trainees and teachers believe that emotional abuse of students is a means of expressing anger or frustration or that it is done because students deserve it. These findings seem to allude to the cultural perceptions of both teacher trainees and teachers in that they view the practice as a way to discipline pupils in schools and not as abuse (Krugman & Krugman, 1984; Shumba, 2002).

It was interesting to note that a large number of pupils believe that some teachers emotionally abuse them "for refusing to have sex with them" and "for refusing to fall in love with the teacher" (see Winters, this volume). Pupils at this stage are between 11- and 13-years-old. The majority of their teachers are between 21- and 40-years-old. Such behavior by teachers is not culturally accepted because teachers act *in loco-parentis* within the school. In other words, they act as on behalf of the actual parents within the school and are expected to protect their pupils against sexual abuse (Shumba, 2001, 2002; Zindi & Shumba, 1999). According to the Public Service (Disciplinary) Regulations, any teacher found having sex with his or her pupil with or without the pupil's consent is supposed to be discharged from the teaching service (Statutory Instrument 65 of the Constitution of Zimbabwe, 1992). In such a situation, the teacher is considered to be abusing his or her authority or power over the pupil (Jones, 1994; Summit, 1983).

The underlying message from both teacher trainees and teachers appears to be that teachers are not aware that emotional abuse is a form of child abuse that has serious consequences on the development of children. It appears that teachers view emotional abuse as responsible in the moulding and shaping of pupils' behavior and that teachers lack alternatives in dealing with pupils who misbehave in their schools. The study also found that some teachers humiliate their pupils to discipline them in class. It appears that most teachers are not aware about what is and is not emotional abuse within the school and its effects on child development.

There are contrasting views from pupils and teachers in terms of the effects of emotional abuse. Most teachers appear to indicate that they verbally abuse pupils as way to discipline them and to control those pupils who misbehave. This implies that such teachers do not view this as abuse but rather as part of child-rearing practices, primarily because scolding of children is acceptable at home (Amdi, 1995; Shumba, 2002). There appears to be a cultural conflict between what goes on in the school and at home because emotional abuse (i.e., verbal abuse) is believed to be part of the child-rearing practices from the Zimbabwean perspective.

These findings seem to be consistent with literature that claims that emotional abuse is a form of child abuse where the perpetrator does not know that he or she is being abusive and where the abuse victim does not know that he or she is being abused (Doyle, 1997; Krugman & Krugman, 1984; O'Brian & Lau, 1995; Shumba, 2002). While some teachers have good intentions, believing that they are moulding the behavior of their pupils from a cultural point of view, there is a negative impact on these children's development (Krugman & Krugman, 1984; O'Hagan, 1995; Rohner, 1975).

It is clear from the above findings that emotional abuse of pupils by teachers is a reality in Zimbabwean primary schools. It appears that most teachers are not aware that they are emotionally abusive; rather, they believe that it is a way to discipline children in school because this is what happens at home (Amdi, 1995; Shumba, 2002).

There is an urgent need for the Ministry of Education, Sport, and Culture to mount awareness workshops, seminars, and conferences for teachers, parents, and pupils where they would discuss what is and is not child abuse within the school context or home, as well as its effects on child development. Laws that protect children against emotional abuse need to be reviewed because those that are available appear to be too lenient to the perpetrators. Such seminars, workshops, and conferences are vital because they would enhance awareness about the effects of emotional abuse on children. It must also be pointed that since this study was retrospective, there is a limitation that both pupils and teacher trainees may have forgotten some of their experiences since they were now in different settings than when the data were collected.

REFERENCES

Amdi, V. (1990). The cause of child abuse and neglect and their effects on the development of children in Samaru Zaria, Nigeria. *Early Child Development and Care, 58,* 31-43.

Bolshakov, V., Carlezon, W., Kandel, E., & Teicher, M. (2000). *McLean researchers document: Brain damage linked to child abuse and neglect.* Retrieved December 14, 2000 from, http://www.mcleanhospital.org/PublicAffairs/20001214_brainchangeslearning.html.

Dean, D. (1979). Emotional abuse of children. *Children Today, 8*(4), 18-20.

Doyle, C. (1997). Emotional abuse of children: Issues for intervention. *Child Abuse Review, 6,* 330-342.

Garbarino, J. (1978). The elusive 'crime' of emotional abuse. *Child Abuse and Neglect, 2,* 89-99.

Hart, S. N. (1987). Psychological maltreatment in schooling. *School Psychology Review, 16*(2), 169-180.

Hart, S. N., & Brassard, M. R. (1991). Psychological maltreatment: Progress achieved. *Developmental and Psychopathology, 3,* 61-70.

Hart, S. N., Germain, R. B., & Brassard, M. R. (Eds.) (1983). *Proceedings summary of the international conference on psychological abuse of children and youth.* Office for the study of the psychological rights of the child, Indiana University.

Jones, J. (1994). Towards an understanding of power relations in institutional abuse. *Early Child Development and Care, 100,* 69-76.

Korbin, J. E. (1980). The cultural context of child abuse and neglect. *Child Abuse and Neglect, 4,* 3-13.

Krugman, R. D., & Krugman, M. K. (1984). Emotional abuse in the classroom: The pediatrician's role in diagnosis and treatment. *American Journal of Diseases of Children, 138,* 284-286.

Melton, G. B., & Corson, J. (1987) Psychological maltreatment and the schools: Problems of the law and professional responsibility. *School Psychology Review, 16*(2), 188-194.

Ney, P. G. (1987). Does verbal abuse leave deeper scars: A study of children and parents. *Canadian Journal of Psychiatry, 32,* 371-378.

O'Brian, C., & Lau, L. S. W. (1995). Defining child abuse in Hong Kong. *Child Abuse Review, 4,* 38-46.

O'Hagan, K. P. (1995). Emotional and psychological abuse: Problems of definition. *Child Abuse and Neglect, 19,* 449-461.

Rohner, R. (1975). *They love me, they love me not: A world study of the effects of parental acceptance and rejection.* New Haven, CT: HRAF Press.

Rohner, R., & Rohner, E. C. (1980). Antecedents and consequences of parental rejection: A theory of emotional abuse. *Child Abuse and Neglect, 4,* 189-198.

Shumba, A. (2002). The nature, extent, and effects of emotional abuse on primary school pupils by teachers in Zimbabwe. *Child Abuse & Neglect: The International Journal, 26,* 783-791.

Shumba, A. (2001). Who guards the guards in schools?: A study of reported cases of child sexual abuse by teachers in Zimbabwean secondary schools. *Sex Education, 1*(1), 77-86.

Shumba, A. (2000). *The epidemiology and aetiology of child abuse by teachers in Zimbabwean primary schools.* Unpublished doctoral thesis, University of the Western Cape, South Africa.

Statutory Instrument 65 of the Constitution of Zimbabwe (1992). *Public Service (Disciplinary) Regulations of 1992,* 423-448.

Summit, R. T. (1983). The child sexual abuse accommodation syndrome. *Child Abuse and Neglect, 7,* 177-193.

Trowell, J. (1983). Emotional abuse of children. *Health Visitor, 56,* 252-255.

Winters, J., Clift, R. J. W., & Maloney, A. (2004). Adult-student sexual harassment in British Columbia high schools. *Journal of Emotional Abuse, 3*(3/4), 177-196.

Zindi, F., & Shumba, A. (1999). The epidemiology and aetiology of child sexual abuse in Zimbabwe's secondary schools. *African Journal of Social Work, 1*(1), 37-50.

School Principal
Mistreatment of Teachers:
Teachers' Perspectives on Emotional Abuse

Jo Blase
Joseph Blase

SUMMARY. This article, the first empirical study of its kind, presents findings from a larger qualitative study of principal mistreatment of teachers. A grounded theory method was used to study a sample of 50 U.S. teachers who were subjected to long-term mistreatment from school principals. The authors discuss descriptive and conceptual findings about principals' actions that, over the long term, teachers define as mistreatment/abuse. In addition, this article briefly describes some of the harmful effects of principal mistreatment/abuse on teachers, psychologically/emotionally and physically/physiologically. Implications of study findings for further research are discussed. *[Article copies available for a fee from The Haworth Document Delivery Service: 1-800-HAWORTH. E-mail address: <docdelivery@haworthpress.com> Website: <http://www.HaworthPress.com> © 2004 by The Haworth Press, Inc. All rights reserved.]*

Address correspondence to: Joseph Blase, PhD, Department of Educational Leadership, College of Education, University of Georgia, 850 College Station Road, Athens, GA 30605 (E-mail: blase@coe.uga.edu).

[Haworth co-indexing entry note]: "School Principal Mistreatment of Teachers: Teachers' Perspectives on Emotional Abuse." Blase, Jo, and Joseph Blase. Co-published simultaneously in *Journal of Emotional Abuse* (The Haworth Maltreatment & Trauma Press, an imprint of The Haworth Press, Inc.) Vol. 4, No. 3/4, 2004, pp. 151-175; and: *Aggression in Organizations: Violence, Abuse, and Harassment at Work and in Schools* (ed: Robert Geffner et al.) The Haworth Maltreatment & Trauma Press, an imprint of The Haworth Press, Inc., 2004, pp. 151-175. Single or multiple copies of this article are available for a fee from The Haworth Document Delivery Service [1-800-HAWORTH, 9:00 a.m. - 5:00 p.m. (EST). E-mail address: docdelivery@haworthpress.com].

KEYWORDS. Emotional abuse, principal-teacher relationships, teacher mistreatment, teacher harassment

Internationally, systematic research on the problem of workplace abuse, notably nonphysical forms of abuse, has increased significantly during the last two decades in countries such as Sweden, Norway, Germany, Austria, Australia, and Britain. Several of these countries have also enacted legislation against workplace abuse and private organizations have been created to help victims of abuse (Björkvist, Österman, & Hjelt-Bäck, 1994; Davenport, Schwartz, & Elliott, 1999; Keashly, 1998; Namie & Namie, 2000). In recent years, scholars in the United States have begun to address the problem; indeed, the emerging national literature suggests that workplace abuse may lead to serious deleterious consequences for both employees and organizations (Baron & Neuman, 1996; Davenport et al., 1999; Hornstein, Michela, Van Eron, Cohen, Heckelman, Sachse-Skidd, & Spenser, 1995; Hornstein, 1996; Keashly, 1998; Keashly, Trott, & MacLean, 1994).

This article is based on a larger qualitative study of school principals' mistreatment/abuse of teachers and the subsequent destructive effects on them, from the perspectives of teachers themselves. The study is the first empirical study of its kind and, as such, it focuses on types of principal behavior that teachers define as "abusive" or "mistreatment" (teachers in our study used both terms synonymously), that is, behaviors teachers experienced as seriously harmful when repeated over the long run. Given space limitations, principal behaviors and the effects such patterns of behavior have on the psychological/emotional and physical well being of teachers are briefly described. For a full description of the behaviors and effects on teachers please refer to *Breaking the Silence: Overcoming the Problem of Principal Mistreatment of Teachers* (Blase & Blase, 2003).

TERMS AND CONSTRUCTS

Using a variety of methods, researchers have used a number of terms in the conceptual, theoretical, and empirical literature to describe the workplace mistreatment/abuse phenomenon including incivility (Andersson & Pearson, 1999), mobbing (Davenport et al., 1999; Leymann, 1990), bullying (Einarsen & Skogstad, 1996; Namie & Namie, 2000), harassment (Björkvist et al., 1994); petty tyranny (Ashforth, 1994), abusive disrespect (Hornstein, 1996), interactional injustice (Harlos & Pinder, 2000), emotional abuse (Keashly, 1998), mistreatment (Folger, 1993; Price Spratlen, 1995), abuse

(Bassman, 1992), aggression (Neuman & Baron, 1998), deviance (Robinson & Bennett, 1995), and victimization (Swedish National Board of Occupational Safety and Health, 1993).

In addition, organizational scholars have developed a variety of empirically grounded constructs to define the workplace mistreatment/abuse phenomenon. To illustrate, the construct of mobbing (or psychical terror), the most common term used in Europe, refers to "hostile and unethical communication that is directed in a systematic way by one or a number of persons toward one individual. . . . These actions take place often, and over a long period (at least six months) and, because of this frequency and duration, result in considerable psychic, psychosomatic, and social misery" (Leymann, 1990, p. 120). Mobbing consists of humiliating, intimidating, and abusive communication, committed directly or indirectly, to confuse, discredit, intimidate, and isolate an individual, to force the individual into submission or out of the workplace (Davenport et al., 1999). Einarsen and Skogstad (1996) define bullying, a term commonly used in the United States and Europe, as ". . . harassment, badgering, niggling, freezing out, offending someone . . . repeatedly over a period of time, and the person confronted . . . [has] difficulties defending him/herself. It is not bullying if two parties of approximately equal strength are in conflict or the incident is an isolated event" (p. 191). Ashforth (1994) developed a measure of tyrannical behavior that consists of six dimensions. He defined a petty tyrant as "an individual who lords his or her power over others . . . acts in an arbitrary and self-aggrandizing manner, belittles subordinates, evidences lack of consideration, forces conflict resolution, discourages initiative, and utilizes noncontingent punishment" (p. 772). Abusive disrespect, a concept developed by Hornstein et al. (1995), is comprised of eight behavioral dimensions of disrespectful supervisory behavior and specifically refers to "transgressions" by bosses that include deceit (i.e., lying), constraint (i.e., controlling subordinates' actions outside of work), coercion (i.e., threatening excessive or inappropriate harm), selfishness (i.e., blaming and scapegoating subordinates), disregard (i.e., violating standards of politeness and fairness, lack of concern for personal lives of subordinates), inequity (i.e., favoritism), cruelty (i.e., harming subordinates through name calling, personal attacks,), and deification (i.e., conduct that communicates a "master-servant" relationship to subordinates).

From a comprehensive review of the workplace mistreatment/abuse literature, Keashly (1998) developed the concept of emotional abuse that subsumes elements of the constructs defined above. Emotional abuse emphasizes the "hostile verbal and nonverbal behaviors . . . directed at gaining compliance from others" (p. 85). Keashly identified emotional abuse with the following: A pattern of abuse (not a single event), behaviors that are unwanted by the target, behaviors that violate norms for appropriate conduct or an individual's rights, behaviors that are intended to harm the target, behaviors that result in harm to the target, and power differences between the abuser and the target of abuse.

MODELS

In addition, empirical research has generated a handful of models of mistreatment in the work setting. For example, Baron and Neuman (1996) constructed the three-factor model of workplace aggression, which includes expressions of hostility, obstructionism, and overt aggression. Expressions of hostility include verbal and symbolic behaviors such as facial expressions, gestures, and verbal attacks like staring, dirty looks, silent treatment, ridicule, unfair evaluations, and gossip. Obstructionism refers to actions that are often passive aggressive in nature, such as withholding a resource or behavior. Some examples are not returning phone calls, refusing to provide needed resources or equipment, and failing to warn an individual of imminent danger. Overt aggression, the third factor, refers to threats or acts of physical violence and theft or destruction of an individual's work equipment.

A typology of workplace deviance, developed by Robinson and Bennett (1995), indicates that workplace behavior varies across two dimensions, minor versus serious and interpersonal versus organizational. Minor forms of deviance were classified into two quadrants including productive deviance (e.g., leaving early, taking excessive breaks) and political deviance (e.g., favoritism, gossiping, and blaming subordinates). More serious forms of deviance were classified as property deviance (e.g., sabotaging equipment, lying about hours worked) and personal aggression (e.g., verbal abuse, sexual harassment, stealing from subordinates, and endangering subordinates).

THEORETICAL WORK

Several scholars have specifically developed theories of boss abuse of subordinates. To illustrate, Hornstein et al., (1995) constructed a theory of supervisory disrespect that draws heavily on symbolic interaction, organizational justice, and the psychological and stress literature. These authors argue that people's feelings of both self-worth and security are affected by how respectfully others treat them; and feelings of self-worth and security, in turn, affect one's mental health and well-being. Hornstein et al. (1995) established validity and reliability for the Boss Behavior Questionnaire (BBQ), which uses measurable constructs of respect and disrespect to examine the eight domains of supervisory disrespectful behavior described above.

Ashforth (1994) developed a model of the antecedents and effects of tyranny on subordinates. He contends that petty tyranny is an interaction between superordinates' predispositions (i.e., beliefs about organizations, subordinates, and self and preferences for action) and situational facilitators (i.e., institutionalized values and norms, power, and stressors). Ashforth argued that tyrannical management causes low leader endorsement and high frustration, stress, and resistance; high helplessness and work alienation; low self-esteem and poor work performance; and low work unit cohesiveness. He emphasized that such affects could trigger a vicious circle that sustains the tyrannical behavior. For instance, the exercise of power may induce a manager to do the following: attribute subordinates' success to him or herself, develop an inflated sense of self-worth, create greater psychological distance from subordinates, and view subordinates as objects of manipulation (Kipnis, 1972).

STUDIES OF WORKPLACE MISTREATMENT/ABUSE

Studies of workplace mistreatment have produced a range of nonverbal and verbal/behavioral types of workplace abuse. Nonverbal behaviors include aggressive eye contact and dismissive behavior (e.g., "dirty looks," staring, snubbing or ignoring, "the silent treatment"), as well as physical gestures (e.g., intrusions into physical space, slamming objects, finger pointing, and throwing objects). Examples of verbal behaviors include sexual harassment, yelling and screaming, put downs, lying, public humiliation, threats of job loss, physical harm, name calling, unfounded criticism of work abilities or personal life, excessive job demands, taking credit for an individual's work accomplishments, blaming, exclusion or isolation, initiating pernicious rumors and gossip, withholding resources, preventing opportunities, favoritism, dismissing an individual's feelings or thoughts, failure to return phone calls, and behavior that implies a master-servant relationship (Björkvist et al., 1994; Brodsky, 1976; Davenport et al.,1991; Einarsen, Hoel, Zapf, & Cooper, 2003; Harlos & Pinder, 2000; Hoel & Cooper, 2000; Hornstein, 1996; Keashly et al., 1994; Leymann, 1990; Lombardo & McCall, 1984; Namie & Namie, 2000; Namie, 2000; Neuman & Baron, 1998; Rayner, Hoel, & Cooper, 2002; Robinson & Bennett, 1995; Ryan & Oestreich, 1991).

In addition, abuse in the workplace is associated with a host of serious adverse effects on an individual's physical health, psychological/emotional health, work performance, and social relationships. Some psychological/emotional effects of abusive workplace behavior are anger, rage, depression, helplessness, powerlessness, distrust and cynicism, self-doubt, guilt, shame, embarrassment, insecurity, poor concentration, disillusionment, lowered self-esteem, revenge, aggressiveness, hypervigilance, panic attacks, and post-traumatic stress disorder (PTSD). Effects on physical health include sleep disorders (e.g., insufficient rest or nightmares), headaches, backaches, exhaustion, hyperactivity, weight changes (e.g., significant increases or decreases), irritable bowel syndrome, skin changes, heart arrhythmia, substance abuse (first time use), ulcers, and suicide; effects of abusive behavior on work performance include decreases in job effort, motivation, commitment, and satisfaction and morale as well as increases in absenteeism, turnover, and attrition; and social effects identified in the literature are loss of friendships and isolation (Björkvist et al., 1994; Brodsky, 1976; Davenport et al., 1999; Einarsen et al., 2003; Harlos & Pinder, 2000; Hoel, 1997; Hornstein, 1996; Keashly et al., 1994; Leymann, 1990; Lombardo & McCall, 1984; Namie & Namie, 2000; Namie, 2000; Pearson, 2000; NNLI, 1993; Rayner et al., 2002; Ryan & Oestreich, 1991).

Research on abusive bosses (versus coworker abuse, for example) has generated a number of disturbing findings. First, abusive conduct by bosses is common in both profit and nonprofit organizations (Hornstein, 1996; Keashly et al., 1994). Second, bosses (e.g., managers, superiors) are more frequently workplace abusers as compared to one's coworkers; in several studies, bosses have been found to engage in abusive conduct toward subordinates between 54% and 90% of the time (Ashforth, 1994; Björkvist et al., 1994; Einarsen & Skogstad, 1996; Einarsen et al., 2003; Hoel & Cooper, 2000; Hornstein, 1996; Keashly et al., 1994; Leymann, 1990; Namie, 2000; Namie & Namie, 2000; NNLI, 1993; Pearson, 2000; Rayner, 1998; Rayner et al., 2002). Third, studies have demonstrated that male and female bosses are equally likely to engage in abusive behavior (Keashly et al., 1994; Harlos & Pinder, 2000), although abusive male bosses tend to use explosive behaviors more frequently than female bosses (e.g., Harlos & Pinder, 2000).

THEORETICAL FRAMEWORK: SYMBOLIC INTERACTIONISM

Indeed, there is some significant scholarly work on the problem of workplace mistreatment/abuse; however, there is no empirical or conceptual work on the school principal mistreatment/abuse problem, and, in particular, none based on a study of victimized public school teachers. The theoretical framework for the present study was symbolic interactionism. This perspective on social inquiry rests on three major premises: (1) individuals act toward things and people on the basis of the meanings that things have for them; (2) the meaning of such things are derived from, or arise out of, the social interaction that individuals have with one another; (3) these meanings are handled in, and modified through, an interpretive process used by individuals to deal with the things and other people they encounter (Blumer, 1969). This theoretical perspective recognizes that although structural factors (e.g., cultural, organizational) affect action, the meanings that people attribute to such factors account for action. In short, an individual's capacity for reflexivity has more influence on action than structural factors. The symbolic interaction perspective views the individual as a social product who is influenced by others but also maintains distance from others and is able to initiate individual action (Blumer, 1969; Mead, 1934). In essence, the Blumer (1969) and Mead (1934) perspective on symbolic interactionism focuses on the study of human subjectivity; that is, it examines the meanings that people construct in their social settings (Schwandt, 1994; Taylor & Bogdan, 1998; Tesch, 1988).

RESEARCH METHOD AND PROCEDURES

Clearly, the study discussed in this article is extremely sensitive and even incendiary in nature, and thus we assumed that school districts would neither grant permission to conduct on-site interviews with teachers victimized by principals, nor would teachers volunteer to participate in a research project of this nature (even if it were authorized) given the potential risks of doing so. Therefore, we employed a snowball sampling technique requiring professors, public school teachers, and administrators throughout the United States to recommend teachers who they believed had experienced long-term, significant abuse by a school principal. We explained the purpose of our research to these individuals and asked them to discuss participation in our study with a victimized teacher. Such sampling techniques are particularly useful in grounded theory research that draws samples from a variety of settings. This technique maximizes variation in the database to generate a large number of categories that describe the phenomenon under study (Bogdan & Biklen, 1982; Glaser, 1978, 1998; Strauss & Corbin, 1998; Taylor & Bogdan, 1998). In this manner, we identified over 50 teachers in the United States who had experienced significant long-term principal mistreatment/abuse.

We then contacted (by telephone) teachers who had expressed an interest in participation, explained our study, responded to questions and concerns, described our backgrounds, and, in general, got to know each teacher. We included in our study only teachers who had experienced long-term and significant abuse (i.e., 6 months to 9 years) by their school principal. Two teachers we contacted had not experienced long term abuse and one decided that talking about her mistreatment experience would be too traumatic. Not surprisingly, teachers were very fearful of possible disclosure; therefore, we employed several safeguards that seemed to alleviate their fears and promote rapport and trust. We explained to teachers that we would maintain their anonymity. We informed teachers that our database (i.e., audiotapes, typed transcripts, official and personal documents, and other related materials) would be destroyed upon completion of our analysis. We explained that all identifiers (including teachers' gender and grade level) would be removed from materials used in any type of presentation of our findings. As a result, we use pseudonyms for the names of people and places. We also shared our general research questions and asked teachers to think about their abuse experience in preparation for the next interview.

The research sample consisted of female (n = 45) and male (n = 5) teachers from rural (n = 14), suburban (n = 25), and urban (n = 11) school locations. Elementary (n = 26), middle/junior high (n = 10), and high school (n = 14) teachers participated. Teachers' average age was 42 and the average number of years in teaching was 16. The sample consisted of tenured (n = 44) and nontenured (n = 6); married (n = 34) and single (n = 16) teachers. Academic degrees held by these teachers included BA/BS (n = 7), MEd/MA (n = 31), EdS (n = 11), and PhD (n = 1). The average number of years working with the abusive principal was 4. Forty-nine (n = 49) teachers lived in the United States and one (n = 1) lived in Canada. Fifteen (n = 15) of the teachers we studied were with an abusive principal at the time of this study; most others had experienced abuse in recent years. Teachers described female (n = 22) and male (n = 28) principals.

Specifically, we used an open-ended format to examine the broad question: How do teachers experience significant long-term mistreatment/abuse by school principals? Interviews are required in qualitative research that focuses on the determination of meanings from the participant's perspective (Bogdan & Biklen, 1982; Glaser & Strauss, 1967; Glaser, 1978, 1992, 1998). We conducted between two and four interviews with each of our research participants; these interviews consisted of unstructured and semi-structured questions. Our initial set of questions included the broad question identified above, followed by additional questions designed to explore basic dimensions of the mistreatment/abuse experience including (1) types of principal behavior/conduct teachers defined as abusive, and (2) the effects of such behavior/conduct on teachers' psychological/emotional well-being, physical/physiological well-being, involvement/performance in the classroom, and involvement/performance in the school. We spent about 135 hours interviewing teachers; this procedure generated about 4,000 pages of transcription for analysis.

We collected personal documents from teachers (e.g., letters, diaries, journal entries) and official documents (e.g., administrators' letters, law briefs, faculty meeting minutes) related to their mistreatment/abuse experiences.

These documents were useful in extending our understanding of the meaning of teachers' mistreatment/abuse experiences (Bogdan & Biklen, 1982; Glaser & Strauss, 1967; Glaser, 1978, 1992, 1998; Taylor & Bogdan, 1998). It should be mentioned that examination of the personal and official documents submitted to us and reports from those who had worked with and referred us to the veteran teachers we studied suggest that they were highly accomplished, creative, and dedicated individuals. In most cases, such teachers had been consistently, formally recognized by their school and district not simply as effective teachers but also as superior teachers; in many cases, such recognition for their exceptional achievements as public educators extended to state levels.

Although interview-based protocols are essential to qualitative studies that focus on meanings (Bogdan & Biklen, 1982; Glaser, 1978, 1992, 1998; Glaser & Strauss, 1967; Strauss & Corbin, 1998; Taylor & Bogdan, 1998), interviewees may present idealized versions of themselves and their situations. To address this and other issues related to trustworthiness and reliability of our findings, we used an inductive-generative approach to data collection and analysis. In addition, we used no priori concepts to direct data collection, developed rapport and trust with study participants, conducted multiple interviews with each participant, audio-taped and transcribed all interviews, probed for detailed responses, inspected data for inconsistencies and contradictions within and between interviews for each participant as well as across participants, compared interview data with available personal and official documents, searched for negative or disconfirming evidence, generated low-inference descriptors, and checked for researcher effects. Finally, as a supplemental validation of our findings, we made comparisons with the existing literature on workplace abuse (Bogdan & Biklen, 1982; Glaser, 1978, 1992, 1998; Glaser & Strauss, 1967; Strauss & Corbin, 1998; Taylor & Bogdan, 1998).

RESULTS: A MODEL OF PRINCIPAL MISTREATMENT

From the beginning, he singled me out for criticism. He criticized me publicly and loudly. He criticized my dress as too casual and told me that I couldn't wear Birkenstocks [shoes] because they were gang-related. He would mock me in front of other teachers in his "in" group, with whom he ate lunch. After a fellow teacher and I pointed out a possible solution to a duty problem, he called me into his office and berated me for over an hour on the proper way to show respect to a principal. He called me a troublemaker and told me that I needed to stop changing things and stop being so smart. He ridiculed me in a faculty meeting as someone who was "too smart for your own good." He said that he would never believe a word that I said; he would always take the word of a parent or student against me anytime. (Victimized teacher)

In essence, we have organized the principal behaviors derived from our database according to level of aggression: Level 1 Principal Mistreatment (indirect, moderately aggressive, Level 2 Principal Mistreatment (direct, escalating aggression), and Level 3 Principal Mistreatment (direct, severely aggressive). Several researchers have conceptualized workplace mistreatment in terms of levels of aggression (e.g., Andersson & Pearson, 1999; Einarsen et al., 2003; Robinson & Bennett, 1995; Ryan & Oestreich, 1991), and our model is generally consistent with these conceptualizations of aggression. Ryan and Oestreich (1991), for example, describe behaviors such as silence and glaring eye contact as abrasive; shouting, angry outbursts, and physical attacks are considered "abusive" behaviors. Robinson and Bennett (1995) view political deviance, including favoritism and gossip, as "minor," while personal aggression (e.g., verbal abuse and sexual harassment) is seen as a more serious form of deviant behavior. It should be stated that our model does not imply that individual Level 1 principal mistreatment behaviors always resulted in less harm to teachers when compared to Level 2 or Level 3 behaviors; to the contrary, the degree of harm related to any single aggressive behavior varied from one victimized teacher to another, as one would expect. In addition, our study focused on long-term mistreatment (6 months to 9 years); therefore, teachers discussed the "cumulative effects" of a multiplicity of principals' continued, systematic mistreatment/abuse. Indeed, the importance of a pattern of mistreatment over the long term, with regard to understanding its devastating effects on victims, and in contrast to isolated or occasional incidents, cannot be overstated (Björkvist et al., 1994; Davenport et al., 1999; Einarsen, Hoel et al., 2003; Einarsen & Skogstad, 1996; Keashly, 1998; Leymann, 1990; Rayner et al., 2002).

Level 1 Mistreatment: Indirect and Moderately Aggressive

Indirect forms of principal mistreatment, as described by teachers in our study, included nonverbal and verbal principal behaviors. Consistent with the work of others, such behaviors are viewed as subtle and discreet as compared to overt forms of mistreatment (Einarsen, 1999; Neuberger, 1999; Neuman & Baron, 1998). This category of principal behaviors was also considered generally less abusive as compared to Level 2 and Level 3 behaviors, and this finding is consistent with studies conducted with the general population (e.g., Keashly, 1998; Neuman & Baron, 1998; Ryan &

Oestreich, 1991). Level 1 behavior was always a part of a more extensive pattern of mistreatment/abuse. At the same time, we found that the frequency of occurrence, timing, amount of negative affect, and the nature of the location in which mistreatment occurred (e.g., public versus private) contributed significantly to the degree of harm teachers incurred from Level 1 behaviors (Keashly et al., 1994; Ryan & Oestreich, 1991). Level 1 behaviors discussed by teachers included discounting teachers' thoughts, needs, and feelings (Principals ignored and snubbed teachers, exhibited insensitivity to personal matters [e.g., illness, death in the teacher's family], and engaged in stonewalling [e.g., failed to respond to written requests]); nonsupport of teachers (Abusive principals failed to support teachers in conflicts with students and/or parents. Principals were "shamelessly unfair," failed to investigate problems, blamed teachers for problems, and frequently reprimanded teachers for problems in the presence of students and/or parents); withholding resources and denying opportunities and credit (Principals unfairly withheld needed instructional resources, denied teachers opportunities for professional development [e.g., to attend conferences], and took credit for teachers' accomplishments [e.g., grant proposals]); favoritism (Principals failed to reward targeted teachers; instead, they routinely rewarded "select" faculty and punished and/or neglected other faculty); and unprofessional personal conduct (Some principals had affairs with other teachers and pursued personal interests during the school day [e.g., working on one's car]).

Level 2 Principal Mistreatment: Direct and Escalating Aggression

Level 2 principal mistreatment behaviors included spying (Principals monitored teachers by situating themselves near classroom doorways, listening in on classes via the intercom, and soliciting the services of "favored" teachers and/or parents as informants); sabotaging (Principals manipulated other faculty to undermine teacher efforts designed to benefit students or colleagues [e.g., directed other teachers not to help targeted teachers]); stealing (Principals were accused of stealing teachers' items such as journals, food, and equipment); destroying teachers' instructional aids (Some principals literally destroyed instructional aids such as reading lofts or ordered them removed from classrooms); making unreasonable demands (Principals overloaded teachers with extra work responsibilities; in several cases, principals forced teachers to do their [the principals'] work); and criticism (Principals routinely and unfairly criticized teachers both privately and publicly for a wide range of reasons. Criticism was often associated with strong negative affect including yelling and pounding a desk. Public criticism of teachers occurred in the presence of others in the front office areas, in hallways, in classrooms, in the lunchroom, and the school parking lot).

Level 3 Principal Mistreatment: Direct and Severely Aggressive

From the foregoing, it is apparent that principals who abused teachers did so in a variety of verbal and nonverbal ways and that such abuse includes Level 1 (indirect, moderately aggressive) and Level 2 (direct, escalating aggression) principal mistreatment behaviors. As devastating as these levels of mistreatment were for teachers, principal mistreatment includes even more aggressive and severe forms of abuse: Level 3 principal mistreatment behaviors, glimpses of which have been foreshadowed in Level 2 behaviors.

According to our data, victimized teachers believed that most of the principals they described "intended to harm" and even "destroy" them and that many such principals were quite aware of the damage they caused. For instance, most principals failed to investigate issues before "attacking" the teacher. And, when teachers confronted abusive principals about their conduct and its destructive effects on them, such principals typically denied all allegations, blamed the teacher, and engaged in further reprisals against them. Most Level 3 forms of principal mistreatment were strongly associated with various forms of deception; that is, with attempts to mislead victimized teachers as well as others (Bok, 1978; Yukl, 1994). They included lying (Principals were accused of "blatant lying," that is, repeatedly making statements that conflicted with the teachers' direct experiences. This form of abuse was commonly associated with principals' nonsupport of teachers in conflict with students and/or parents and with unfounded criticism, among other things); explosive behavior (During face-to-face interaction with teachers, many principals engaged in loud verbal abuse [e.g., yelling] and negative affect [e.g., pounding fists on a table]); threats (Principals directly threatened individuals and groups of teachers in order to change students' grades, for example; they also threatened teachers for expressing opinions that disagreed with the principal's opinions and for confronting a principal for his/her abusive conduct); unwarranted written reprimands (Some principals "wrote [teachers] up" for "almost anything," including conduct toward students, a stolen video camera, and going into a storage closet, when there was no wrongdoing by teachers); unfair evaluations (In all cases, teachers worked in school districts that required that principals complete "objective" teacher evaluations. According to teachers, abusive principals typically included flagrantly false information on their evaluations. It should be mentioned that, with the exception of beginning teachers, all but one experienced teacher had received superior evaluations from principals before mistreatment began.); mistreating students (Principals who mistreated students engaged in name-calling, racism, and even physical abuse of students, particularly special education students who the principals described as "misbehaving"); forcing teachers out of their jobs (abusive principals engaged in a variety of unfair actions against teachers such as unilateral reassignments, transfers, and termination); preventing teachers from leaving (Some principals obstructed teachers' attempts to leave a school by failing to forward applications [within a district] and writing negative letters of reference); sexual harassment (Several female teachers accused their principals of ongoing, long-term sexual harassment. Teachers viewed the principal's sexual harassment as obvious assertions of power and control); and racism (Teachers defined six principals, three Caucasians and three African Americans, as racists).

Thus far, the results section of this article has described what teachers define as "abusive" principal conduct. In addition, and in contrast to the existing conceptual literature on boss abuse (Robinson & Bennett, 1995; Neuman & Baron, 1998; Ryan & Oestreich, 1991), we have conceptualized abusive conduct as a model comprised of three levels of aggression: Level 1 principal mistreatment behaviors (indirect and moderate aggression), Level 2 principal mistreatment behaviors (direct and escalating aggression), and Level 3 principal mistreatment behaviors (direct and severe aggression). The individual behaviors we describe are similar to what others have found in studies of abusive bosses conducted throughout the world (Björkvist et al., 1994; Brodsky, 1976; Davenport et al., 1999; Harlos & Pinder, 2000; Hoel & Cooper, 2000; Hornstein, 1996; Keashly et al., 1994; Leymann, 1990; Lombardo & McCall, 1984; Namie & Namie, 2000; Namie, 2000; Neuman & Baron, 1998; Rayner et al., 2002; Robinson & Bennett, 1995; Ryan & Oestreich, 1991).

With respect to our findings, Buss's (1961) model of human aggression is particularly relevant to the aforementioned findings. Buss described three dimensions of aggression: Physical forms of aggression refer to overt actions against one individual; verbal aggression, in contrast, is exhibited through language. Active types of aggression involve the performance of a behavior, and passive types of aggression refer to withholding some behavior from a target. Direct aggression refers to harm aimed directly at the target, whereas indirect aggression refers to acts conveyed through another person or by attacking something the target values. Ridiculing an individual during face-to-face interaction illustrates active and direct aggression, and withholding recognition or needed resources are examples of indirect, passive aggression.

As noted, our inductively derived model of principal mistreatment described above consists of three major levels of aggression and a total of 21 categories of abusive behaviors. Level 1 describes low intensity, subtle, and somewhat discreet forms of verbal and non-verbal behavior. According to Buss's (1961) framework, all five categories of Level 1 behavior are passive and indirect, although non-support of teachers contains some active and direct behaviors as well. All Level 2 behaviors are considered active and direct with the exception of sabotaging and destroying teachers' instructional aids, which are active and indirect. Level 3 mistreatment consists of behaviors that are predominately active and direct; only mistreatment of students can be described as active and indirect. In essence, according to our data, principal mistreatment of teachers is predominately active and direct. By comparison, in a study of 178 full time employees who worked in a range of private and public organizations, Neuman and Baron (1996) found that aggression was primarily passive and direct. Neuman and Baron studied the incidence of mistreatment in general, not boss abuse in particular. The immense power differential (i.e., power distance [Hofstede, 1984]) existing between school principals and public school teachers may account, in part, for the greater use of more direct and aggressive forms of mistreatment with teachers.

Effects on Teachers: A Brief Description

> I would go home every day and soak in the tub. I probably soaked my skin off those last four years. At home, I would lose my temper over nothing. I lost the joy of teaching and I wasn't enjoying the journey. I didn't sleep. I tossed and turned in bed. I didn't eat. I was depressed and tried not to show it at school. That is probably what affected my marriage. I have been married for 23 years, but for four years things were very rocky. I don't know if we would have stayed together if we didn't have a son. I was totally wiped out every day. My sex life was nil. Other teachers were depressed too. If it had not been for having a child and loving my husband to death, I would have split; I was at that point. To tell you the honest truth, there was a time I would go to the grocery store at night and sit in the parking lot. I remember sitting one time in the parking lot wondering if I had enough money and could leave and not come back. It took me a year to recover from the nervousness after I left that school. (Victimized teacher)

In addition to teachers' early responses to mistreatment (i.e., shock, disorientation, humiliation, self-doubt, and low self-esteem), and beyond collateral damage on teachers' relationships in schools, their classroom work, their participation in decision making, and on their family life (discussed in Blase & Blase, 2003), mistreated teachers experienced a range of very severe and often chronic psychological/emotional effects.

Fear is considered a primary human emotion and as such has a "profoundly noxious quality" (Izard & Youngstrom, 1996, p. 35); it is essentially an awareness of psychological distress and is considered the most toxic of all human emotions (Tomkins, 1962). Our study revealed that intense and chronic fear and anxiety were among teachers' primary long-term responses to principal mistreatment. There were several reasons for this: First, teachers viewed the various forms and patterns of principal mistreatment as extremely threatening and punishing, and they perceived themselves to be particularly vulnerable. Second, teachers tended to internalize their fears and this provoked a chronic state of anxiety, of apprehension, obsessional thinking, and hyper vigilance regarding the possibility of further mistreatment. Third, fear of mistreatment provoked an array of powerful secondary fears, such as fear of losing one's job, losing one's reputation, being ostracized by colleagues, expressing one's opinion, receiving poor evaluations, lack of support from the central office, and failing one's students instructionally and socially. Fourth, fear was experienced as pervasive: It permeated all aspects of a victimized teacher's work life; for many, it also profoundly and adversely affected the quality of their personal and family lives. Said differently, fear dominated teachers' entire "sense of being" for long periods of time ranging from several months to many years. Some terms that teachers used to denote chronic fear and anxiety states were "fear," "scared," "afraid," "dread," and "paranoid."

Also considered a primary human emotion, anger is a more or less primitive response to "being either physically or psychologically restrained from doing what one intensely desires to do" (Izard, 1977, 329-330). Hence, anger motivates people to prepare their bodies for real or imagined battles and to defend themselves with vigor and strength. Ekman and Friesen (1975) stated that the major provocation to anger is "frustration resulting from interference with [one's] activity or the pursuit of [one's] goals" (p. 78). They noted, "your anger will be more likely and more intense if you believe that the agent of interference acted arbitrarily, unfairly, or spitefully" (p. 78). Indeed, Averill (1982) asserted (as did Aristotle) that anger involves an appraisal that another person has intentionally and unjustifiably wronged one.

All of the teachers we interviewed also expressed strong feelings of anger and rage, both explicitly and implicitly. For most teachers, anger was chronic; it was a dominant emotion throughout their mistreatment experiences and, for many, continued long after mistreatment ended. Teachers' anger always included strong feelings of indignation, a form of anger due to the unjust and unfair nature of their victimization by principals. Teachers used many strong words such as "bitter," "hate," "furious," "angry," "enraged," "outraged," "appalled," "disgusted," "despise," "resent," and "hot" to convey the intensity of their anger.

Many teachers admitted that because of their victimization by principals, they harbored feelings of anger towards school administrators in general. Predictably, teachers felt compelled to suppress their anger, given the power differences between themselves and principals; the principals' inclination to use power in abusive ways; and the failure of school district offices, boards of education, and unions to provide help.

A depressive state refers to pervasive, absorbing, and chronic feelings of being out of control. As described above, anxiety is a kind of "mobilization" response to a future threat that may be developing or coming and that, one hopes, can be avoided. On the other hand, depression is a "demobilization" response to a loss, a "static or unlikely-to-vary situation that can no longer (with any hope) be avoided because it has already developed or come to pass" (Riskind, 1997, p. 687).

Most of the teachers who participated in our study also reported being chronically depressed throughout their mistreatment experience. In describing feelings, teachers used terms such as "depressed," "futile," "helpless," "hopeless," "devastated," "beaten down," "paralyzed," "broken," "worn out," "defeated," "disoriented," "distraught," "trapped," "isolated," "sad," "down," "humiliated," and "despair." Clearly, for most victimized teachers, going to work as well as being at work was a "constant struggle to survive each day." Many teachers' depression was so severe that they sought counseling or psychiatric care for therapy and medication.

In addition, feeling isolated, trapped, and unmotivated was strongly associated with feelings of depression. For example, to avoid further mistreatment, teachers usually withdrew both emotionally and physically (when possible) from social and professional activities (e.g., faculty meetings, committee work, sponsorship of student activities, professional associations). They refused, for example, to volunteer for committee work and sponsorships; when required to attend certain events they did not participate. According to our findings, teachers' protective actions may have inadvertently exacerbated their feelings of isolation and depression. Other factors typically associated with principal mistreatment, showing favoritism, being ostracized by other teachers, and lack of viable opportunities for recourse (e.g., from central office, unions), also contributed to a targeted teacher's sense of isolation.

Like psychological/emotional problems, physical and physiological problems were typically chronic; they began with the onset of mistreatment and usually ended when mistreatment terminated. In some cases, problems persisted for several months and even several years later. The seriousness of these problems appears to be related to the longevity of teachers' mistreatment, at least in part. The most frequently identified physical/physiological problems were chronic sleep disorders (e.g., insomnia, nightmares, obsessive thinking), chronic fatigue, stomach aches, nausea, weight gain or loss, neck and back pain, and headaches or migraines. Examples of other severe physical/physiological problems teachers experienced included diarrhea, high blood pressure, blurred vision, nausea or vomiting, respiratory infections, hives, vertigo, heart palpitations, gum disease, auditory impairment, panic attacks, chest pains, and frequent colds and allergies. Our data indicate that in addition to the psychological/emotional problems discussed earlier, individual teachers simultaneously experienced, on average, at least four of the physical/physiological problems previously described throughout their mistreatment experience. Roughly two-thirds of the teachers we studied sought medical treatment for their problems.

In sum, beyond the teachers' responses of shock and disorientation, humiliation, self-doubt, and injured self-esteem, principal mistreatment seriously damaged in-school relationships, damaged classrooms, and frequently impaired school-wide decision-making. In addition, principals' mistreatment/abuse of teachers resulted in psychological/emotional problems, including severe, chronic fear and anxiety, anger, depression, a range of physical/physiological discussed in the general empirical literature on boss abuse (Björkvist et al., 1994; Brodsky, 1976; Davenport et al., 1999; Einarsen et al., 2003; Harlos & Pinder, 2000; Hoel, 1997; Hornstein, 1996; Keashly et al., 1994; Leymann, 1990; Lombardo & McCall, 1984; Namie & Namie, 2000; Namie, 2000; NNLI, 1993; Pearson, 2000; Ryan & Oestreich, 1991; Rayner et al., 2002).

DISCUSSION

Although we used no a priori concepts to control data collection (Blumer, 1969; Glaser & Strauss, 1967; Glaser, 1978, 1992, 1998; Taylor & Bogdan, 1998), a comparison of our findings with Keashly's (1998) definition of "emotional abuse," constructed from a comprehensive review of the workplace abuse literature, indicates that teachers' experiences of abuse and, in particular, the conditions under which teachers define a principal's behavior as mistreatment or abusive are consistent with what appears in the available literature. According to Keashly, individuals will tend to define a superior's behavior as abusive if there is a pattern of verbal and nonverbal abuse, behaviors are unwanted, behaviors violate norms for appropriate conduct or an individual's rights, behaviors are intended to harm the target, behaviors result in harm, and there are power differences between the abuser and the target of abuse.

Several dimensions of Keashly's (1998) definition of workplace abuse (discussed earlier) require discussion in the context of the present study. The statement that abusive conduct constitutes a pattern of repeated actions against a targeted individual over the long term (6 months to 9 years in terms of our data base) is critical to understanding the degree of harm teachers incurred as a result of principal mistreatment/abuse. Taken together, such factors produced a set of internal dynamics that had devastating outcomes for teachers. For instance, although we found that one category of principal behaviors (i.e., Level 1) was considered less abusive when compared to other categories (i.e., Levels 2 and 3), and this finding is consistent with the results of other studies (Keashly, 1998; Neuman & Baron, 1998; Ryan & Oestreich, 1991), the individual behaviors contained in Level 1 (e.g., ignoring) cannot be understood in isolation. To begin, less aggressive and less abusive principal behaviors were often accompanied by more aggressive and more abusive behaviors; thus, we found that through simple association, less abusive behaviors could ignite strong emotional responses in teachers. Moreover, a long-term pattern of mistreatment/abuse produced "chronic" emotions in teachers including fear, anger, and depression. Consequently, any abusive behavior by a school principal at any time had the potential to precipitate seriously adverse effects on teachers; strong human emotions such as fear have a particularly long half-life and have the capacity to defy the boundaries of time or place (Harlos & Pinder, 2000), and thus have the potential to reinforce preexisting adverse psychological, physical, and behavioral responses in teachers.

Our data also suggest that other factors such as location or timing account, in part, for the degree of harm teachers experience from principal mistreatment. We found, for example, that a single instance of public ridicule had long-lasting, harmful effects on teachers; such behavior generated additional considerations for the teacher including embarrassment, loss of professional reputation, and reactions of others that do not accompany other behaviors such as direct criticism. We also found that timing could be an important factor in understanding the harmful effects of mistreatment. For example, being targeted for repeated classroom observations and evaluations during personal life tragedies (e.g., death, divorce) significantly intensified the degree of harm teachers experienced as a result of such observations and evaluations.

In many respects, public education in the United States has been strongly influenced by the principles of equity and fairness (Cusick, 1983; Dreeben, 1970); indeed, teachers take very seriously violations of norms of appropriate conduct and human rights, particularly by school principals (Blase, 1988; Lortie, 1975). Many researchers have pointed to the significance of fairness to productive school principal-teacher interaction in schools (Blase, 1988; Blumberg & Greenfield, 1986; Lightfoot, 1983). Thus, it was not surprising to discover that teachers victimized by abusive principals primarily experienced "moral outrage" (anger from indignation) in response to the unjust and unfair treatment they received (see Folger, 1993); such forms of outrage were reinforced because classroom instruction and students in particular suffered as a result of principals' abusive conduct toward them.

Intentionality with regard to a victim's experience of abuse is considered the weakest aspect of Keashly's (1998) definition of emotional abuse (Hoel et al., 1999). However, it should be mentioned that in the context of the present study, teachers' attributions of principals' intent to harm were typically slow in coming. Teachers' responses to being mistreated/abused during the early stages of their experience included disorientation, confusion, self-doubt, and self-blame ("What's wrong with me?" or "What have I done?"). Teachers blamed principals directly and concluded that their actions were intentional only after "repeated attacks" and repeated attempts on their part to address the problem (see pp. 41-42).

The significance of power differences between teachers and school principals in accounting for the degree of harm experienced by teachers cannot be overstated. Keashly (1998) points out that administrators in organizations generally have both reward and coercive power; among other things, administrators control performance evaluations, professional development opportunities, and promotions. Indeed, our data demonstrate that abusive principals have access to these as well as other sources of formal and informal power; clearly, the power distance (Hofstede, 1984) between principals and teachers is substantial, and this accounts for teachers' vulnerability and inability to reciprocate when mistreated (Keashly & Nowell, 2003). The wide range of different abusive behaviors exhibited by principals, both verbal and nonverbal, that emerged from our data, support this conclusion. Even in situations governed by union contracts, teachers reported significant mistreatment/abuse experiences by principals. In fact, we found that teachers rarely complained to district level administrators because they expected to receive "no help" and because they "feared" reprisals. This is consistent with other research that had demonstrated that victims' complaints about abusive bosses typically result in (a) no action (no response) from upper management, (b) efforts to protect abusive bosses, (c) reprisals against victims who complain (Bassman, 1992; Davenport et al., 1999; Hornstein, 1996; Keashly, 1998; Keashly et al., 1994; Leyman, 1990; Martin, 1986; Namie, 2000; Namie & Namie, 2000; Pearson, 2000; Rayner, 1998). The lack of legal protections for most forms of workplace abuse (with the exception of racial discrimination, sexual harassment, and, in reference to the present data, stealing) (Yamada, 2000) may also explain teachers' reluctance to file formal complaints against abusive principals.

IMPLICATIONS FOR FURTHER RESEARCH

This study of principal mistreatment has generated new descriptive and conceptual knowledge in the general area of workplace mistreatment; this is the first phenomenological report of the actual experiences of abused teachers, and, as such, emphasizes the verbal and nonverbal behaviors that constitute principal mistreatment and some of its common effects on teachers. Yet, although we have begun to illuminate this problem, it nevertheless requires much more investigation. For example, we suspect that principals' mistreatment of teachers is contingent on a multitude of internal (i.e., personality) and external (i.e., organizational) factors (Hornstein, 1996; Rayner et al., 2002). Useful research could focus on the relationships among abusive principals' personalities, preparation, and school contexts. Studies focusing on race, gender, and ethnicity of school principals and victimized teachers would be valuable. Qualitative and quantitative studies can provide descriptions beyond those provided here (i.e., beyond forms of abuse, effects, and how abuse is perceived by victims) to include the extent to which abusive principals recognize the effects of abuse, abusive principals' intentions, and how and under what contextual conditions abusive relationships evolve.

Quantitative studies using random samples of teachers are critical to understanding the pervasiveness of the principal mistreatment problem. Victims' interpretations of abusive principals' behaviors, the degree to which the victims may contribute to the abuse, when and how victims are willing to challenge abuse, victims' coping skills, and the exorbitant costs of abuse, e.g., related to investigations of complaints, teachers' time, legal fees, union representation, health insurance claims, hiring, training, and teachers' performance and productivity (Field, 1996) should also be studied.

CONCLUSION

Katzenmeyer and Moller (1996) note that, "Today we face the frustrating task of making massive changes in America's schools while working within an educational system that was never designed for today" (p. 1). In spite of the second wave of school reform efforts in the United States that focused on school effectiveness and recommended a move away from top-down approaches to school improvement (Carnegie Forum, 1986; Holmes Group, 1986; and National Governors' Association, 1986), researchers have found that "variants of structural-functionalism continue to maintain a strong grip on the field of educational administration" (Heck & Hallinger, 1999, p. 145) and that school principals tend to resist relinquishing power and persist in authoritarian and control-oriented approaches to leadership (Blase, Blase, Anderson, & Dungan, 1995; Drury, 1999). Thus, many school principals operate as managers, (as opposed to school leaders (Bennis, 1997); they stubbornly maintain this bureaucratic-rational perspective and the status quo, and they effectively block organizational change as well as the on-going growth and development of people and institutions necessary for success (Kouzes & Posner, 1987).

In addition, research confirms the critical nature of the principal's role in school effectiveness and improvement (Sheppard, 1996; Smith & Andrews, 1989); however, principals in general have not broadly realized the recommended development of professional environments for teachers and the decentralization of authority intended to lead to democratic and transformational forms of school leadership that emerged from research published during the 1990s (Blase & Blase, 1997; Maeroff, 1988; Lambert, 1998; Schlecty, 2001).

The failure of school principals and school restructuring efforts to achieve the promise once held for school effectiveness and improvement is due also to the difficult challenges they confront related to school safety and violence, drugs, diversity, inadequate facilities and instructional materials, and disillusioned faculties (Olson, 1999; Rusch, 1999; Steinberg, 1999). Such difficulties and challenges notwithstanding, the American public, and in particular parents, teachers, principals and school board members, must confront the corrosive problem of principal mistreatment in our schools, a problem that, most assuredly, compounds the manifold difficulties faced by educators and undermines the potential of our youth. Such mistreatment undermines opportunities for principals and teachers to work together collaboratively to reinvent schools. To be sure, collaboration is possible only when school principals build trust, not fear and anger, with and among teachers; trust, in turn, serves as a foundation for open, honest, and reflective professional dialogue; problem solving; innovative initiatives; and, more directly, the development of the school as a powerful community of learners willing to take responsibility for and capable of success (Blase & Blase, 2001).

REFERENCES

Andersson, L.M., & Pearson, C.M. (1999). Tit for tat? The spiraling effect of incivility in the workforce. *Academy of Management Review, 24*(3), 452-471.

Baron, R. A., & Neuman, J. H. (1996). Workplace violence and workplace aggression: Evidence on their relative frequency and potential causes. *Aggressive Behavior, 22,* 161-173.

Bassman, E. S. (1992). *Abuse in the workplace: Management remedies and bottom line impact.* New York: Quorum.

Beatty, B. R. (2000). The emotions of educational leadership: Breaking the silence. *International Journal of Educational Leadership, 3*(4), 331-357.

Bennis, W. (1997). *Managing people is like herding cats.* Provo, UT: Executive Excellence Publishing.

Björkvist, K., Österman, K., & Hjelt-Bäck, M. (1994). Aggression among university employees. *Aggressive Behavior, 20,* 173-184.

Blase, J. (1988). The politics of favoritism: A qualitative analysis of the teacher's perspective. *Educational Administration Quarterly, 24*(2), 152-177.

Blase, J., & Blase, J. (2001). *Empowering teachers* (2nd ed.). Thousand Oaks, CA: Corwin Press.

Blase, J., & Blase, J. (1997). *The fire is back! Principals sharing school governance.* Thousand Oaks, CA: Corwin Press.

Blase, J., Blase, J., Anderson, G.L., & Dungan, S. (1995). *Democratic principals in action: Eight pioneers.* Thousand Oaks, CA: Corwin Press.

Blumberg, A., & Greenfield, W. (1986). *The effective principal: Perspectives on school leadership.* Boston: Allyn & Bacon.

Blumer, H. (1969). *Symbolic interactionism: Perspective and method.* Englewood Cliffs, NJ: Prentice Hall.

Bogdan, R. C., & Biklen, S. K. (1982). *Qualitative research for education: An introduction to theory and methods* (2nd ed.). Boston: Allyn & Bacon.

Bok, S. (1978). *Lying: Moral choice in public and private life.* New York: Random House.

Brodsky, C. M. (1976). *The harassed worker.* Lexington, MA: Lexington Books.

Buss, A. H. (1961). *The psychology of aggression.* New York: John Wiley.

Carnegie Forum on Education and the Economy (1986). *A nation prepared: Teachers for the 21st century.* Washington, DC: Carnegie Forum on Education and the Economy.

Cusick, P.A. (1983). *The egalitarian ideal and the American high school: Studies of three schools.* London: Longman.

Davenport, N., Schwartz, R. D., & Elliott, G. P. (1999). *Mobbing: Emotional abuse in the American workplace.* Ames, IA: Civil Society Publishing.

Dreeben, R. (1970). *The nature of teaching: Schools and the work of teachers.* Glenview, IL: Scott, Foresman, & Co.

Dreeben, R. (1968). *On what is learned in school.* Reading, MA: Addison-Wesley.

Drury, D. W. (1999). *Reinventing school-based management: A school board guide to school-based improvement.* Alexandria, VA: National School Boards Association.

Einarsen, S. (1999). The nature and causes of bullying. *International Journal of Manpower, 20,* 16-27.

Einarsen, S., Hoel, H., Zapf, D., & Cooper, C. (2003). *Bullying and emotional abuse in the workplace: International perspectives in research and practice.* London: Taylor & Francis.

Einarsen, S., & Skogstad, A. (1996). Bullying at work: Epidemiological findings in public and private organizations. *European Journal of Work and Organizational Psychology, 5*(2), 185-201.

Evans, R. (1996). *The human side of school change.* San Francisco: Jossey-Bass.

Folger, R. (1993). Reactions to mistreatment at work. In J. K. Murningham (Ed.), *Social psychology in organizations: Advances in theory and research* (pp. 161-183). Englewood Cliffs, NJ: Prentice Hall.

Ginsberg, R., & Davies, T. (2001, April). *The emotional side of leadership*. Paper presented at the annual meeting of the American Educational Research Association, Seattle.

Glaser, B. G. (1978). *Theoretical sensitivity: Advances in the methodology of grounded theory.* Mill Valley, CA: Sociology Press.

Glaser, B. G. (1992). *Emergence vs. forcing: Basics of grounded theory.* Mill Valley, CA: Sociology Press.

Glaser, B. G. (1998). *Doing grounded theory: Issues and discussions.* Mill Valley, CA: Sociology Press.

Glaser, B. G., & Strauss, A. L. (1967). *The discovery of grounded theory: Strategies for qualitative research.* Chicago, IL: Aldine.

Harlos, K. P., & Pinder, C. C. (2000). Emotion and injustice in the workplace. In S. Fineman (Ed.), *Emotion in organizations* (2nd ed., pp. 255-276). Thousand Oaks, CA: Sage.

Heck, R. H., & Hallinger, P. (1999). Next Generation Methods for the Study of Leadership and School Improvement. In J. Murphy, & K.S. Louis (Eds.), *Handbook of research on educational administration* (2nd ed., pp. 141-162). San Francisco: Jossey-Bass.

Hoel, H. (1997). Bullying at work: A Scandanavian perspective. *Institution of Occupational Safety and Health Journal, 1,* 51-59.

Hoel, H., & Cooper, C. (November, 2000). *Destructive conflict and bullying at work.* University of Manchester Institute of Science and Technology, Manchester, UK.

Hofstede, G. (1980). *Culture's consequences: International differences in work-related values.* Newbury Park, CA: Sage.

Holmes Group (1986). *Tomorrow's teachers: A report of the Holmes Group.* East Lansing, MI: Holmes Group.

Hornstein, H. A. (1996). *Brutal bosses and their prey.* New York: Riverhead Books.

Hornstein, H. A., Michela, J. L., Van Eron, A. M., Cohen, L. W., Heckelman, W. L., Sachse-Skidd, M., & Spencer, J. L. (1995). *Disrespectful supervisory behavior: Effects on some aspects of subordinates' mental health.* Teachers College, Columbia University. Unpublished manuscript.

Izard, C. E., & Youngstrom, E. A. (1996). The activation and regulation of fear and anxiety. In R. A. Dienstbier & Hope, D. A. (Eds.), *Perspectives on anxiety, panic, and fear* (pp. 1-59). Lincoln: University of Nebraska Press.

Katzenmeyer, M., & Moller, G. (1996). *Awakening the sleeping giant: Leadership development for teachers.* Thousand Oaks, CA: Corwin Press.

Keashly, L. (1998). Emotional abuse in the workplace: Conceptual and empirical issues. *Journal of Emotional Abuse, 1*(1), 85-117.

Keashly, L., & Nowell, B. L. (2003). Conflict, conflict reduction, and bullying. In S. Einarsen, D. Zapf, & C. Cooper (Eds.), *Bullying and emotional abuse in the workplace: International perspectives in research and practice* (pp. 339-358). London: Taylor & Francis.

Keashly, L., Trott, V., & MacLean, L. M. (1994). Abusive behavior in the workplace: A preliminary investigation. *Violence and Victims, 9*(4), 341-357.

Kouzes, J. M., & Posner, B. Z. (1987). *The leadership challenge: How to get extraordinary things done in organizations.* San Francisco: Jossey-Bass.

Lambert, L. (1998). *Building leadership capacity in schools.* Alexandria, VA: Association for Supervision and Curriculum Development.

Leymann, H. (1993). *Mobbing* (N. Davenport, Trans.). Hamburg: Rowohlt Taschenbuch Verlag GmbH.

Leymann, H. (1990). Mobbing and psychological terror at workplaces. *Violence and Victims, 5*(2), 119-126.

Lombardo, M. M., & McCall, Jr., M. W. (January, 1984). The intolerable boss. *Psychology Today,* 44-48.

Lortie, D. (1975). *Schoolteacher: A sociological study.* Chicago: University of Chicago Press.

Maeroff, G. I. (1988). Blueprint for empowering teachers. *Phi Delta Kappan, 69*(7), 473-477.

Martin, J. (1986). When expectations and justice do not collide: Blue-collar visions of a just world. In H. W. Bierhoff, K.L. Cohen, & J. Greenburg (Eds.), *Justice in social relations* (pp. 317-335). New York: Plenum.

Mead, G. H. (1934). *Mind, self, and society.* Chicago: University of Chicago Press.

Namie, G. (2000). *U.S. hostile workplace survey 2000.* Benicia, CA: Campaign Against Workplace Bullying.

Namie, G., & Namie, R. (2000). *The bully at work: What you can do to stop the hurt and reclaim your dignity on the job.* Naperville, IL: Sourcebooks.

National Governors' Association (1986). *Time for results.* Washington, DC: National Governors' Association.

Neuberger, O. (1999). *Mobbing: Playing bad games in organizations* (3rd ed.). Munich and Mering: Hampp.

Neuman, J. H., & Baron, R.A. (1997). Aggression in the workplace. In R. A. Giacalone, & J. Greenberg (Eds.), *Antisocial behavior in organizations* (pp. 37-67).

Neuman, J. H., & Baron, R. A. (1998). Workplace violence and workplace aggression: Evidence concerning specific forms, potential causes, and preferred targets. *Journal of Management, 24*(3), 391-419.

Northwestern National Life Insurance Company (1993). *Fear and violence in the workplace.* Minneapolis, MN: Author.

Olson, L. (1999, March). Demands for principals growing but candidates aren't applying. *Education Week, 18*(20), 20.

Pearson, C. (2000). *Workplace "incivility" study.* Chapel Hill: University of North Carolina.

Rayner, C. (1998). *Bullying at work.* Stoke-on-Kent, UK: Staffordshire University Business School.

Rayner, C., Hoel, H., & Cooper, C. (2002). *Workplace bullying: What we know, who is to blame, and what can we do?* New York: Taylor & Francis.

Robinson, S. L., & Bennett, R. J. (1995). A typology of deviant workplace behaviors: A multidimensional scaling study. *Academy of Management Journal, 38*(2), 555-572.

Rusch, E. A. (1999). The experience of the piñata: Vexing problems. In F. K. Kochan, B. L. Jackson, & D. L. Duke (Eds.), *A thousand voices from the firing line: A study of educational leaders, their jobs, their preparation, and the problems they face* (pp. 29-43). (UCEA Monograph Series). Columbia, MO: University Council for Educational Administration.

Ryan, K. D., & Oestreich, D. K. (1991). *Driving fear out of the workplace: How to overcome the invisible barriers to quality, productivity, and innovation.* San Francisco: Jossey-Bass.

Schlechty, P. C. (2001). *Shaking up the schoolhouse.* San Francisco: Jossey-Bass.

Schwandt, T. A. (1994). Constructivist, interpretivist approaches to human inquiry. In N. Denzin, & Y. S. Lincoln (Eds.), *Handbook of qualitative research* (pp. 118-137). Thousand Oaks, CA: Sage.

Sheppard, B. (1996). Exploring the transformational nature of instructional leadership. *The Alberta Journal of Educational Research, 42*(4), 325-344.

Steinberg, J. (1999, November 14). Federal funds for teachers reveal surprising hurdles. *New York Times,* 18.

Strauss, A. L., & Corbin, J. (1998). *Basics of qualitative research: Techniques and procedures for developing grounded theory* (2nd. ed.). Thousand Oaks, CA: Sage.

Taylor, S. J., & Bogdan, R. (1998). *Introduction to qualitative research methods: A guidebook and resource* (3rd ed.). New York: Wiley.

Tesch, R. (1988, April). *The contribution of a qualitative method: Phenomenological research.* Paper presented at the annual meeting of the American Educational Research Association, New Orleans, LA.

Yamada, D. C. (2000). The phenomenon of 'workplace bullying' and the need for status-blind hostile work environment protection. *The Georgetown Law Journal, 88*(3), 475-536.

Yukl, G. (1994). *Leadership in organizations* (3rd ed.). Englewood Cliffs, NJ: Prentice Hall.

Adult-Student Sexual Harassment in British Columbia High Schools

Jason Winters
Robert J. W. Clift
Anne Maloney

SUMMARY. To determine the prevalence and impact of adult-student sexually harassing behavior in British Columbia high schools, the High School Experiences Questionnaire was distributed to 449 undergraduate psychology students at the University of British Columbia. Thirty-seven and one-half percent of students reported being sexually harassed by school adult employees. There was no significant difference in the proportion of male and female students that experienced potentially sexually harassing behavior. However, female students were more upset than male students by sexually harassing behaviors. Overall, high school SES and type of school (public versus private) were not related to sexual ha-

Address correspondence to: Jason Winters, Department of Psychology, University of British Columbia, 2136 West Mall, Vancouver, BC, Canada V6T 1Z4 (E-mail: jwinters@interchange.ubc.ca).

During the time this research was conducted, Robert J. W. Clift was supported by the National Science and Engineering Research Council of Canada. Anne Maloney was supported by Race & Company, Squamish, British Columbia.

[Haworth co-indexing entry note]: "Adult-Student Sexual Harassment in British Columbia High Schools." Winters, Jason, Robert J. W. Clift, and Anne Maloney. Co-published simultaneously in *Journal of Emotional Abuse* (The Haworth Maltreatment & Trauma Press, an imprint of The Haworth Press, Inc.) Vol. 4, No. 3/4, 2004, pp. 177-196; and: *Aggression in Organizations: Violence, Abuse, and Harassment at Work and in Schools* (ed: Robert Geffner et al.) The Haworth Maltreatment & Trauma Press, an imprint of The Haworth Press, Inc., 2004, pp. 177-196. Single or multiple copies of this article are available for a fee from The Haworth Document Delivery Service [1-800-HAWORTH, 9:00 a.m. - 5:00 p.m. (EST). E-mail address: docdelivery@haworthpress.com].

rassment. An evaluation of reporting and discipline indicates that overall 1.4% of cases concluded with formal discipline of the perpetrator. *[Article copies available for a fee from The Haworth Document Delivery Service: 1-800-HAWORTH. E-mail address: <docdelivery@haworthpress.com> Website: <http://www.HaworthPress.com> © 2004 by The Haworth Press, Inc. All rights reserved.]*

KEYWORDS. Sexual harassment, high school, prevalence, rates, reporting, socio-economic status, public school, private school, sex

Courts in Canada and the United States have defined two types of sexual harassment. The first is quid pro quo sexual harassment, for which sexual activity is required in exchange for a reward (e.g., a promotion or good grade). The second is sexual harassment that creates a "hostile environment" or a "poisoned environment" (e.g., sexual behavior, pictures, and comments). American school officials have been held liable for both (Kopels & Dupper, 1999). The Supreme Court of Canada has avoided such a distinction. The Canadian definition of sexual harassment is: "Unwelcome conduct of a sexual nature that detrimentally affects the work environment or leads to adverse job-related consequences for the victims of the harassment" (*Janzen v. Platy Enterprises*, 1989). American and Canadian law both recognize sexual harassment as a form of sexual discrimination. While the Supreme Court in Canada has specifically addressed sexual harassment in the workplace, it has not heard cases in which students have brought suits against school districts. Still, Canadian school districts are also open to sexual harassment lawsuits.

In British Columbia, 37 teachers have been disciplined by the British Columbia College of Teachers (BCCT) for professional misconduct related to incidents with students since June 1998 (BCCT, 2003). Of those cases, 24 involved inappropriate sexual relationships with students. The disciplinary actions taken by the College ranged from one-month suspensions to cancellation of teaching certification (BCCT, 2003). Between 1989 and 1996, the Ontario Teacher's Federation investigated over 100 sexual misconduct cases (OAG, 2001). Reported numbers of sexual misconduct cases and inappropriate relationships may not accurately reflect the true prevalence of these types of behaviour. As with other forms of abuse against children (e.g., Finkelhor & Hashima, 2001), the sexual harassment of students by adult school employees (e.g., teachers, sports team coaches, counselors, club leaders, etc. . . .) may be underreported and therefore it is possible that the number of teachers committing these offences is higher (see Shumba, this volume).

One Canadian case is worth describing in more detail because it illustrates the poor way in which sexual harassment cases have been handled in the past. In Ontario, civil suits were brought against a teacher, Kenneth DeLuca, his school board, various school board officials, and others. The plaintiffs claimed that the school board, and certain officials and employees, failed to take reasonable steps to prevent misconduct when they knew, or should have known, of the assaults, harassment, and invasions of privacy by DeLuca (OAG, 2001). DeLuca's misconduct took place over twenty years between 1972 and 1993, involving fourteen victims at five different schools. Complaints had been received about him from as early as 1973. Unfortunately, the various authorities' responses were inadequate. At times, they accused students of lying and they warned parents of the deep pockets of the school board and the teachers' union should parents decide to take legal action. Also, they forced students to confront DeLuca with their allegations in the presence of the principal (OAG, 2001). DeLuca was sentenced to forty months in prison in 1994. The civil suits were settled for an undisclosed amount in 1998 (OAG, 2001).

Adult-student sexual harassment can have deleterious effects on its victims. Bagley and Bolitho (1997) found a positive correlation between experiencing verbal, physical, or sexual assault (including sexual harassment), and suicidal ideation and emotional problems (i.e., sexual harassment as sexual-emotional abuse). Other responses to harassment include absenteeism, decreased quality of schoolwork, skipping or dropping classes, as well as mental health symptoms including loss of appetite, nightmares (or disturbed sleep), feelings of isolation, of sadness, of anger, and of nervousness (American Association of University Women, 1993; Yaffe, 1995). The impact of harassment and other forms of sexual abuse is often less correlated with the severity or intrusiveness of the sexual behaviour than with the pre-abuse victim relationship to the abuser, the vulnerability of the victim, or the response to the disclosure of the abuse. Merely an inappropriate comment, then, could be potentially devastating to a student (OAG, 2001). This is especially important to note, since the vast majority of harassment may appear from the outside to be mild (e.g., inappropriate jokes, staring, or comments).

AMERICAN INCIDENCE STUDIES

Several American studies have done in depth analyses of adult-student sexual harassment. Balenger and Sedlacek (1992) collected data on: (1) the prevalence of sexual harassment in high school; (2) the perceptions the participants had of sexual harassment experiences of other students; (3) what incidents students believe constitute sexual harassment; and (4) ratings of the seriousness of various incidents that might be considered sexual harassment. Their sample consisted of 317 incoming first-year undergraduate students at the University of Maryland, College Park (148 male and 169 female, with a mean age of 17.7). The survey used was a modified version of a questionnaire used by Mazer and Percival (1989), which in turn was largely drawn from a survey developed by Reilly, Lott, and Gallogly (1986). The items were divided into those which described incidents that occurred in the classroom context and incidents that occurred outside the classroom. Balenger and Sedlacek (1992) found that 61% of students reported that their teachers had made jokes that put down women and 52% reported that their teachers had made jokes that put down men. Less than 1% of participants reported that their teachers had attempted to kiss or fondle them outside of class. This behavior goes beyond sexual harassment and may fall within the rubric of sexual assault. Male and female students tended to agree that most incidents occurring outside of the classroom constituted harassment. There were two areas of gender differences. Females were more likely than males to consider: (a) pressure for social contact by teachers and (b) sexual activity resulting in positive incentives offered by the teacher, to be sexual harassment.

In another study, Wishnietsky (1991) surveyed both superintendents and recent high school graduates in an effort to determine the rates of and responses to sexual harassment in North Carolina high schools. Survey items included insulting comments, insulting looks or gestures, unwanted sexual touching, expected socializing, and expected sexual activity. One hundred and forty surveys were sent to superintendents. Sixty-five were returned (46%), of which 18 (28%) indicated that a teacher or administrator had been disciplined for sexual harassment in that area during the past 3 years. Twenty-six incidents were reported in total. Wishnietsky (1991) then mailed the same survey to 200 female and 100 male high school graduates who had graduated in June 1989 from 30 different high schools across the state (10 students were randomly selected from the graduating class of each school). One hundred and five female students responded (52.5%) and 43 male students responded (43%). Twenty incidents of sexual intercourse were reported. Of the 19 occurrences in which male teachers had intercourse with female students, it is unclear how many teachers and how many students were involved. It is possible that one female student had sex 19 times with the same male teacher. Wishnietsky likely has this information on the returned surveys, but did not include it in his manuscript. The sampling procedures used in the study ensured a random selection of participants. However, the low response rate may make the findings tenuous.

Shakeshaft and Audrey (1995) spent four years compiling information for their study of the sexual harassment and sexual abuse of students by teachers or other school employees. They sent letters to 764 superintendents in New York State inquiring whether or not they had ever dealt with an incident of sexual abuse of a student by an employee. Forty-three percent responded, 192 of whom indicated "yes" and that they were willing to discuss the incident(s). One hundred and eighty-four superintendents were interviewed; 41 others who had also expressed willingness to discuss their experiences were added from other parts of the country. From those interviews, Shakeshaft and Audrey (1995) examined 225 reported cases in which students were sexually harassed by teachers or other professional staff members. Ten cases were selected to investigate in detail. In doing so, Shakeshaft and Audrey (1995) interviewed superintendents, school attorneys, parents, and teachers in New York State.

Shakeshaft and Audrey (1995) classified levels of sexual abuse that were reported: (a) Level I non-contact abuse (visual), such as showing pornography; (b) Level II non-contact abuse (verbal), such as commenting on the specific body parts of students; (c) Level I contact sexual abuse, such as pinching or fondling; and (d) Level II contact sexual abuse, such as fellatio or intercourse. Ninety-six percent of the perpetrators in the study were male and 76% of the students who were abused were female. Interestingly, when women were the perpetrators, their targets were mostly female also (86% female versus 14% male). Males were more likely to be abused, or to report abuse, in elementary school, while females reported equal amounts of abuse at all grade levels. School district responses to the teacher's behavior included attempts to terminate employment, and formal and informal disciplinary action. Fifty-four percent of accused perpetrators resigned, left the district, retired, or were fired. Superintendents reported that 16% of the perpetrators were teaching in other schools and that they did not know what had become of the other 84%. Sometimes the accused teacher turned up in another district without that district knowing of the allegations against him or her, an occurrence that superintendents referred to as "passing the trash." Superintendents seemed to consider the abuse of males a more serious offense. They "discussed cases involving male victims at greater length and knew more details about them, and reported that they pursued these investigations more energetically" (Shakeshaft & Audrey, 1995, p. 520). Male accusers were seldom suspected of lying, which was not true for female accusers. Homosexual acts were taken more seriously than heterosexual acts; same-sex complaints were more likely to be believed and judged as more serious than opposite-sex abuse. Superintendents reported that they could sympathize with the abuser, but only when the accuser was female. Seven and a half percent of the superintendents reported that some allegations turned out to be untrue or were not serious enough to be considered sexual abuse, though the authors state that many of these incidents were indeed against the law. It is notable that superintendents reported a low frequency of "false" or "not serious enough" allegations. Shakeshaft and Audrey's (1995) study is interesting in that it attempts to trace the responses of the school districts to allegations of abuse.

Corbett, Gentry, and Pearson (1993) surveyed 185 introductory sociology undergraduate students about sexual harassment in high school. The survey provided a definition of sexual harassment, and then requested participants to estimate the seriousness and frequency of these behaviors in their high schools. Participants were asked to report knowledge and a description of harassment experienced by someone other than themselves (i.e., friends or other students). A series of questions followed regarding what the participants had experienced. Lastly, participants were asked if they knew of any sexual relationships between students and high school teachers. Ninety-three (50.2%) participants described incidents in which other students had been treated inappropriately; 29% reported knowledge of affairs or dating between students and high school teachers. Although consensual dating would not fall within the rubric of sexual harassment since there is no upset, it would still be illegal in most jurisdictions. For example, in Canada, teacher-student dating is legally considered sexual exploitation (Section 153, Canadian Criminal Code, 1985). Twelve (6%) reported having been treated inappropriately themselves, mostly in the form of unwanted sexual remarks or touching. There are limitations to Corbett et al.'s (1993) findings. Many of the incidents reported happened to students other than the respondent. It is possible that several respondents reported the same story. Additionally, participants' reports about other students may have been based on hearsay.

However, Corbett et al.'s (1993) study was novel in that it measured student attitudes about the reported behaviors. Many students excused the teachers' behaviors when the behaviors occurred in the context of affairs or dating. These students did not seem to realize that by law, any intimate relationship between a person in power and a juvenile is non-consensual. Corbett et al., (1993) note that students often do not have the experience or the sense of empowerment to be able to recognize and label all sexually harassing behavior. Therefore, provision of a procedure to report and investigate sexual harassment may not be enough. In other words, schools need to make clear to students, through education, the nature of all types of sexually harassing behavior, in addition to providing the framework for report and investigation.

It is apparent that reported rates of adult-student sexual harassment vary across studies. There are a few factors that may contribute to the inconsistent results. First, varied definitions of sexual harassment are used. Low report rates are expected when a stringent definition of sexual harassment is used. The opposite is expected for less rigorous definitions. Second, there is a lack of uniformity in the content of survey questions themselves. Some surveys in-

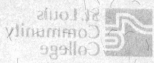

St. Louis Community College

#500 03-19-2012 12:02PM
Item(s) checked out to p19501699.

TITLE: Aggression in organizations : vio
BARCODE: 300080006248578
DUE DATE: 04-09-12

quire only about behaviors at the more severe end of the sexual harassment spectrum and leave out entirely the milder forms of behavior, such as staring or leering. Also, the wording of the questions may influence results. Questions that are more complex in nature may elicit different responses than those that are more transparent. Third, the temporal nature of the surveys may lead to different report rates. The results from studies that are retrospective in nature may be confounded by forgetting. Fourth, sampling methods that allow for potential participants to self-select themselves out of the sample may influence report rates. Fifth, findings from studies that ask students to recall experiences of others' may be inflated due to rumors or gossip. Also, it is possible that several students (especially when participants are from the same area) may relate the same incident, causing an inflation of report rates.

The purpose of our study was to examine prevalence rates of adult-student sexual harassment in British Columbia high schools, and the effects of those behaviors, while addressing problems associated with previous adult-student sexual harassment research. Rather than having students endorse items that use legal definitions of sexual harassment, we felt that it would be clearer for students to provide a list of example behaviors ranging from relatively mild (e.g., staring) to extreme (e.g., rape). Additionally we believed that it was essential to determine the level of upset associated with the various experiences, as legal definitions of harassment require that the behavior be unwanted and causes upset. While our sample pool was limited to one university, the students themselves came from geographically, economically, and ethnically diverse communities. We attempted to avoid self-selection problems by not relating the exact nature of the survey during the recruitment phase. Our study is retrospective; however, the vast majority of our participants were in high school within the previous three years.

METHOD

Participants

Notices requesting participants were posted on bulletin boards in the Department of Psychology at the University of British Columbia in Vancouver, Canada. The notice directed potential participants to a box, located in the psychology department, from which they could obtain a survey. Researchers also went to first-year psychology classes and made announcements. Surveys were distributed to students who expressed interest. Participants were offered course credit in exchange for completed surveys. The researchers attempted to control for self-selection by avoiding specific references to sexual harassment when recruiting participants. Two copies of an informed consent form were attached to the front of the survey. One was to be kept by the participant and the other was to be returned to the lab along with the completed surveys. When surveys and consent forms were submitted, participants were given a debriefing form which included phone numbers for counseling services.

A total of 449 surveys were distributed and 373 were completed and returned (83% return rate). Participants ranged in age from 18 to 71, but were mostly 18-21 (average age = 20.1). Most respondents identified themselves as Asian (n = 215; 59.6%), European (n = 101; 27.9%), or South Asian/Indian (n = 23; 6.4%). Although the majority of psychology students at the University of British Columbia (UBC) are Asian, the sample's ethnic proportions were significantly different than those of students that graduated from the UBC psychology undergraduate program in the last five years (χ^2 = 12.410, df = 2, p < .05).

Most students indicated that they had gone to school in British Columbia (224/239; 93.7%). A small proportion of students attended school in other parts of Canada (11/139; 4.6%) or elsewhere in the world (4/239; 1.7%). It became apparent that some participants had not understood the questions, perhaps due to difficulties with the English language. Some participants did not identify their gender. For these reasons, 10 of the surveys were deemed invalid and left out of the data analysis: 2 unknown sex, 1 white female, 4 Asian females, 1 Middle Eastern female, 1 South Asian (Indian) male, and 1 Asian male. Data from 266 women and 96 men were analyzed.

Measures

Demographics. A demographics questionnaire included the following items: age, sex, ethnicity, family income; nature of the school that the participant attended (i.e., public or private), and the socioeconomic status of the attended school. A small number of subjects reported having attended more than one school. In those cases, the school at which they had spent the majority of their time, or the school that they had attended most recently (when dates were unknown), was the school that was recorded. After data was collected from the first 122 participants, an additional question was added inquiring the about the location of the participants' high school.

High School Experiences Questionnaire (HSEQ). The HSEQ is an as-yet unpublished survey by Fitzgerald and Collinsworth (2000). It was adapted from the Sexual Experiences Questionnaire (SEQ; Fitzgerald, Gelfand, & Drasgow, 1995). The HSEQ is comprised of two sections; student-student behaviors and adult-student behaviors. For the purposes of this study, only adult-student behaviors were used. A complete list of the items can be found in Table 1.

TABLE 1. Items from the High School Experiences Questionnaire (HSEQ) and Number, Percent, and Sex of Students That Experienced Each Behavior

Item	Female Students (n = 262)	Male Students (n = 97)
1. "gotten in your face," trying to intimidate you	59 (22.5%)	23 (23.7%)
2. struck you	2 (0.8%)	3 (3.1%)
3. told you sexual stories or jokes that you didn't want to hear	29 (11.1%)	11 (11.3%)
4. said sexual things to you or others in front of you	32 (12.2%)	15 (15.5%)
5. stared at you or parts of your body	56 (21.4%)	3 (3.1%)**
6. cornered, leaned over, or followed you	34 (13.0%)	3 (3.1%)*
7. said offensive things about your body or how you looked	16 (6.1%)	6 (6.2%)
8. showed, used, or handed out sexual pictures, stories or cartoons	12 (4.6%)	6 (6.2%)
9. said things to put you down because you were male or female (for example, said you shouldn't be doing something because of your sex)	49 (18.7%)	9 (9.3%)
10. made sexual or obscene gestures	8 (3.1%)	10 (10.3%)*
11. kept asking you out even after you had said "no"	7 (2.7%)	1 (1.0%)
12. hinted or said something bad would happen if you didn't go along with something sexual (for example, that you would lose a grade or recommendation)	0 (0.0%)	0 (0.0%)
13. made sexual remarks about you to others or called you sexual names	3 (1.1%)	2 (2.1%)
14. hinted or said that something special would happen if you went along with something sexual (for example, get a better grade or be moved up to a better position)	0 (0.0%)	0 (0.0%)
15. touched you in a way that made you feel uncomfortable (for example, put an arm around your shoulder)	57 (21.8%)	4 (4.1%)**
16. made sexual remarks about your gender (for example, "all women are bitches" or "men are dicks")	28 (10.7%)	10 (10.3%)
17. tried to stroke your leg or other body part	6 (2.3%)	1 (1.0%)
18. made forceful attempts to have sex with you	0 (0.0%)	0 (0.0%)
19. called you an offensive name for a homosexual	1 (0.4%)	2 (2.1%)
20. treated you badly for refusing to have sex	0 (0.0%)	0 (0.0%)
21. gave you any sexual attention you did not want	8 (3.1%)	1 (1.0%)
22. kissed or hugged you when you did not want it	17 (6.5%)	5 (5.2%)
23. spread sexual rumors about you	0 (0.0%)	0 (0.0%)
24. made you do something personal you didn't want to (for example, listen to personal problems or stories about his/her sex life)	8 (3.1%)	1 (1.0%)

TABLE 1 (continued)

Item	Female Students (n = 262)	Male Students (n = 97)
25. hinted or said you would receive gifts if you had sex with the person	0 (0.0%)	0 (0.0%)
26. pulled your clothing down or off	1 (0.4%)	0 (0.0%)
27. tried to have sex with you while you were under the influence of drugs or alcohol	0 (0.0%)	0 (0.0%)
28. tried to get sex by pressuring or arguing with you, but did NOT succeed	0 (0.0%)	0 (0.0%)
29. had sex with you without your consent or against your will	0 (0.0%)	0 (0.0%)
30. raped you	0 (0.0%)	0 (0.0%)

Note: Items 1 and 2 were not included in data analysis, as they are not specifically sexually motivated.

The HSEQ includes a variety of items ranging from general harassment to sexual assault and rape. Participants were asked to indicate the frequency (never, once, twice, or more), the gender of the person who had acted against them (male, female, or both), the position of the offender (teacher or other), and the participants' reactions to the behavior (not upset, slightly upset, moderately upset, very upset) for each of the behaviors listed. Items 1 ("gotten in your face, trying to intimidate you") and 2 ("struck you") were left out of analysis because they identify behaviors that are aggressive, but are not specifically sexually motivated behaviors.

HSEQ Follow-Up. Following the HSEQ were open-ended and checklist-style questions which asked participants to: elaborate on any endorsed behavior items; describe any behaviors that had not been included in the list but that had occurred; and indicate what actions the subjects had taken in response to the behavior (ignored the behavior, played along, confronted, told friends, family, counselor/teacher, told principal, police, or "other"). Participants were then asked if telling anyone had resulted in "some sort of formal investigation by the school or by the authorities"; whether or not the offending student or adult had been disciplined and what had happened; whether or not the subjects felt they had been sexually harassed; and whether or not they were aware of these incidents happening to anyone else in their schools. Some of the questions were open-ended and not all participants chose to fill them out.

Marlowe-Crowne Scale. After finishing the survey, participants completed the Marlowe-Crowne Scale (Crowne & Marlowe, 1960), an indicator of socially desirable responding. It utilizes items about behaviors that are culturally sanctioned and approved of, but unlikely to occur (e.g., "I never hesitate to go out of my way to help someone in trouble"). Items have minimal pathological implications if responded to in either direction. The test has a high internal consistency coefficient (Kuder-Richardson formula 20 is 0.88) and high test-retest correlation (.89 at one month). We chose to delete one item from the Marlowe-Crowne Scale. The item requested participants to identify if they had ever been dishonest. We decided that participants who may have disclosed experiences of sexual abuse this might find this item judgmental.

RESULTS

On the Marlowe-Crowne Scale for social desirability, the sample scored a mean of 14.2 ($SD = 5.3$) which is significantly greater than that of a sample of depressed patients (12.3; $t(327) = 6.528$, $p < .001$) but is significantly lower than that of sample female Peace Corps volunteers (16.4; $t(327) = -7.482$, $p < .001$; Paulhus, 1991). This indicates that as a sample, there was no trend for participants to present themselves in a socially desirable manner. However, scores on the Marlowe-Crowne Scale correlated negatively and significantly ($r = -.106$, $p < .05$) with reported behaviors. When the sexes were analyzed separately, the relationship was not significant for male students ($r = -.016$, $p > .05$) but was for their female counterparts ($r = -.133$, $p < .05$). This indicates that there may have been a slight trend for female students to underreport experiences due to social desirability. Consequently, reported rates for female students may be conservative estimates of actual behavior experienced.

Overall, 47.4% (163/344) of the participants surveyed reported that they had experienced at least one of the behaviors listed on the HSEQ. Of those 163 participants, 79.1% (129/163) reported that at least one experience had upset them. Thus, 37.5% (129/344) of the sample had experienced adult-student sexual harassment, as legally defined. However, of those students who experienced sexual harassment and responded to the question "Were you sexually harassed?" only 13.0% (15/115) responded in the affirmative. When all students were included, the proportion of students that felt they had been sexually harassed was 4.4% (15/344). Participants had experienced, on average, 1.3 of the behaviors listed ($SD = 1.9$), with a range from 0 to 11. The modal number of behaviors experienced was 0. Of those participants that had experienced at least one behavior, they were upset by an average of 1.9 experienced behaviors ($SD = 1.9$), with a range from 0 to 10. Ten of 28 items were not endorsed by any of the participants (items 12, 14, 18, 20, 23, 25, 27, 28, 29, and 30).

There was no significant difference between the proportion of male students (42.9%; 39/91) and the proportion of female students (49.0%; 124/253) that had experienced any of the listed behaviors ($\chi^2 = 1.256$, df = 1, $p > .05$).

However, significantly more female students (42.6%; 112/263) than male students (23.7%; 23/97) had experienced at least one of the listed behaviors and had been upset by that experience ($\chi^2 = 11.382$, df = 2, $p < .001$). Similarly, for those participants that had experienced at least one behavior, a significantly larger proportion of female students (85.5%; 106/124) than of male students (63.9%; 23/39) had been upset ($\chi^2 = 12.630$, df = 1, $p < .001$).

Male students experienced, on average, 1.0 ($SD = 1.7$) of the behaviors listed, with a range from 0 to 8 and a mode of 0. Female students experienced, on average, 1.4 ($SD = 2.0$) of the behaviors listed, with a range from 0 to 11 and a mode of 0. There was no significant difference in the average amount of behaviors experienced by male and female students, $F(1, 342) = 3.351$, $p > .05$.

More female than male students experienced behaviors described in items 5 ($\chi^2 = 18.600$, df = 2, $p < .001$), 6 ($\chi^2 = 7.444$, df = 2, $p < .05$), and 15 ($\chi^2 = 15.520$, df = 2, $p < .001$). More male students experienced behavior outlined in item 10 ($\chi^2 = 6.319$, df = 2, $p < .05$). When a Bonferonni adjustment for multiple comparisons was applied, the differences for items 6 and 10 became nonsignificant ($p > .002$). When level of upset was taken into account, responses to item 5 indicated that females (mean upset = 1.77, $SD = .874$) were more upset than males (mean upset = .33, $SD = .577$) if they experienced the described behavior, $t(57) = -2.798$, $p < .01$. On the other hand, males (mean upset = 2.00, $SD = .000$) were more upset than females (mean upset = 1.71, $SD = .889$) if they experienced item 15 behavior, $t(55) = -2.406$, $p < .05$. For the rest of the items, there were no sex differences in reported prevalence rates. For a detailed list, and the proportions of male and female students that endorsed each item, please see Table 1.

When degree of upset was collapsed into "not upset" versus "any upset," a greater proportion of female than male students were upset when they experienced behaviors described in items 3, 4, 5, 6, 9, 16, 17, and 21 (see Table 2). After a Bonferonni adjustment for multiple comparisons was conducted, the only difference that remained significant was for item 9 ('said things to put you down because you were male or female').

Participants that went to low socio-economic status schools experienced, on average, 1.4 ($SD = 2.0$) of the behaviors listed, with a range from 0 to 7 and a mode of 0. Participants that went to medium socio-economic status schools experienced, on average, 1.4 ($SD = 2.0$) of the behaviors listed, with a range from 0 to 11 and a mode of 0. Participants that went to high socio-economic status schools experienced, on average, 1.0 ($SD = 1.7$) of the behaviors listed, with a range from 0 to 9 and a mode of 0. Participants that went to extremely high socio-economic status schools experienced, on average, 1.8 ($SD = 2.7$) of the behaviors listed, with a range from 0 to 10 and a mode of 5. There was no signifi-

TABLE 2. Items from the High School Experiences Questionnaire (HSEQ) and Number, Percent, and Sex That Experienced Each Behavior and Were Upset

Item	Female Students		Male Students	
	Not Upset	Upset	Not Upset	Upset
3. told you sexual stories or jokes that you didn't want to hear	6 (20.7%)	23 (79.3%)	8 (72.3%)	3 (27.3%)*
4. said sexual things to you or others in front of you	17 (52.1%)	15 (46.9%)	14 (93.3%)	1 (6.7%)*
5. stared at you or parts of your body	7 (11.9%)	52 (88.1%)	2 (66.7%)	1 (33.3%)*
6. cornered, leaned over, or followed you	5 (14.7%)	29 (85.3%)	2 (66.7%)	1 (33.3%)*
7. said offensive things about your body or how you looked	5 (31.3%)	11 (68.7%)	1 (16.7%)	5 (83.3%)
8. showed, used, or handed out sexual pictures, stories, or cartoons	7 (58.3%)	5 (41.7%)	5 (83.3%)	1 (16.7%)
9. said things to put you down because you were male or female (for example, said you shouldn't be doing something because of your sex)	3 (6.1%)	46 (93.9%)	5 (55.6%)	4 (44.4%)**
10. made sexual or obscene gestures	3 (37.5%)	5 (62.5%)	6 (66.7%)	3 (33.3%)
11. kept asking you out even after you had said "no"	1 (14.3%)	6 (85.7%)	0 (0.0%)	1 (100.0%)
12. hinted or said something bad would happen if you didn't go along with something sexual (for example, that you would lose a grade or recommendation)	0 (0.0%)	0 (0.0%)	0 (0.0%)	0 (0.0%)
13. made sexual remarks about you to others or called you sexual names	3 (100.0%)	0 (0.0%)	1 (50.0%)	1 (50.0%)
14. hinted or said that something special would happen if you went along with something sexual (for example, get a better grade or be moved up to a better position)	0 (0.0%)	0 (0.0%)	0 (0.0%)	0 (0.0%)
15. touched you in a way that made you feel uncomfortable (for example, put an arm around your shoulder)	5 (8.8%)	52 (91.2%)	0 (0.0%)	4 (100.0%)

TABLE 2 (continued)

Item	Female Students		Male Students	
	Not Upset	Upset	Not Upset	Upset
16. made sexual remarks about your gender (for example, "all women are bitches" or "men are dicks")	7 (25.0%)	21 (75.0%)	7 (70.0%)	3 (30.0%)*
17. tried to stroke your leg or other body part	0 (0.0%)	6 (100.0%)	1 (100.0%)	0 (0.0%)*
18. made forceful attempts to have sex with you	0 (0.0%)	0 (0.0%)	0 (0.0%)	0 (0.0%)
19. called you an offensive name for a homosexual	1 (100.0%)	0 (0.0%)	1 (50.0%)	1 (50.0%)
20. treated you badly for refusing to have sex	0 (0.0%)	0 (0.0%)	0 (0.0%)	0 (0.0%)
21. gave you any sexual attention you did not want	1 (12.5%)	7 (87.5%)	1 (100.0%)	0 (0.0%)*
22. kissed or hugged you when you did not want it	4 (23.5%)	13 (76.5%)	2 (40.0%)	3 (60.0%)
23. spread sexual rumors about you	0 (0.0%)	0 (0.0%)	0 (0.0%)	0 (0.0%)
24. made you do something personal you didn't want to (for example, listen to personal problems or stories about his/her sex life)	3 (37.5%)	5 (62.5%)	1 (100.0%)	0 (0.0%)
25. hinted or said you would receive gifts if you had sex with the person	0 (0.0%)	0 (0.0%)	0 (0.0%)	0 (0.0%)
26. pulled your clothing down or off	0 (0.0%)	1 (100.0%)	0 (0.0%)	0 (0.0%)
27. tried to have sex with you while you were under the influence of drugs or alcohol	0 (0.0%)	0 (0.0%)	0 (0.0%)	0 (0.0%)
28. tried to get sex by pressuring or arguing with you, but did NOT succeed	0 (0.0%)	0 (0.0%)	0 (0.0%)	0 (0.0%)
29. had sex with you without your consent or against your will	0 (0.0%)	0 (0.0%)	0 (0.0%)	0 (0.0%)
30. raped you	0 (0.0%)	0 (0.0%)	0 (0.0%)	0 (0.0%)

Note: Items 1 and 2 were not included in data analysis, as they are not specifically sexually motivated.
Note: *Pearson Chi-Square, $p < .05$, **Pearson Chi-Square, $p < .001$.

cant difference in the average amount of behaviors experienced by students from schools of different socio-economic status, $F(3, 338) = 2.052, p > .05$. There was also no significant difference between the proportion of participants who had experienced at least one listed behavior and that had attended schools of low (50.0%; 13/26), medium (51.7%; 91/176), high (39.1%; 45/115), and extremely high (52.0%; 13/25) socio-economic status ($\chi^2 = 4.745$, df = 3, $p > .05$). Likewise, there was no significant difference between the proportion of students that had attended schools of low (92.3%; 12/13), medium (84.6%; 77/91), high (71.1%; 32/45), and extremely high (61.5%; 8/13) socio-economic status who had experienced at least one listed behavior and had been upset ($\chi^2 = 7.319$, df = 3, $p > .05$).

Public school students experienced, on average, 1.3 ($SD = 2.0$) of the behaviors listed, with a range from 0 to 11 and a mode of 0. Private school students experienced, on average, 1.3 ($SD = 1.9$) of the behaviors listed, with a range from 0 to 7 and a mode of 0 and 0. There was no significant difference in the average amount of behaviors experienced by private and public school students, $F(1, 337) = .033, p > .05$. Additionally, there was no significant difference between the proportion of participants who had experienced one of the listed behaviors ($\chi^2 = .552$, df = 2, $p > .05$) and had attended public school (47.6%; 141/296), private school (45.5%; 20/44) or both (66.7%; 2/3). Likewise, there was no significant difference in the proportion of public school students (79.4%; 112/141), private school students (75.0%; 15/20) or students who had attended both a private school and a public school (100.0%; 2/2), that had experienced at least one behavior and were upset ($\chi^2 = .742$, df = 2, $p > .05$).

In response to the HSEQ follow-up question inquiring about the actions the students took if they had experienced one of the behaviors listed in the HSEQ (see Table 3), 47.0% (79/168) indicated that they ignored the behavior, 13.1% (22/168) indicated that they played along with the adult(s)'s behavior, 5.4% (9/168) indicated that they confronted the adult, 0.6% (1/168) indicated that they engaged in a relationship with the adult(s), 29.8% (50/168) indicated that they told friends, 10.1% (17/168) indicated that they told family, 4.8% (8/168) indicated that they told a school counselor or another teacher in the school, 1.8% (3/168) indicated that they told the school principal, 0% (0/168) indicated that they told the police, and 1.2% indicated that they told someone else. For a break-down of responses by sex, please see Table 3. Of those students that indicated that they took action, 1.2% (2/85) reported that their actions led to an investigation. In both cases, the perpetrator was disciplined. Of the 132 students that responded to the question, "Are you aware of any of these incidents happening to other students in your school?" 46 (38.4%) responded in the affirmative.

TABLE 3. Student Responses to Adult Sexually Harassing Behavior

Response	n Total ($n = 168$)	n Female Students ($n = 129$)	n Male Students ($n = 39$)
Ignored the behavior	79 (47.0 %)	61 (47.3%)	18 (46.2%)
Played along with the adult's behavior	22 (13.1%)	12 (9.3%)	10 (25.6%)
Confronted the adult	9 (5.4%)	9 (7.0%)	0 (0.0%)
Engaged in a relationship with the adult	1 (0.6%)	1 (0.8%)	0 (0.0%)
Told friends	50 (29.8%)	45 (34.9%)	5 (12.8%)
Told family	17 (10.1%)	17 (13.2%)	0 (0.0%)
Told school counselor or another teacher in school	8 (4.8%)	8 (6.2%)	0 (0.0%)
Told principal	3 (1.8%)	3 (2.3%)	0 (0.0%)
Told police	0 (0.0%)	0 (0.0%)	0 (0.0%)
Told other	2 (1.2%)	2 (1.6%)	0 (0.0%)

DISCUSSION

Nearly half (47.4%) of students surveyed reported that they had experienced at least one behavior that was listed on the HSEQ. Of those, 79.1% reported being upset by one or more experiences. Consequently, the experiences of 37.5% of students (41.9% of female students and 27.5% of male students) met the legal criteria for sexual harassment. These rates of high school adult-student sexual harassment are substantially greater than those found in previous studies conducted in the United States. The AAUW (1993) survey indicated that of the students sampled, 25% of female students and 10% of male students reported being sexually harassed by adults in their schools. Stratton and Backes (1997) found that in their sample, only 9.6% of female students and 6.9% of male students reported sexual harassment by teachers and coaches. In a sample of almost 1200 students, McCormack (1985) found that 17% of female students and only 2% of male students had been sexually harassed by school staff. There are two possible reasons why our findings are different. The first explanation is that adult-student sexual harassment may be more prevalent in British Columbia high schools than in American high schools. The second, and more probable explanation, is that previous surveys asked students directly if they had experienced sexual harassment perpetrated by adults in their schools, whereas the survey we used listed endorsable behavioral items that would constitute sexual harassment if they caused upset. This did not require students to formulate their own opinions about the nature of sexual harassment. In support of the second explanation, our data show that only a small minority of female students (13%), and no male students that were upset by adult sexually harassing behaviors actually felt they had been sexually harassed. This proportion is more on par with the prevalence rates reported in previous studies.

No items were endorsed that had a sexually coercive or reward element (items: 12, 14, 18, 20, 23, 25, 27, 28, 29, and 30). However, students did experience, on average, 1.3 of the other behaviors listed. This indicates that many students will go through school experiencing a behavior that has the potential to meet the criteria for sexual harassment. This, in combination with the finding that only 13% of female students and no male students believed that their upsetting experiences were instances of sexual harassment, suggests that students do not understand the legal definition of sexual harassment. This is an issue that should be addressed by school boards, teachers, and staff. Also, other researchers in the area should keep this in mind when doing studies of prevalence rates.

Surprisingly, there was no significant difference in the proportion of male (42.9%) and female (49.0%) students that had experienced one or more of the listed behaviors. Similarly, there were no significant differences in the average amount of behaviors experienced by female and male students (1.4 and 1.0, respectively). However, more female students were upset by their encounters than their male counterparts, indicating that the experiences of more females met the legal criteria for sexual harassment. The greater prevalence of female upset may be related to the different types of behaviors experienced by male and female students. For example, a larger proportion of female than male students experienced behaviors described in items 5 ('stared at you or parts of your body') and 15 ('touched you in a way that made you feel uncomfortable'). These items have an underlying sexually aggressive quality. Male students did not report experiencing these types of experiences as much as their female counterparts. Regardless, the vast majority of both sexes were generally upset by the behaviors when they occurred (85.5% of female students and 63.9% of male students).

Unexpectedly, school socio-economic status (SES) and school type (public versus private) did not relate to prevalence of sexual harassment. This contradicts stereotypes which suggest that adult-student sexual harassment is more common in low SES public schools. Researchers may want to pursue this surprising finding in future studies.

Data from the HSEQ follow-up indicate that most students (47.0%) ignore sexually harassing behavior by school adults. The next most common response was to tell friends (29.8%). Only 4.7% of students reported to teachers or school counselors, while 1.8% reported to their principals. When male and female reporting patterns were analyzed separately, some interesting differences surfaced. A small proportion of female students confronted the adult (7.0%), and more female students opted to tell their family (13.2%) than other adults in the school (6.2%) or the principal (1.8%). Female students accounted for all reports to adults ($n = 19$). Only one female student reported that she engaged in relationship with a teacher. On the other hand, male students opted to ignore the behavior (46.2%), play along (25.6%), or tell friends (12.8%). No male students reported to adults.

In general, very few students chose to report sexually harassing behavior to any adult. Considering the number of students that were bothered by their experiences (79.1%), we suspect the low report rate, and the differences in report rates between male and female students, to be attributed to seven possible reasons: (a) students may have been bothered, but not bothered enough to report; (b) students may have chosen not to report due to personal reasons such as being shy or feeling ashamed, guilty and/or weak; (c) students may have feared the adult perpetrators, especially in more severe cases (e.g., sexual assault); (d) students may not have realized that there were means by which to report; (e) students may not have known the legal definition of sexual harassment, and therefore did not realize their experiences fit the criteria; (f) it is possible that students may have felt that there would be negative repercussions associated with reporting, such as being graded unfairly or being teased by other students; and (g) students may have felt that they would not be believed if they reported their experiences, especially considering the power differential between students and adults. Future research should focus on elucidating the causes underlying low reporting rates.

Regardless, the data suggest that many incidents of sexual harassment go unreported. This dramatic underreporting should be addressed by the education system. A good way to disseminate information about sexual harassment, for example, would be to include a module in the sexual education curriculum. We suggest that by educating students about sexual harassment, more students may come forward to report sexually harassing behaviors. Further, different educational approaches may be more effective for male and female students.

REFERENCES

American Association of University Women (1993). Hostile hallways: The AAUW survey on sexual harassment in America's schools. *Women's International Network News*, 9(3), 74-76.

Bagley, C., & Bolitho, F. (1997). Sexual assault in school, mental health, and suicidal behaviors in adolescent women in Canada. *Adolescence*, 32(126), 361-377.

Balenger, V. J., & Sedlacek, W. E. (1992). Sexual harassment during the high school years: Experiences and perceptions of incoming university students. *Counseling Center Research Report #4.* University of Maryland, College Park.

Bermann, H., McKenna, K., Traher Arnold, C., Taylor, G., & MacQuarrie, B. (2000). Sexual harassment: Everyday violence in the lives of girls and women. *Advances in Nursing Science, 22*(4), 32-46.

British Columbia College of Teachers (2001). *News releases.* Retrieved April 25, 2001 from http://bcct.bc.ca/newsreleases_archive.html.

British Columbia Teachers' Federation (2001). *Code of ethics.* Retrieved April 29, 2001 from, http://www.bctf.bc.ca/About/MembersGuide/code.html.

Canadian Criminal Code §153 (1985).

Corbett, K., Gentry, C., & Pearson, W. (1993). Sexual harassment in high school. *Youth and Society, 25*(1), 93-103.

Crowne, D. P., & Marlowe, D. (1960). A new scale of social desirability independent of psychopathology. *Journal of Consulting Psychology, 24*(4), 349-354.

Finkelhor, D., & Hashima, P. Y. (2001). The victimization of children and youth: A comprehensive overview. In S. O. White (Ed.), *Handbook of youth and justice: The Plenum series in crime and justice* (pp. 49-78). Dordrecht, Netherlands: Kluwer Academic Publishers.

Fitzgerald, L. F., Gelfand, M. J., & Drasgow, F. (1995). Measuring sexual harassment: Theoretical and psychometric advances. *Basic and Applied Social Psychology, 17*(4), 425-445.

Hall, E. R., Howard, J. A., & Boezio, S. L. (1986). Tolerance of rape: A sexist or antisocial attitude? *Psychology of Women Quarterly, 1*(0), 101-118.

Hendrie, C. (1998). Cost is high when schools ignore abuse. *Education Week on the Web.* Retrieved April 22, 2001 from, http://www.edweek.org/ew/vol-18/15handle.h18.

Janzen v. Platy Enterprises Ltd. (1989) 1 S.C.R. 1252, 10 C.H.R.R. D/6205, as cited in Joanis, S.T. (1999). *Human rights law in B.C.: Sexual harassment.* CHRR memorandum. Retrieved April 29, 2001 from, http://www.canlii.org/ca/cas/scc/1989/1989scc 47.html.

Joanis, S.T. (1999). *Human rights law in BC: Sexual harassment.* CHRR memorandum. Retrieved April 29, 2001 from http://www.bchrc.gov.bc.ca/text_ only/HRLawSexual Harassment.asp.

Kopels, S., & Dupper, D. R. (1999). School-based peer sexual harassment. *Child Welfare, 78*(4), 435-461.

Loredo, C., Reid, A., & Deaux, K. (1995). Judgments and definitions of sexual harassment by high school students. *Sex Roles, 32*(1/2), 29-45.

Mazer, D. B., & Percival, E. F. (1989). Students' experiences of sexual harassment at a small university. *Sex Roles, 20*(3-4), 1-22.

Ontario Office of the Attorney General (2001). *Protecting our students: Executive summary and recommendations.* Retrieved February 5, 2001 from, http://www.attorney general.jus.gov.on.ca/html/robins/robinsrvw.htm.

Reilly, M. E., Lott, B., & Gallogly, S. M. (1986). Sexual harassment of university students. *Sex Roles, 15*(7-8), 333-358.

Shumba, A. (2004). Emotional abuse in the classroom: A cultural dilemma? *Journal of Emotional Abuse, 4*(3/4), 139-149.

Stratton, S. D., & Backes, J. S. (1997). Sexual harassment in North Dakota public schools: A study of eight high schools. *High School Journal, 80*(3), 163-173.

Wishnietsky, D. (1991). Reported and unreported teacher-student sexual harassment. *Journal of Educational Research, 84*(3), 164-169.

Yaffe, E. (1995). Expensive, illegal, and wrong: Sexual harassment in our schools. *Phi Delta Kappan, 77*(3), 1-8.

Early Responses to School Violence: A Qualitative Analysis of Students' and Parents' Immediate Reactions to the Shootings at Columbine High School

Nikki A. Hawkins
Daniel N. McIntosh
Roxane Cohen Silver
E. Alison Holman

SUMMARY. On April 20, 1999, two angry students attacked Columbine High School. The unprecedented murder/suicide resulted in 15 deaths, more than 20 injuries, and thousands of psychologically traumatized individuals. We present a qualitative analysis of interviews conducted two weeks after the incident with 4 Columbine High School students and 7 parents who were directly and indirectly affected. Findings highlight both similarities and variability in immediate emotional, cognitive, and social responses to the mass violence. Helpful and unhelpful support attempts are noted. Implications of the media's heavy in-

---

Address correspondence to: Daniel N. McIntosh, PhD, Department of Psychology, University of Denver, Denver, CO 80208 (E-mail: dmcintos@edu).

The authors thank Tera Beaber for her assistance in transcribing the interviews.

Project support provided by a grant from the National Hazards Research Center of the University of Colorado and NSF grant BCS-9910223 to Roxane Cohen Silver.

[Haworth co-indexing entry note]: "Early Responses to School Violence: A Qualitative Analysis of Students' and Parents' Immediate Reactions to the Shootings at Columbine High School." Hawkins, Nikki A. et al. Co-published simultaneously in *Journal of Emotional Abuse* (The Haworth Maltreatment & Trauma Press, an imprint of The Haworth Press, Inc.) Vol. 4, No. 3/4, 2004, pp. 197-222; and: *Aggression in Organizations: Violence, Abuse, and Harassment at Work and in Schools* (ed: Robert Geffner et al.) The Haworth Maltreatment & Trauma Press, an imprint of The Haworth Press, Inc., 2004, pp. 197-222. Single or multiple copies of this article are available for a fee from The Haworth Document Delivery Service [1-800-HAWORTH, 9:00 a.m. - 5:00 p.m. (EST). E-mail address: docdelivery@haworthpress.com].

Digital Object Identifier: 10.1300/J135v04n03_12   *197*

volvement in sensational traumas are discussed, emphasizing important considerations for future research on the psychological effects of school violence. *[Article copies available for a fee from The Haworth Document Delivery Service: 1-800-HAWORTH. E-mail address: <docdelivery@haworthpress.com> Website: <http://www.HaworthPress.com> © 2004 by The Haworth Press, Inc. All rights reserved.]*

KEYWORDS. School violence, workplace violence, terrorist attacks, coping, media, adjustment, traumatic events, social support

On April 20, 1999, in a middle-class suburb of Denver, Colorado, two youths attacked Columbine High School. Before taking their own lives, they killed 12 classmates, one teacher, and injured more than 20 others using sawed-off shotguns, assault rifles, pistols, and 30 bombs (Bartels, 2002). Because the motive of the perpetrators appears to have been to punish the members of the school community for perceived years of teasing (Adams & Russakoff, 1999; Weintraub, Hall, & Pynoos, 2001), we see their attack as a dramatic attempt at emotional abuse.

The Columbine attack far exceeded the magnitude of previous school violence, and it remains America's deadliest school assault (Yettick, 2002). Over 2,000 people work and learn at Columbine. In addition to the 15 fatalities and over 20 severe injuries, many were traumatized through witnessing killings, seeing killed or injured peers, and seeing, smelling, and hearing indications of the attack. About 300 people were trapped in the school for hours while their families waited for news. Over 8,000 individuals were potentially eligible for victim assistance, with 9,000 estimated to be in the "high-risk" group for psychological difficulties (Weintraub et al., 2001, p. 147). Indeed, exposure to such violence is linked with distress, intrusive thoughts, difficulties concentrating, and social concerns, among other reactions (Buka, Stichick, Birdthistle, & Earls, 2001; Howard, Feigelman, Li, Cross, & Rachuba, 2002).

Those exposed to the incident were challenged with recovering from a trauma that was new to them and to most people who assisted in their coping efforts. The mental health community responded in large numbers to aid the victims and their families. In the first three days, the county mental health center spent 1,600 staff hours helping Columbine students, families, and staff; the number and type of interventions provided by local, state, and national organizations and individuals is inestimable (Weintraub et al., 2001). However, due to the unprecedented nature of mass school violence, these workers were necessarily functioning with less information and context than they needed

(Weintraub et al., 2001). In our discussions with mental health workers in the community, we repeatedly heard frustration about the need for more information that could help mental health professionals understand the experiences of individuals victimized by mass violence. Similar frustration has been expressed by those working to help victims of the September 11th terrorist attacks (Sealey, 2001). Moreover, community members felt their experiences were not adequately represented by the media presentations on the survivors' responses, nor reflected in the public comments made by vocal members of the mental health profession.

This report provides qualitative information from individuals interviewed in the immediate aftermath of the attack on Columbine. By documenting the experiences of some victims, we intend to give voice to the variety of experiences of victims of mass violence and allow for more informed study of responses to such events. Especially with the increased likelihood of terrorist attacks in the U.S., we must advance research that is sensitive to the experiences of victims of mass violence so as to provide consistent and genuinely helpful assistance in its wake.

The literature on coping with trauma is replete with studies on responses to many types of traumatic events (Norris et al., 2002). Our study adds to this body of research in three ways. First, reacting to traumatic events is a dynamic process in which responses are influenced by individual and social variables (Kaniasty & Norris, 1995; Lepore, Silver, Wortman, & Wayment, 1996; Tait & Silver, 1989; van der Kolk, 1996). The dynamic nature of responses requires early information on reactions, but few studies have collected such data (see Holman & Silver, 1998; Shalev et al., 1996, for exceptions). We focused on obtaining immediate responses (within two weeks of the event). Second, much of the literature on the effects of traumatic violence focuses on the minority of individuals who display signs of acute or posttraumatic stress disorders. In contrast, our investigation focused on a group of individuals who were not necessarily in need of, or desirous of, professional help. We set out to document a range of normal responses to an abnormal event. Third, we were particularly interested in the social context in which responses to trauma occur, and we recognize that providing social support to others can be a stressful experience (Cohler & Lieberman, 1980). The Columbine attack provided an opportunity to examine the effects on, and responses of, key members of the primary victims' social networks: Their parents.

Our intent was to glean from the adolescents and their parents insight into immediate psychological effects of their experiences with mass violence. We focused on understanding emotional and cognitive responses, feelings about talking to others about their experiences, and the larger context of general social responses. We considered these issues at the intersection of the victim's subjective experience and the support of the social network as crucial to understanding psychosocial adjustment after traumatic or stressful events (Holman & Silver, 1996; Pritchard & McIntosh, 2003; Silver & Wortman, 1980; Tait & Silver, 1989). Discussing traumatic experiences with a supportive audience can also facilitate long-term adjustment (Lepore et al., 1996; Pennebaker, 1989), whereas an unsupportive environment may exacerbate the maladaptive tendency to focus one's attention on the past (Holman & Silver, 1998; Holman & Zimbardo, 2003; Lepore et al., 1996; Tait & Silver, 1989). The dynamics and experience of such interactions may be affected by the type of trauma (Norris et al., 2002). Thus, we specifically considered our respondents' social experiences.

Moreover, as noted to us by community members, the media often focus on reactions that are dramatic and negative, omitting the heterogeneity of responses. Perhaps due to the lack of data on acute responses, the common use of clinical samples, and inaccurate portrayals by the media, laypeople and professionals hold several unsubstantiated beliefs about coping (Wortman & Silver, 1987, 1989, 2001). In analyzing our interviews, we examined two of these assumptions: (1) an expectation of uniformly strong negative emotions, with little expectation of positive emotions, and (2) a belief that talking or grief counseling immediately after a loss is a demonstrably useful intervention. Here, we consider the validity of these beliefs through interviews with individuals who did not seek immediate help from professionals following this trauma. In all areas, we wanted to hear what was important to our respondents, and present this as a guide for future research.

METHOD

Participants

We interviewed four female Columbine High School students ages 15 to 17, and seven parents (six female) ages 41 to 49. All students had one participating parent. Three Columbine High School parents did not have participating children. To increase confidentiality, we do not distinguish reports of the father from those of the mothers; moreover, there were no clear gender differences.

Procedures

Participants responded to flyers distributed the week after the attacks at a community memorial service, a local mall, and the makeshift memorial grounds adjacent to the school. The flyers invited Columbine High School students and parents to participate in research on coping with the attack. To take part, students had to be at school on the day of the shootings. Parents had to have a child in attendance that day. All who volunteered participated in a structured interview with a trained interviewer in their own home or a quiet setting of their choice. Interviewers had been previously unknown to participants. Interviews lasted approximately one hour and were tape-recorded.

Unfortunately, a series of negative events in the Columbine area after the shootings (e.g., community reactions to media intrusion, pending litigation involving the Board of Education, an Internet threat resulting in another closure of the school, and the shooting deaths of two Columbine students) led to premature termination of data collection.

Measures

The interviews consisted of closed-ended and open-ended questions developed to assess cognitive responses (e.g., ruminative thinking, searching for meaning in the event, undoing, or counterfactual thinking), emotional responses (frequency and intensity of specific positive and negative emotions), and social adjustment (interpersonal support and conflict, frequency of ventilation with different social contacts) in the immediate aftermath of the shootings. Data used in this report primarily come from the open-ended questions. Examples of questions include, "What meaning have you found in this experience?" "Since the shootings, have other people done things that have been particularly helpful to you as you have tried to cope with the shootings?" and, "If so, what have they done?" Additionally, we asked whether the shootings had an effect on family, then friends, and then community relationships, and, if so, what effect they had.

Analysis

The interview audiotapes were transcribed. Responses to closed-ended questions were entered into a statistical program and analyzed to detect similarities, differences, and general trends in the reported experiences of students and parents. Responses to the open-ended questions were also entered into a database for coding, filing, memoing, and diagramming of the data. We coded the data specifically for content pertaining to cognitive responses, emotional responses, and social adjustment of students and parents. Below, we summarize these findings and highlight unanticipated themes that emerged from the open-ended responses.

RESULTS AND DISCUSSION

Exposure

Student exposure. All students heard bombs exploding, and most could smell smoke from the explosions. Two heard or saw guns fired. When the attack began, two were in classrooms. Of these, one heard screams in the hallway, but neither knew what was happening until after they evacuated the building. Once outside, they learned of the ongoing attack and were told to flee. Although these two were not aware of the danger until they were outside the school, their experiences were intense and traumatic [quotations have been edited to enhance confidentiality]:

> (Student) We were just standing around and all of the sudden we heard an explosion and we could see it across the street over by the parking lot and the cafeteria. We were like, "ok, this is serious." Kids were really crying and word started spreading around that people had been shot. People started looking for friends and starting to panic . . . It really started hitting home when we heard another explosion . . . And we just bolted into the neighborhood . . . I started freaking out then because I couldn't find my little brother. (Student) And we heard something, we didn't know what it was but I think now it was probably like a pipe bomb . . . We saw more kids running so we ran, all the way to [the] park and there we just kind of didn't know what was going on. One of my other friends was crying very hard . . . She had seen [a teacher] bleeding, he was shot and he was bleeding and she was very scared about that. I saw a lot of people out there. There were a lot of rumors going around about what had happened. From there, the whole group started running into the neighborhood, I don't know why, but we did.

Two students were not able to escape the building before knowing of the attack. One was in the cafeteria (where the shooting started) when the attack began, and the other was in the library (where most fatalities occurred). The student in the cafeteria said her first warning was from a student who yelled, "Someone has a gun" and a janitor who told everyone to "get down." She escaped to a room where she could hear gunshots and bombs exploding where she had been. This student fled the building with friends and stayed with them at a nearby public library.

The student who had been in the school library when the shootings began had the most direct exposure. This student hid under a table and witnessed the killing of several students:

> I was in the library and we started hearing gunfire outside and everyone kept working. I assumed it was construction, that's what it sounded like

to me. So everyone kept working and then a teacher came in and she started yelling "get on the floor there are students with guns" and she got on the phone and we got under the table and I just got under the table assuming it was probably some kid walking around thinking he was cool you know and had just pulled it out of his backpack or something. So I was just under the table talking to some kids I knew and we were just talking you know and we started hearing gunfire downstairs and people were screaming and it got pretty scary. They came into the library and started shooting people . . . and they shot the black kid because he was black . . . They shot people in the library and then they left, I don't know why.

When the shooters left the library, this student fled the building.

After escaping, all but one of the students congregated in homes of people they did not know. They watched television coverage of the attack, and tried to telephone their parents:

The basement was full, the first floor was full and we turned on the news and started to watch what was going on . . . everybody started to try and use the phones to call their parents because it was all over TV and we didn't want them to be, like, freaking out. But the lines were totally jammed; you couldn't get out. You kept getting busy signals. Even people's cell phones weren't ringing.

Although each student had a different experience, all shared a sense of confusion, chaos, and terror in response to the events. Information was scarce and largely inaccurate, students were unsure about what to do, and they were unclear about why they were doing the things they were doing. Many had difficulty finding parents and getting back to their homes. When they learned what had happened and who had been affected, all realized that they knew at least one person who had been injured and three realized that someone they knew had been killed.

Parent exposure. Five of the seven parents were at work when they learned of the shootings; two were at home. Most parents were notified of the attack by friends or relatives who telephoned them. The others learned through television or radio. Learning about the attack was stressful; six had to wait some length of time before hearing that their child was okay. None were in any danger from the shootings, but several were indirectly exposed. One heard gunshots from home and performed first aid on severely injured students. Another was in a hospital where students were being treated. Another witnessed a child being rescued by officers crouched down covering the child for protection while running to safety. Of the parents not exposed in such direct ways, all but one reported being halted by road-blocks in route to meeting their children.

Negative Emotional Responses

Immediate reactions. All students and most parents said their initial reactions entailed confusion and disbelief. After learning more, however, most students and parents felt scared and panicked. Those who did not feel extremely panicked said they kept their minds on some particular task. For one student, that task was getting herself and her friends away from immediate danger. One parent indicated that she did not feel anxious because she was focused on helping injured students and paramedics stationed near her house. Whereas intensely focusing on tasks prevented these respondents from feeling panicked, others indicated that they were not able to focus on specific tasks because panic had overtaken them.

In the days after the shootings, respondents reported experiencing an array of emotions. Almost all reported feeling devoid of emotion or "numb" immediately after the shootings. However, during the days immediately following the events, feelings of numbness began to subside. With time, students and parents reported thinking more about the effects of the events and they became increasingly aware of their emotions, which were often intensely negative. "I'm finding it more difficult to carry on now than I did in the immediate crisis," said one parent almost two weeks after the shootings; "I'm finding out that I do really well in the moment of crisis and in the aftermath . . . but [now] it's harder for me."

Most experienced many intense negative feelings in the first two weeks, and nine of eleven reported that these feelings were more prevalent than positive feelings. Half the students reported that the negative emotions were overwhelming at times and prevented them from functioning; half said that the negative emotions were never very strong. All parents indicated that overwhelming negative feelings had prevented them from normal functioning at times.

Respondents reported how often they experienced nervousness, misery, guilt, and irritability. Nine experienced all these, even if only momentarily, during the first two weeks. Among the students, the most common negative feeling was nervousness; among the parents, it was misery and irritability. Some students reported being nervous specifically about returning to school, a place filled with reminders of their proximity to a life-threatening incident.

Nervousness and anxiety. Nervousness related to returning to the site of the event is particularly important in school and workplace violence, because victims are often re-exposed to the site after the incident. Although an attack in the school or workplace may allow victims to avoid the site for a short period, it often necessitates a return some days later. Work and school are arenas in which individuals must function well. Nervousness related to the introduction of a violence-related stimulus after some delay may be an unusual aspect to consider when evaluating the ongoing impact of such violence.

Aside from nervousness regarding returning to school, students experienced nervousness that they could not attribute to any source. This free-floating anxiety infiltrated other emotions and activities:

> Sometimes getting out and trying to have fun helps, but I find that I'm really tense and nervous at times. Like, I went out on a date with my old friend that I hadn't talked to in a long time who had called. And I was, like, trying to be happy because I'm just totally optimistic about things but there were times when I just got really tense and weird.

Irritability. Almost all respondents reported feeling extremely irritable during the two weeks following the incident. Parents, especially, said that they felt irritable quite often and with extreme intensity. In some cases, these feelings were directed toward parenting responsibilities. Parents who had other children commented that they felt "preoccupied and not as attentive" to the other children as they would normally have been. Some reported that they had little or no energy left for their other children, and as a result, many reported feeling irritated when they needed attention. These feelings of irritation led to feelings of guilt for several parents:

> I've been more irritated with my younger [children . . .]. [I'm] having less patience with them and their questions and [I'm] just really not wanting to be available to them at all. And, I have a lot of guilt there . . . I have a lot of guilt and issues with that.

Parents also felt irritation with spouses, friends, and co-workers. One said that co-workers had not been supportive the day of the shootings and this parent felt extremely irritated with them for their lack of support. This parent now felt annoyed by almost anything they did:

> Just anyone saying anything I don't like, it really irritates me. I just can't control it, and I've always been able to control my irritability with people and be nice and now it's like, I don't care. Even my boss, I don't care. They irritate me. [They're] bothersome, and their complaints are petty. I have no patience.

This increased irritation among survivors and their primary caretakers is notable due to its potential consequences for social support. At a time when the survivors and their caretakers may obtain benefit from the support and assistance of others, their expressions of irritability and impatience may lead members of their potential support network to retreat from engaging them.

Friction between potential support providers and the victims may complicate social support provision following a trauma (Coyne, Wortman, & Lehman, 1988; Herbert & Dunkel-Schetter, 1992). Here, we find that this problem applies not only to direct witnesses of violence but also to their supporters. Thus, normal support networks may be strained severely, especially during large-scale events. One question raised by these interviews is whether, in the case of mass violence, the shared experience of the attack increases or decreases the availability of support. Notable in our interviews were reports of difficulty with social relationships *outside* the affected community (old friends, non-Columbine parents, co-workers). Might the social nature of mass violence provide a ready-made support network? Or, might the shared nature of the attack serve to severely strain and damage support networks that have been affected? We suggest future work examine specifically the types of support, and types of social friction, that occur among differing groups (e.g., co-workers, spouses, family, friends) following such violence.

Positive Emotional Responses

Although negative feelings dominated much of the respondents' experiences after the shootings, students and parents also reported experiencing positive feelings. In fact, all reported many positive feelings in the first weeks after the events, including happiness, vigor, affection, and satisfaction. The most common and intense positive emotion reported by the respondents was affection. One parent expressed intense feelings of affection for a daughter who had escaped gunfire:

> I didn't want to let her out of my sight. I wanted to be holding her all the time or hugging her or be around her or comfort her or be around her. I couldn't do enough for her, pick up after her, whatever I could do to make her life better.

Feelings of affection were also strikingly prevalent among the students. Students reported feeling affectionate just as often as they felt nervous (the most common negative feeling), and affection was the most intense of *all* feelings reported in the two weeks after the shootings.

Although some have noted the occurrence of early positive emotions in survivors of various types of trauma and loss (Silver, 1982; Wortman & Silver,

1987; see also Tedeschi & Calhoun, 1995), there remains an almost exclusive emphasis in the literature on negative emotions and negative reactions soon after a trauma. Positive emotions soon after a traumatic event also continue to be relatively unexpected by laypeople and the popular media who commonly judge those displaying positive feelings as reacting inappropriately (e.g., von Fremd, 2002). Finding that our respondents all experienced an array of positive emotions very soon after experiencing the shootings should be taken as an important reminder of this relatively understudied, and unexpected, but apparently common phenomenon.

Variability in Emotional Experience

Almost all respondents recognized losses and gains because of the events. Students lost friends and a sense of security in their everyday routine and parents lost the trust that they had in the protection of the school. All recognized gain in the emotional closeness that they developed with family, friends, or others in the surrounding community following the shootings. The emotions reported in the two weeks after the tragedy reflected this range of outcomes. Sometimes respondents felt intense pain over the threat and loss from the events, and other times they felt happy that they had survived and were able to experience the resulting emotional closeness. ". . . [Y]ou have good days and bad days; and when they're bad, they're really bad and when they're good they're only ok," said one student.

Documenting our respondents' range of emotions is particularly important. Although negative emotions prevailed for most, all experienced positive emotions, and the most intense emotion reported by most was positive. Further, the negative emotions were broader than might have been expected. Although nervousness was dominant among those most directly affected (the students), irritability was also prominent, and most experienced a wide range of negative emotions. Further, irritability was more prevalent among the parents than among the students.

Coping occurs in a social context, and our interviews highlight that potential supporters should be aware of the probable variability in the targets of their assistance. Ironically, the traumatized individual's emotional response to the event may hinder social assistance (Silver, Wortman, & Crofton, 1990). This is especially true if the support network is not aware of the typical range and variability in emotional responses. Survivors who are not acting appropriately in the eyes of potential helpers (e.g., not sad enough, too happy, too irritable) may receive less support. Members of the victim's social network may be confused by the desire for a hug at one moment, and an irritated reply at another. Many emotions can be viewed as normal reactions to the abnormal occurrence. Future work should examine expectations of others regarding the emotional sequelae of victimization, and their responses to the emotional variability among survivors.

Cognitive Responses

Rumination. All respondents reported unpleasant thoughts about the shootings or their aftermath two weeks later. These ruminative thoughts were troubling and largely undesired, and only one student and one parent said they were able to prevent the ruminations. Among those who could not control them, all had trouble doing other things because the vivid memories, thoughts, and pictures of the attack played repeatedly in their minds.

Although all reported some rumination, the frequency of rumination varied substantially between individuals. For example, one student reported that the ruminations occurred only rarely and blocking them from her mind was not difficult. In contrast, one parent experienced constant ruminations and could not block them at all. Interestingly, the frequency of rumination was unrelated to the objective level of exposure to the attack. Those who faced the least direct exposure generally reported experiencing ruminations just as often as did those who had been directly exposed to guns, blood, and explosions. This finding is consistent with work by Silver, Holman, McIntosh, Poulin, and Gil-Rivas (2002), who found that the degree of psychological effects of a major trauma (i.e., the September 11th terrorist attacks) are not predicted simply by objective measures of exposure to or loss from the event.

Whereas level of exposure was not associated with the amount of time respondents ruminated, those most directly exposed spent more time and energy trying to *block* their unpleasant thoughts and memories. This suggests that either the ruminations themselves were more intense or these individuals were more troubled by the ruminations than were the others. This discrepancy underscores the importance of considering the content and nature of ruminations. Ruminative thoughts categorized broadly may not adequately explain the amount of distress incurred by them. These findings also emphasize the need to examine more thoroughly which responses might vary by exposure (e.g., perhaps content of ruminations, or response to ruminations) and which might not (e.g., the amount of rumination).

As a group, parents reported more frequent ruminations, more attempts to block them, less success in doing so, and more interference because of them than did the students. This was unexpected, as one might predict that students, who had more direct exposure to the attack, would consequently think more about their proximity to disaster. Developmental differences between adults and adolescents are one plausible explanation for this difference. This observed difference emphasizes the importance of developmentally-informed research on responses to traumatic events, as there may be age differences in processes of adjustment to such events (Compas, Connor-Smith, Saltzman, Thomsen, & Wadsworth, 2001).

Content of cognitions. Besides thinking about the event itself, respondents also reported spending considerable amounts of time thinking about ways that the shootings could have been avoided or how it could have been worse. For many, these counterfactual thoughts dominated their ruminations, which were themselves considered a source of trauma to the survivors:

> Probably one of the hardest parts was [thinking about] if [my other child] had been there. [That child] is a [part of a group targeted by the shooters], and would have been in the cafeteria. So the "what if's?"...
> By the grace of God, if [that child] hadn't [been absent], [that child] would have been there. And knowing my [child] as well as I do, [my child] probably would have tried to do something. So the "what if's" are even more so than what had happened. So, you know, the thought of "gee I could have lost [my other child]" was really traumatic.

Most said they thought about things others could have done to prevent the incident. Two students and two parents also reported thinking about what they, personally, could have done to prevent it. Both students who reported having these feelings also reported having had contact with one or both of the perpetrators before the attack. The parents who reported these feelings did not report having any prior contact with them; however, they were the parents of the students who reported thinking about what they could have done to stop the attack. It is unclear whether the feelings of personal responsibility displayed by the parents reflect an extension of the contact between their children and the perpetrators or a style of personal control shared by the parents and children. Future work should examine factors that influence assumption of potential personal control over a traumatic event, and the degree of association between a parent and child's responses to negative life events.

Aside from ruminations and counterfactuals, several other cognitive responses were noted. For example, all felt that the results of the shooting were unfair.

> (Student) It was like all the kids that never said anything [mean] to anybody ... that were totally sweet and were those who everybody loved. It's just funny how that always happens. The kids that never would have said two [mean] words to these people. That was really hard to deal with.

> (Parent) It was just the unfairness of it all, the way they got hurt. And you know the kids [in the hospital] that could be permanently paralyzed. It's just the randomness of things that's so scary.

Vulnerability. Although no respondent was physically injured in the events, more than half felt personally cheated because of the incident. They felt stripped of a sense of security in their surroundings. Some reporting losing a sense of certainty in the future, and others reported a lost sense of control. A common feeling was that of surprise and disbelief that the shooting had happened in their neighborhood, previously believed to be immune from this type of incident:

> (Parent) Well, it shook me that it could happen here. I did feel really safe and protected in that neighborhood. I still feel good about the kids, the area, and the school . . . but, you know the safety . . . I was like, "wow."

> (Student) You know if it could happen here it could happen anywhere although it seems like Columbine was like a really extreme case. It's kind of like, we used to joke around [by saying] "Columbine 90210" because even the shooters drove like BMW's, we have a friend with a [very expensive car] that's brand new that he got when he turned 15 and it's just . . . maybe it's more extreme than other places.

It is common for trauma survivors to experience a surprising sense of vulnerability. According to Janoff-Bulman (1989), most non-victimized people operate their day-to-day lives holding to several fundamentally positive assumptions about themselves and their environment. These assumptions, known collectively as an "illusion of invulnerability," consist of three beliefs: (1) the world is benevolent, (2) the world is meaningful, and (3) the self is worthy. When individuals experience a traumatic event, these assumptions can be seriously challenged or shattered. The reactions of the respondents in our sample indicate that the shootings posed a significant threat to their feelings of invulnerability and their illusions of the world as a benevolent and fair place.

Finding meaning. When assumptive frameworks are sundered, successful coping may depend on the victim's ability to interpret the event in meaningful terms and to integrate this information into a new coherent, stable, and adaptive conceptual framework (McIntosh, 1995; McIntosh, Silver, & Wortman, 1993; Tait & Silver, 1989). By the second week after the attack, some respondents had already made progress in rebuilding their assumptive frameworks.

By the second week, all reported having tried to make some sense of the events. However, the importance of finding meaning in the events varied notably. For some, making sense of it was very important; for others, it was less so. Only one indicated that the search for meaning in the event was not at all important. In terms of time devoted to finding meaning, the respondents' answers ranged from thinking about it only rarely to thinking about it all the time. Among the five who said that they had spent considerable time trying to make sense of the shootings, one student and two parents reported that they had been able to do so. These three each expressed unique perspectives on the meaning they had found; however, in all their accounts there existed a similar sense of understanding and identification with the shooters:

> (Student) Well, I can understand why they did it, I guess. That's not an excuse and that's a horrible thing to do, but I can kind of understand.

> (Parent) During church that morning I reflected on what it means to be on the outside–because that's what I felt. And that's when I really had a reflection on the two killers, and what it must be like for them. To be on the outside all the time, be told you can't, you can't do this, you can't do that, or you can't belong or you can't be part of it.

> (Parent) I can understand the pain, the rage, and the feelings of powerlessness that those boys must have felt. I felt some of the same pain when I was in high school . . . so, I can understand.

In addition to understanding the perpetrators' motivations, one student said she also made sense of the experience by believing that God let it happen to encourage growth and closeness in the survivors and the community. One parent made sense of it by believing that the shooters' parents and the police department were negligent and guilty of allowing the situation to occur.

Despite the success achieved by these respondents in their search for meaning, other respondents said they had searched and been unable to find answers:

> (Student) I mean . . . can you even visualize yourself doing that? I can't make sense of it. Never mind that I think it came out because they had a diary, they had been planning it for a year. That really blew everybody's mind. For most people, you get mad at somebody and it's gone 10 minutes later. You're like, "Oh, I hate them," and then it goes away. Imagine saying that for a year and then killing people. Nobody can understand.

Several who had not been able to make sense of the events expressed an *in*ability to identify with the attackers. They held the shooters responsible for their behavior:

> (Student) And when I think back on that I guess I can see how those kids didn't fit in. But it was, like, self-inflicted. They just, like, separated themselves on their own. I know they got teased, but everyone gets

teased, and I know it wasn't an everyday thing because it wasn't like, "Hey, let's pick on those kids."

Forgiveness. For several respondents, forgiveness was something that they were not ready to consider or did not think they would ever be able to extend. However, over half were trying to forgive the assailants within the first two weeks after the attack. One student had already forgiven them. As a group, respondents who expressed a desire to forgive were not more invested in finding meaning, more able to make sense of the incident, or more religious or spiritual than were those who were uninterested in forgiving the shooters. Instead, forgiveness appeared to be an independent decision made by each individual who had been affected, either directly or indirectly.

Helpful Social Responses

Those recovering from traumatic events frequently benefit from being involved in an informal social support system (Norris et al., 2002). Respondents cited many instances in which support from others was helpful. Most found it helpful spending time talking with both people who had experienced the event and those who had not. Just spending time talking and being with friends and family was the support most often mentioned as helpful. This appreciation of talking is consistent with findings on its value (Lepore et al., 1996; Pennebaker, 1989). Several said that they especially liked calls and visits from people with whom they had not spoken recently. One parent said it was helpful to know that old friends still cared.

Approximately half the respondents mentioned being greatly helped by feeling that there was a larger network of community support that had become cohesive and was supportive of them. One student felt encouraged by seeing others in the community wearing shirts and ribbons that represented the school. Many mentioned visits to the community-sponsored memorial grounds as helpful. At the memorial, it was possible to experience support from the community visually in the collections of posters, cards, flowers, and the like. The gestures mentioned as helpful fit with research suggesting that collective grieving is helpful because it allows victims to express solidarity and thus unity and collective action (Norris et al., 2002).

Quite a few respondents spontaneously mentioned their appreciation of being hugged, being close, and being held by others. One student explained her appreciation of the increased physical affection: "To actually physically hold someone and be like, 'Oh, you're still here.'" Previous research on coping with trauma has not closely examined the role of physical affection in social support, which may be particularly important to some individuals early after a trauma.

For parents, especially, tangible forms of support were greatly appreciated. Childcare, prepared meals, and towels and sheets (given to replace ones donated to treat victims of the attack) were particularly helpful. Several students mentioned appreciation of sentimental gifts, such as stuffed animals. The parents also valued these; however, they reported gifts that relieved some normal responsibilities to be more helpful.

Unhelpful Involvement of Others

Social networks can have negative consequences, particularly when people fail to fulfill expectations for aid (Belle, 1991). This was seen in our respondents' networks. Some were disappointed by the level of support from close others, even immediately after the attack. Four parents indicated that they wanted to talk to their children about the events more than their children did, and one student indicated that family and friends did not always want to listen to what she had to say. One student wanted to talk to her parents about the events, but found that their conversations were unhelpful because they became angry so quickly. One parent said there had been less spousal emotional support than usual. "My [spouse] and I have tracked differently through this, so, we haven't been the kind of comfort we normally would be to one another."

Smothering. When respondents did receive support, it was not always perceived as helpful. Most unhelpful support could be classified as gestures that were uninvited and too restrictive of the respondents' coping efforts. For example, one student complained that her sibling tried to protect her by screening her calls. She understood her sibling was trying to help but reported that it was more frustrating than helpful because she *wanted* to talk to people. Such acts of smothering appear to be a typical response by supporters of a partner in crisis. Support given by close others who become overbearing, albeit with good intentions, can be a detriment to the well-being and recovery of the support recipient (Coyne, Wortman, & Lehman, 1988).

Structured counseling. Several respondents mentioned that structured counseling activities offered through school and the emergency response systems were not helpful. In fact, some reported these activities to be unhelpful and irritating:

> (Student) That nice little counseling activity was pretty retarded . . . limiting time on how long you can speak and making it so structured. That [counseling] activity and that day was so structured and everybody is telling everybody what to do and how to handle everything, it just doesn't work, especially when so many kids are in so many different

spots recovering. Kids who weren't even there aren't taking it as hard as the kids who were in the cafeteria, like my friend [who was] watching [the shooters] reload. It's not helping. They're trying to treat everyone necessarily the same way . . . And it was just like so hard because they're making us talk about it and, I guess that was "good" for us but it was hard.

(Parent) I remember a fireman came in and said "we need to get somebody to talk to these kids" and they did call an advocate and she came and she was probably the least helpful person there that whole day. She was *not* very effective.

These responses underscore the importance of evaluating the efficacy of post-traumatic interventions. Without such evaluation, well-intentioned interventions may do more harm than good. Programs that may be helpful to individuals who have sought professional services after a trauma may not be appropriate as community or mandatory interventions. This is consistent with work examining "confrontative" strategies for grief, in which survivors are encouraged to think about their relationship with the loved one or how the death occurred; these often portend subsequent difficulties (Archer, 1999). Some therapies show empirical evidence of success (e.g., Foa & Rothbaum, 1997; Resick & Schnicke, 1992); thus, we advocate research on *which* interventions are helpful for those experiencing violence, and on *whom* these interventions are likely to help. As our respondents' reactions point out, not all interventions will be experienced as helpful by everyone.

Too much talking. The quote above suggests that the counseling activity was aversive to the student in part because it required talking when she did not want to talk. Several parents also expressed their frustration with being asked to talk too much. "Constant interviews [were annoying]. Having to retell the story on the phone, over and over and over, to people. Rediscussing it, and rediscussing it, and rediscussing it."

This frustration with talking too much about the incident is surprising, as much social support literature contends that trauma victims want to talk openly about an event during the first two weeks (Pennebaker & Harber, 1993), and that they often desire *more* contact and support than others are willing or able to lend (Herbert & Dunkel-Schetter, 1992; Janoff-Bulman, 1992). This complaint is especially notable, as only people who *volunteered* to speak with an interviewer were in our sample. As such, this feeling may have been more prominent among those who did not volunteer. Further, in general, our respondents said that talking with others was helpful.

There are several possible explanations for the difference between our findings and the well-documented findings of the coping literature. For one, our interviews were conducted very soon after the trauma. At this time, the incident was new and our respondents may not have talked to many friends and relatives about the events more than once. It is possible that our respondents experienced the more typical pattern of disinterest and avoidance from their support networks as time passed. In fact, research that has found dwindling or inadequate social support following severe crises has often been conducted a considerable time (several months) after the tragic event occurred (e.g., Bowler, Mergler, Huel, & Cone, 1994).

A second factor that may help explain the heightened interest of friends and family in this instance is the nature of this trauma. In contrast to other events, which may be devastating but relatively common, the Columbine attack was unprecedented. People are drawn to the unusual and unfamiliar and, thus, the phenomenal nature of violence like this may create a unique context in which supporters are more interested in hearing about the events in the immediate aftermath. Consequently, dramatic incidents of violence may have a unique effect on the type of support victims of these events receive from others.

Third, we believe that the contradiction can be reconciled by focusing on the victim's desires. The talking that was reported as aversive was initiated by others (i.e., friends, family, and counselors) who requested information and discussion. Voluntary talking was experienced as very helpful. This discrepancy suggests that it may be most helpful to present opportunities to talk, but not actually request or require discussion. Negotiating this line is likely to be difficult, and we encourage careful work examining this distinction.

Reactions to media involvement. The Columbine attack received worldwide media attention. One media representative stated, "The town was flooded with reporters, and students and their family members were inundated with flowers, fruit baskets, and good wishes on behalf of famous journalists seeking 'the get'" (Trigoboff, 2000). The media normally are not considered as components of a victim's social network; however, our respondents repeatedly talked about the media when asked about the social consequences of the events.

In the immediate aftermath of the shootings, respondents seemed to be helped by the media coverage. Several parents were notified of the situation by news programs. Students who quickly found their way to a television set after being abruptly escorted from the school learned of the complexity of the situation and of the methods advocated by police for reuniting with family members. Despite these preliminary advantages, however, students and parents experienced frustration with the inaccuracy (especially the exaggeration) of media reports:

> (Student) They hardly ever wore those trench coats. I mean, like they called themselves the trench coat mafia but they hardly ever wore them.

They made it to be like this huge deal in the media, which was just kind of retarded.

(Student) I was getting my hands on any piece of news I could, which became really disappointing because a lot of it was inaccurate. The local media did an awesome job, but I don't know . . . the national was pretty crappy. Reading it, reading how much of it was wrong, it was just kind of a letdown.

Irritation with media inaccuracy persisted three years later, as many reportedly considered media reports about their school to be "completely and utterly ridiculous" (Bartels, 2002, p. 8S).

As the hours after the incident progressed, respondents experienced many instances in which intense media involvement served as unhelpful and even hurtful social interaction. Several mentioned media intrusion being particularly unhelpful at the makeshift memorial park. As one parent expressed, it was particularly troublesome "not being able to go to the park and grieve without having a camera stuck in our faces." Others expressed irritation with being asked repeatedly to give interviews while they tried to pay their respects at the park.

(Student) The first guy who stopped me, he had a tape recorder and he was from a newspaper. He's like, "I have a casualty list do you want to see it?" and I'm like "yes" and I grabbed it from him and he's like, "I don't know if it's spelled right." And that's when I saw [a close friend of mine] was dead, which is someone I have in [class] who has been a really good friend of mine . . . Looking back on it, I got really mad because you know he showed me that just for a reaction. I didn't get halfway through the list; I was just bawling. [. . . We] just all hugged and the media was right there with their cameras just going away. They interviewed us and were just asking questions like "What were these kids like?" you know, and "How does this reflect on the school?" It was just really horrible. And so I talked to like all these media, and I got up to where I wanted to pay my respects to my friends and, um, there was a ring of 20 cameras and I had to walk through them to get to the flowers to lay them down and I didn't feel like I could stay there. I'm like "this doesn't really . . . you know . . . it's kind of something that you want to be like a private thing." So I laid them down and as soon as I did they're like, "Who are you laying those flowers down for?" You know, like one person starts talking to you and they've got a camera in your face and then five people put a camera in your face because they want it too and they don't have to ask the question. I mean it happened the whole way back and it was just totally awful.

Several complained about media following them to their homes. One parent said members of the media knocked on the door at all times of the day and night requesting interviews and that this lasted for nearly two weeks. "They'll get your name," said one student who reported receiving calls from a number of major media sources, "and it's all over."

In sum, media played an influential role in the events following the Columbine attack. The widespread attention given the events contributed to supportive gestures from the non-involved public. However, as is often the case with highly publicized traumas, support from outsiders was short-lived and resented by some (Norris et al., 2002; Trigoboff, 2000). Intrusive media involvement may exacerbate the trauma of victims of mass violence. Media influence on victims' should be studied in future investigations. The sensational nature of large-scale events is likely to generate a heavy media presence whenever they occur.

Impact on Relationships

We asked respondents whether events related to the shootings and their aftermath had an impact on any relationships, and all said the events had affected their relationships with family members, friends, and others. All students believed the events had strengthened their social ties. Students felt closer and more affectionate with their parents, they believed their relationships with their friends had grown stronger, and they reported finding a new respect for, and closeness with, others in the community. These reports of positive effects on relationships vary from descriptions of disturbances in relationships reported by adolescents who had directly experienced or witnessed interpersonal violence and who showed strong signs of PTSD (Layne, Pynoos, & Cardenas, 2001). Whether it is the mass nature of the Columbine attack, the selection of a community vs. clinical sample, or both, the factors that contribute to potential varying effects on relationships cannot be disentangled. Clearly, further work on mass violence specifically, and non-clinical samples generally, is warranted to avoid possible inappropriate generalizations.

Among the parents, the impact on relationships was less uniform. Whereas three said the incident had brought their families closer together, four felt differently. Several suggested that the events had, at least temporarily, made relationships feel more strained or distant. Some felt less patient and more irritated with loved ones, while others felt less secure and more distant from them. In terms of relationships with friends, similar differences emerged. Two felt closer with friends, three felt less close, and two were closer with some friends but more distant with others. These latter two believed that the experience had served to weed out "real" friends from more superficial ones. All parents reported feeling increased closeness with others in the community.

CONCLUSIONS AND IMPLICATIONS

A key finding from this study is that there exists important variation in responses during the earliest period after a traumatic event. Models of reactions and strategies of intervention that do not consider such individual variation will fall short. In particular, emotional reactions were quite variable during the first two weeks after this trauma. Although numbness was common early, there was soon variation within and between individuals. Perhaps most striking, negative emotions were not uniformly more prominent than positive ones; indeed the most intense emotion reported was affection. The importance of making sense of the event varied notably between individuals, and the desire and ability to do this was not uniform. The importance individuals place on finding meaning in a traumatic life event may moderate the implications of not finding meaning (Downy, Silver, & Wortman, 1990). Future research should examine this possibility more closely.

Regarding social support, respondents noted that talking and being with friends and family was most often helpful. However, we noted an important limitation to this: Being asked or forced to talk was perceived by several as harmful. Consistent with the within-person variability in emotions, the social needs of the respondents varied over time. At times, they desired interaction with others, and at other times, they found interactions were annoying. It is important to consider this variability in the context of normal coping responses, especially when assessing the merits of psychological interventions to people coping with mass trauma.

Coping with school and workplace violence. One theme that emerged from our interviews was the difficulty the students were having returning to the scene of the attack. Responses to school and workplace violence may differ in important ways from those that occur at chance locations. Individuals who are victimized by school and workplace violence are often initially prevented from returning, and then are forced to return, or make a significant change in their lives. In the case of the Columbine attack, many students chose to finish high school at a different school because "theirs was too burned, too bloody, too spooky" (Bartels, 2002; p. 2S). The institution had to make changes, also. Balloons are banned, and the cafeteria no longer serves the meals that were on the menu on the day of the attack (Bartels, 2002; Yettick, 2002). Our respondents reported being conflicted about returning in the immediate aftermath of the attack. Indeed, half the employees working at Columbine during the attack (and all administrators but the principal) have left, resulting in an unusually high level of turnover for the district (Curtin & Aguilera, 2002; Yettick, 2002). Future research should examine the impact of school and workplace violence on functioning within the institution, as well as the effects on, and of, post-attack attrition. Although high rates of turnover may be common after such an event, the impact on long-term functioning may be *less* than expected in some cases. For example, although a psychologist predicted in May, 1999 that Columbine High School would subsequently become dysfunctional for the students, this has not been the case according to various educational measures since then (Weintraub et al., 2001; Yettick, 2002).

Future Research

Our analysis highlights several issues in responding to mass violence and examines similarities and differences in the experiences among students and their parents. Overall, we stress the importance of considering the emotional, cognitive, and social impact of this type of event on adolescents and their caregivers. We do not intend these data to provide firm conclusions about the psychological effects of coping with mass violence (the sample is small, and almost exclusively female), nor do we wish to evaluate the experiences or coping efforts of the individuals we interviewed. Instead, this investigation informs the ongoing pursuit to better understand the psychological aftermath of mass violence. We suggest several areas for future research.

Responses across time. In some instances (e.g., desire to talk), our respondents' comments contradicted findings from studies using data collected more than two weeks post event. Our findings underscore the importance of collecting information very early after events occur. We believe that "time since event" is a crucial consideration in examining responses (Pennebaker & Harber, 1993).

Due to the early termination of data collection, we were unable to address the influence of the interval of time since the event on the reactions of interest. Coping is a process, and rates and interrelationships of responses are likely to change over time (Benight et al., 2000; Holman & Silver, 1998; Silver et al., 2002). In combination with the necessity of longitudinal studies to address the plausibility of certain causal claims (e.g., whether coping responses matter, see Silver et al., 2002), we advocate studies that begin immediately after the occurrences of violence, and continue at regular intervals for substantial amounts of time thereafter.

New topics. Qualitative studies uncover issues of importance to those who experience trauma. Two such topics emerged here. First, individuals who were able to find meaning in this event often appeared to do so by empathizing with the perpetrators. As Norris et al. (2002) point out, coping with human-caused events involves different psychological processes than coping with natural disasters. Here, we have uncovered one way the process may differ. Future work should examine the prevalence, predictors, and outcomes of empathizing with perpetrators.

Finally, the social and psychological effects of the media deserve careful consideration. Although the media provided help early in the process to those most directly involved in the trauma, the media quickly became a significant problem. In the wake of the attack, the massive onslaught of media intrusion received a fair amount of attention by the media itself; however, the psychological effects of media intrusion after a crisis remain generally unknown and unstudied. It is important for researchers and mental health professionals to recognize the magnitude of impact that the media can have on victims and to explore further the consequences of heavy media involvement in the aftermath of sensational trauma.

REFERENCES

Adams, L., & Russakoff, D. (1999, June 12). Dissecting Columbine's cult of the athlete. *Washington Post*. Retrieved September 5, 2002, from http://www.washington post.com/wp-srv/national/daily/june99/columbine12.htm.

Archer, J. (1999). *The nature of grief: The evolution and psychology of reactions to loss*. London: Routledge.

Bartels, L. (2002, April 13). Columbine 2002: The Last Class. *Rocky Mountain News, S*.

Belle, D. (1991). Gender differences in the social moderators of stress. In A. Monat, & R. S. Lazarus (Eds.), *Stress and coping: An anthology* (3rd ed.), pp. 258-274. NY: Columbia University Press.

Benight, C. C., Freyaldenhove, R. W., Hughes, J., Ruiz, J. M., Zoschke, T. A., & Lovallo, W. R. (2000). Coping self-efficacy and psychological distress following the Oklahoma City bombing. *Journal of Applied Social Psychology, 30*, 1331-1344.

Bowler, R. M., Mergler, D., Huel, G., & Cone, J. E. (1994). Psychological, psychosocial, and psychophysiological sequelae in a community affected by a railroad chemical disaster. *Journal of Traumatic Stress, 7*, 601-624.

Buka, S. L., Stichick, T. L., Birdthistle, I., & Earls, F. J. (2001). Youth exposure to violence: Prevalence, risks, and consequences. *American Journal of Orthopsychiatry, 71*, 298-310.

Cohler, B. M., & Lieberman, M. A. (1980). Social relations and mental health: Middle-aged and older men and women from three European ethnic groups. *Research on Aging, 2*, 445-469.

Compas, B. E., Connor-Smith, J. K., Saltzman, H., Thomsen, A. H., & Wadsworth, M. E. (2001). Coping with stress during childhood and adolescence: Problems, progress, and potential in theory and research. *Psychological Bulletin, 127*, 87-127.

Coyne, J. C., Wortman, C. B., & Lehman, D. R. (1988). The other side of support: Emotional overinvolvement and miscarried helping. In B. B. Gottlieb (Ed.), *Marshaling social support: Formats, processes, and effects* (pp. 305-330). Newbury Park, CA: Sage.

Curtin, D., & Aguilera, E. (August 18, 2002). Fleeing the pain. *Denver Post*, A-01.

Downey, G., Silver, R. C., & Wortman, C. B. (1990). Reconsidering the attribution-adjustment relation following a major negative event: Coping with the loss of a child. *Journal of Personality & Social Psychology, 59*, 925-940.

Foa, E. B., & Rothbaum, B. O. (1997). *Treating the trauma of rape*. NY: Guilford.

Herbert, T. B., & Dunkel-Schetter, C. (1992). Negative social reaction to victims: An overview of responses and their determinants. In L. Montada, S. H. Filip, & M. J. Lerner (Eds.), *Life crises and experiences of loss in adulthood* (pp. 497-518). Hillsdale, NJ: Erlbaum.

Holman, E. A., & Silver, R. C. (1996). Is it the abuse or the aftermath: A stress and coping approach to understanding long-term responses to incest. *Journal of Social & Clinical Psychology, 15*, 318-339.

Holman, E. A., & Silver, R. C. (1998). Getting "stuck" in the past: Temporal orientation and coping with trauma. *Journal of Personality & Social Psychology, 74*, 1146-1163.

Holman, E. A., & Zimbardo, P. (2003). *The social language of time: Trauma, time perspective, and social relationships*. Manuscript under revision.

Howard, D. E., Feigelman, S., Li, X., Cross, S., & Rachuba, L. (2002). The relationship among violence victimization, witnessing violence, and youth distress. *Journal of Adolescent Health, 31*, 455-462.

Janoff-Bulman, R. (1992). *Shattered assumptions: Towards a new psychology of trauma*. NY: Free Press.

Kaniasty, K., & Norris, F. H. (1995). Mobilization and deterioration of social support following natural disasters. *Current Directions in Psychological Science, 4*, 94-98.

Layne, C. M., Pynoos, R. S., & Cardenas, J. (2001). Wounded adolescence: School-based group psychotherapy for adolescents who sustained or witnessed violent injury. In M. Shaifii, & S. L. Shafii (Eds.), *School violence: Assessment, management, prevention*. Washington DC: American Psychiatric Association.

Lepore, S. J., Silver, R. C., Wortman, C. B., & Wayment, H. A. (1996). Social constraints, intrusive thoughts and depressive symptoms among bereaved mothers. *Journal of Personality and Social Psychology, 70*, 271-282.

McIntosh, D. N. (1995). Religion as schema, with implications for the relation between religion and coping. *The International Journal for the Psychology of Religion, 5*, 1-16.

McIntosh, D. N., Silver, R. C., & Wortman, C. B. (1993). Religion's role in adjustment to a negative life event: Coping with the loss of a child. *Journal of Personality & Social Psychology, 65*, 812-821.

Norris, F. H., Friedman, M. J., Watson, P. J., Byrne, C. M., Diaz, E., & Kaniasty, K. (2002). 60,000 disaster victims speak: Part I. An empirical review of the empirical literature, 1981-2001. *Psychiatry, 65*, 207-239.

Pennebaker, J. W. (1989). Confession, inhibition, and disease. In L. Berkowitz (Ed.), *Advances in experimental social psychology* (Vol. 22, pp. 211-244). San Diego, CA: Academic Press.

Pennebaker, J. W., & Harber, K. D. (1993). A social stage model of collective coping: The Loma Prieta earthquake and the Persian Gulf War. *Journal of Social Issues, 49*, 125-145.

Pritchard, M. E., & McIntosh, D. N. (2003). What predicts adjustment among law students? A longitudinal panel study. *Journal of Social Psychology, 143*(6), 727-745.

Resick, P. A., & Schnicke, M. K. (1992). Cognitive processing therapy for sexual assault victims. *Journal of Consulting & Clinical Psychology, 60*, 748-756.

Sealey, G. (2001, November 5). Fragile psyches: Mental health counselors gear up for potential crisis in New York. *ABCNews.com.* Retrieved September 6, 2002, from http://abcnews.go.com/sections/us/DailyNews/STRIKE_nypsyche011005. html.

Shalev, A. Y., Peri, T., Canetti, L., & Schreiber, S. (1996). Predictors of PTSD in injured trauma survivors: A prospective study. *American Journal of Psychiatry, 153*, 219-225.

Silver, R. L. (1982). *Coping with an undesirable life event: A study of early reactions to physical disability.* Unpublished doctoral dissertation, Northwestern University, Evanston, IL.

Silver, R. C., Holman, E. A., McIntosh, D. N., Poulin, M., & Gil-Rivas, V. (2002). Nationwide longitudinal study of psychological responses to September 11th. *Journal of the American Medical Association, 288*, 1235-1244.

Silver, R. L., & Wortman, C. B. (1980). Coping with undesirable life events. In J. Garber & M. E. P. Seligman (Eds.), *Human helplessness: Theory and applications* (pp. 279-340). NY: Academic Press.

Silver, R. C., Wortman, C. B., & Crofton, C. (1990). The role of coping in support provision: The self-presentational dilemma of victims of life crises. In B. R. Sarason, I. G. Sarason, & G. R. Pierce (Eds.), *Social support: An interactional view* (pp. 397-426). NY: Wiley.

Tait, R., & Silver, R. C. (1989). Coming to terms with major negative life events. In J. S. Uleman, & J. A. Bargh (Eds.), *Unintended thought* (pp. 351-382). NY: The Guilford Press.

Tedeschi, R. G., & Calhoun, L. G. (1995). *Trauma and transformation: Growing in the aftermath of suffering.* Thousand Oaks, CA; Sage.

Trigoboff, D. (2000). Lessons of Columbine: Newspeople, recalling the horrors of Littleton, are learning to put saving lives first. *Broadcasting & Cable, 130*, 26-31.

van der Kolk, B. A. (1996). The complexity of adaptation to trauma: Self-regulation, stimulus discrimination, and characterological development. In B. A. van der Kolk, A. C. McFarlane, & L. Weisaeth (Eds.), *Traumatic stress: The effects of overwhelming experience on mind, body, and society* (pp.182-213). NY: Bruner/Mazel.

Von Fremd, M. (2002, July 3). Doubts on Death Row: Was Texas Death Row mom wrongly convicted? *Good Morning America.* Retrieved 8/2/2002, from http://abcnews.go.com/sections/GMA/GoodMorningAmerica/GMA020703Texas_death row_mom. html.

Weintraub, P., Hall, H. L., Pynoos, R. S. (2001). Columbine High School shootings: Community response. In M. Shaifii, & S. L. Shafii (Eds.), *School violence: Assessment, management, prevention.* Washington DC: American Psychiatric Association.

Wortman, C. B., & Silver, R. C. (1987). Coping with irrevocable loss. In G. R. VandenBos, & B. K. Bryant (Eds.), *Cataclysms, crises, and catastrophes: Psychology in action* (Master Lecture Series, Vol. 6) (pp. 189-235). Washington, DC: American Psychological Association.

Wortman, C. B., & Silver, R. C. (1989). The myths of coping with loss. *Journal of Consulting & Clinical Psychology, 57,* 349-357.

Wortman, C. B., & Silver, R. C. (2001). The myths of coping with loss revisited. In M. S. Stroebe, R. O. Hansson, W. Stroebe, & H. Schut (Eds.), *Handbook of bereavement research: Consequences, coping, and care* (pp. 405-429). Washington DC: American Psychological Association.

Yettick, H. (April 20, 2002). Columbine: Three years later: Echoes of a tragedy. *Rocky Mountain News,* 1B, 3B.

School-Wide Bullying Prevention Program for Elementary Students

Elizabeth A. Rock
Marsha Hammond
Sandra Rasmussen

SUMMARY. Bullying is a serious problem affecting students nationwide with up to 15% reporting regular bullying. This article discusses the characteristics of bullies and the impact of bullying on victims. "No Bullying Allowed Here" is a school-wide program for elementary schools. Lesson plans cover characteristics of bullies and victims, responding techniques, problem solving, perspective taking, and empathy. Students completed surveys prior to instruction and at the end of the year. Chi-square analysis shows significant changes in the reported frequency of bullying and associated behaviors. Changes in frequencies across all categories are distributed in a manner that is significantly different from what would be expected in the population. Students reported far less bullying and fear about being bullied after instruction in prevention techniques. *[Article copies available for a fee from The Haworth Document Delivery Service: 1-800-HAWORTH. E-mail address: <docdelivery @haworthpress.com> Website: <http://www.HaworthPress.com> © 2004 by The Haworth Press, Inc. All rights reserved.]*

Address correspondence to: Elizabeth A. Rock, PhD, Park County School District #1, 160 North Evarts, Powell, WY 82435 (E-mail: earock@park1.k12.wy.us).

[Haworth co-indexing entry note]: "School-Wide Bullying Prevention Program for Elementary Students." Rock, Elizabeth A., Marsha Hammond, and Sandra Rasmussen. Co-published simultaneously in *Journal of Emotional Abuse* (The Haworth Maltreatment & Trauma Press, an imprint of The Haworth Press, Inc.) Vol. 4, No. 3/4, 2004, pp. 223-237; and: *Aggression in Organizations: Violence, Abuse, and Harassment at Work and in Schools* (ed: Robert Geffner et al.) The Haworth Maltreatment & Trauma Press, an imprint of The Haworth Press, Inc., 2004, pp. 223-237. Single or multiple copies of this article are available for a fee from The Haworth Document Delivery Service [1-800-HAWORTH, 9:00 a.m. - 5:00 p.m. (EST). E-mail address: docdelivery@haworthpress.com].

Digital Object Identifier: 10.1300/J135v04n03_13

KEYWORDS. Bullying, perspective taking, empathy, victims, violence prevention, elementary students

Victimization or bullying by peers has been identified as an area of major concern for school students (Kochenderfer & Ladd, 1996). Approximately 30% of children are involved with bullying as victims, aggressors, or at times taking both roles (National Resource Center for Safe Schools, 2001). Estimates of the number of students regularly being victimized in some way by peers are as high as 15% (Egan & Perry, 1998; Olweus, 1993; Skiba & Fontanini, 2000). Bullies systematically harass certain groups or individuals using physical or psychological aggression with the intention of causing harm (Hoover & Oliver, 1996; Olweus, 1993). Adults often fail to identify bullying because they are unfamiliar with most of the dynamics involved (Skiba & Fontanini, 2000). Conflicts between students are seen as a normal part of growing up.

Bullies use a variety of negative actions, such as physical attacks or threats, verbal abuse such as teasing and humiliation, and forms of social isolation known as relational aggression (Crick & Bigbee, 1998; Hoover & Oliver, 1996; Olweus, 1993). While some bullies may be rejected or avoided by peers because of their aggressive behaviors, many are popular and become leaders within a portion of their peer group (Coie & Dodge, 1998). This may be related to their ability to offer protection or to provide a sense of status and affiliation to less confident peers (Charlesworth, 1996). They are proactive and thus gain dominance in many situations. Their self-confidence is strong and gained through the use of their power and ability to dominate others (Staub, 1999). They enjoy hurting others and obtaining control over them with their aggressive actions.

Victims of bullies suffer not only the immediate harm of hurt feelings, embarrassment, and physical injury, but also are more likely to suffer from anxiety, depression, have lowered academic scores due to concentration problems, and may avoid school altogether (Hodges, Malone, & Perry, 1997; O'Connell, Pepler, & Craig, 1999; Olweus, 1993). Victimization also has an impact on social development for children (Colvin, Tobin, Beard, Hagan, & Sprague, 1998; Hodges & Perry, 1999). Victims of bullying often lack the interpersonal skills needed to develop friendships that protect them against victimization (Kochenderfer & Ladd, 1996). Children who are victimized may limit their friends to others who experience similar problems or engage in inappropriate behaviors that invite bullying or victimization (Finnegan, Hodges, & Perry, 1996; Olweus, 1992). Victims are seen by some peers as the cause of their own problems and therefore are not given the support by their non-aggressive peers that other children might receive (Hodges, Boivin, Vitaro, & Bukowski, 1999; Huesmann & Guerra, 1997).

Some victimized children have been shown to engage in a type of aggressive behavior that places them at even greater risk for further attack by peers (Olweus, 1991; Perry, Perry, & Kennedy, 1992). This aggressive behavior is meant as retaliation for victimization, but a lack of planning and self-regulation of emotions makes the children ineffective in their aggression (Schwartz, Proctor, & Chien, 2001). These children engage in behaviors that actually provoke the bully. These include disrupting activities, being argumentative, and attempting to bait the bully with aggressive actions such as verbal taunts (Olweus, 1993; Perry, Perry, & Kennedy, 1992). This type of victim can also be highly emotional and quick to become angry (Schwartz, Dodge, Petit, & Bates, 1997). These children are called provocative victims (Olweus, 1993). Adults and peers can easily mistake this behavior for actual bullying.

DEFICITS IN EMOTIONAL COMPETENCE

A lack of emotional competence places children at risk and makes them attractive targets for bullies (Olweus, 1993). These children do not have the skills necessary to decide on a behavior that is efficacious in a bullying situation (Saarni, 1999). These skills include the ability to know one's own feelings, to be able to label them, to rely on them to guide behavior, and to be able to control emotional responses in a manner that helps achieve a goal (Park & Park, 1997). It is also critical to be able to recognize feelings in others and to use that information to accurately interpret actions and predict behaviors (Park & Park, 1997; Saarni, 1999). Children who cannot do this become likely victims of bullies because they engage in behaviors that are rewarding in some way for the bully (Hodges et al., 1997). Specifically, they cry easily, may appear fearful, have few friends, and can be made to submit quickly (Schwartz, Dodge, & Coie, 1993).

Lack of ability to self-regulate emotional responses is also seen as lack of emotional competence. Adults see children who have limited self-regulation of their emotions as unable to engage in prosocial behaviors (Eisenberg, Fabes, Murphy, Jones, & Guthrie, 1998; Zahn-Waxler, Radke-Yarrow, Wagner, & Chapman, 1992). This can lead to the assumption that antisocial behaviors manifested by a child represent pathology and results in efforts to force the child to conform to a predetermined manner of response (Chess & Thomas, 1999). This undermines the child's own ability to interact with and gain mastery over the environment. Additionally a child's inappropriate behaviors may be labeled as bullying when these behaviors actually represent a lack of specific skills for responding to social situations.

RESPONSE TO SOCIAL SITUATIONS

Complex cognitive activity shapes the response to social interactions with peers (Bengtsson & Johnson, 1992). The behavioral response is based on a series of steps in cognitive processing (Dodge, Pettit, McClaskey, & Brown, 1986). Children (a) interpret cues, (b) determine what their options are for behavior, and (c) then make a choice about the action to be taken. A child who is socially rejected by peers tends to attribute hostile intent to the actions of others (Dodge & Frame, 1982; Dodge & Somberg, 1987). This child's choice of actions may be aggressive rather than productive (Saarni, 1999). Failure of an action to resolve a situation increases the tendency of the child to attribute negative intent to the actions of others (Dorsch & Keane, 1994). Thus inappropriate behaviors that the child has learned continue to place him or her in situations that elicit negative or hostile actions from peers.

The cognitive process children use to respond to a variety of social situations is a factor that impacts the behavior of victims of bullying and bystanders observing it (Cowie & Sharp, 1994). For this reason, direct intervention in the form of some type of cognitive skills training would be desirable in the school setting. There are a variety of bullying prevention programs available, such as "Expect Respect" (Safe Place, 2001), "Bully Busters" (Guzman, 2001), and "Olweus Bullying Prevention" (Olweus, 1991). The available programs focus on middle school and high school populations and include information on how to handle sexual harassment, physical aggression, and anger management. There are also recommendations for group discussions for students in need of assistance. A strong component, directed at the cognitive processes of elementary students that are still forming, is not included.

ASPECTS OF A COMPREHENSIVE INTERVENTION

A program to prevent bullying behavior in an elementary school setting needs several critical components to be effective. First, comprehensive intervention needs to be done at the school-wide level (Atlas & Pepler, 1998; Skiba & Fontanini, 2000). It is critical that the school adopts policies against bullying and makes it clear that bullying will not be tolerated. Consequences need to be clearly defined and consistently applied. If the administration and staff of the school encourage intervention against bullying, then more bystander students are likely to feel empowered to take action on behalf of fellow students (Smith & Sharp, 1994).

A second component is staff training. A lack of knowledge and understanding about bullying prevents adults from detecting bullying, recognizing victims, and taking action when they see it happening (U.S. Department of Education, 1998). It is important for adults to become familiar with what constitutes bullying behavior, the characteristics of bullies and victims, and the techniques the children will be instructed to use with bullies. Adults will function much like a coach to students who do need to seek assistance. Adequate training for staff and their visibility and support of the no-bullying policy will help to mobilize the large group of students who are neither victims nor bullies. Their support and intervention is an important aspect of a successful program (Banks, 2000).

Elementary-age children typically prefer to handle conflict situations without adult intervention (Newman, Murray, & Lussier, 2001). Well-adjusted and socially skilled children do this because they perceive seeking intervention as inappropriate avoidance. Children who perceive themselves as unpopular seek help possibly because they lack confidence about what to do in situations. Most children in response to a conflict situation want to reestablish control or in some manner correct an injustice and for this reason seek adult assistance.

Even socially skilled children, however, do not always know the most effective response to bullying behavior. Current decisions about a behavior response are based on past experience with the effectiveness of a response (Huesmann, 1998). Children working independently to resolve conflict tend to be aggressive or passive (Newman et al., 2001). These response styles lack effectiveness in dealing with bullying behavior to self or others. Aggression results in further aggression since it is provocative for the bully, and passiveness can make the children seem like an easy target for the bully (Olweus, 1991). Children may also experience conflict within themselves regarding what appropriate behavior should be. When unsure, many children may elect non-intervention as the perceived safe action (Cowie & Sharp, 1994). This can actually have the effect of making the child feel somewhat like a victim without any power to prevent what is happening or knowledge of how to correct it.

A third component of an effective program is specific instruction in concepts, skills, and rehearsal that supports development of a school belief system that bullying is not acceptable and that support of each other is critical and important to overall school climate. Children's beliefs about aggressive types of behaviors are in flux in the early years of school and do not take on any stability until about the fourth grade (Huesmann & Guerra, 1997). At the beginning of any encounter with peers that has potential hostility or conflict, children with a tendency to believe aggression is acceptable will attribute more hostile intent to the actions of others. The higher the level of arousal, as in children with poor self-regulation of their emotions, the greater is the likelihood of negative bias on the part of the child (Dodge & Somberg, 1987). Thus the child pulls up behavioral scripts for aggressive behaviors. Instead of continuing to rely on old scripts, children can learn new techniques for responding to bully behavior and for interpreting the behavior of others.

Essential to the development of new scripts is the skill of problem solving. Children learn to evaluate their existing scripts against a new model or manner of behaving. Use of this approach as part of a total school program has been especially effective with elementary students (Howard, Flora, & Griffin, 1999). Children are taught to identify the key issues of a problem situation and then to review all of the available alternatives for response. These alternatives are taught as part of the bullying prevention program. This skill of problem solving is taught using a group activity that allows for interchange of ideas. Students then have the opportunity to share solutions with the class group and receive further feedback on the process they are using.

Existing bullying prevention programs contain many of these critical elements, but each had limitations when the structure of the program was applied to the elementary school setting. Instruction in specific strategies, and the cognitive skills needed to problem solve and select appropriate strategies was not included in the programs. Most programs recommended school-wide policies for addressing the problem of bullying based on recommendations from research done by Olweus (1993). Staff training was included, as was the recommendation to develop clear policies regarding non-tolerance of bullying behaviors. Although some of the programs stated that they were acceptable for use at all grade levels, the lack of specific instruction or cognitive training was seen as a deficit for use with elementary students. Elementary-age children's thinking and cognitive skills are still in formation and thus subject to change depending upon the response that a child receives from others. Specific instruction on how to respond as well as the opportunity to practice new skills were not part of the programs reviewed. Other programs were clearly aimed at older students, high school or middle school, and addressed as a major issue how to deal with sexual harassment.

THE PREVENTION PROGRAM: "NO BULLYING ALLOWED HERE"

The school site where this program was developed began to identify a need to make adjustments in the school discipline program to address the issue of bullying. It is a program specifically developed for use in grades 3-5. Classroom teacher participation in the instruction and follow-up actions as well as support from the school site administrator are critical. The students served by this program are 98% Anglo with the remainder having Hispanic surnames. None of these students were identified as limited English speaking. The population in the community is primarily middle class. Parents work in a variety of occupations including farming, ranching, construction and related trades, and professional roles.

Program Goals

The goals for this program addressed students, staff, and parents. Development of goals in this manner fit with the already existing school philosophy of working as a team to meet the needs of all those involved. The goals of the program are listed in Table 1.

Program Content

This program is designed for use in grades three through five. The lessons present the basic concepts of bullying and strategies for responding to it through the use of lecture, demonstration, role-playing, cooperative groups, and discussion. A critical aspect of this program is helping students learn to speak and listen to each other. Through this experience, the students begin to develop empathy for their peers and recognize their responsibility as a member of the school community to assist and support classmates in dealing with bully behavior.

The instructional component for students includes: (a) perspective taking, (b) communication skills to assist in better expressing their feelings, (c) problem solving, and (d) conflict resolution. These skills are taught through a variety of activities that vary with the grade level. Older students participate in role-playing, cooperative learning groups, and group discussions addressing actual events from their school day experience. Other activities include making posters to "advertise" the no bullying ideas, group games using problem solving skills, and discussion groups. All students work together to develop class rules regarding bullying. These rules help the students identify the need to include everyone in their activities as a major tool to prevent bullying, as well as general statements that bullying will not be tolerated.

Also included in this program is an emphasis on working together as a community to help each other. Students are encouraged to listen to their peers and aide those they see being victimized. Teachers will be encouraged to listen to students with a new perspective that recognizes that apparent antisocial behavior may be learned responses on the part of a child with good intentions. They may also consider that some children need changes in the environment

TABLE 1. Goals of the "No Bullying Allowed Here" Program

Goals for Students

   1. Students will learn that bullying includes all behaviors that are hurtful to others such as teasing, name calling, interfering with work, and exclusion from games.

   2. Students will learn what to do when confronted by a bully.

   3. Students will learn what they can do when they see someone else being bullied.

   4. Student will develop a sense of the class and school as a community that respects the rights, feelings, and uniqueness of each person.

Goals for Staff

   1. Staff will learn what bullying is and to recognize when it is happening at school both in the classroom as well as other areas.

   2. Staff will learn to support students in their efforts to stop bullying through coaching, supervision, and discussion with them about how to apply the skills learned.

   3. Staff will learn to respond and intervene appropriately to student complaints about bullying behaviors.

Goals for Parents

   1. Parents will learn the techniques that are being taught to their children at school for responding to bullying behavior toward themselves and others.

   2. Parents will learn how to help their child apply the skills being learned.

---

and expectations for their behavior in order function at their best and learn new patterns of behavior.

Parents are provided with support materials for use at home as needed. They are kept informed of the progress of the program through the school newsletter. Parents are encouraged to talk with their children about bullying issues and to report incidents to the school administration. They can also ask for assistance for themselves or their child in dealing with specific issues that arise.

The lesson plans are presented with a statement of objectives, a sequence of activities for each lesson, and the basic materials needed in the form of student handouts. An example presented in Table 2 is a session on techniques they can use to respond to bullying behavior either directed at themselves or at other students.

These lessons are not scripted. They are designed to allow flexibility in the actual discussions of the students to foster greater growth through their communication and interaction with each other. The sequence in which the skills are taught can be altered if needed. Extra lessons may also be included to address areas of need identified as the program progresses. There are no written tests to assess student progress. Rather, assessment is accomplished through

TABLE 2. Sample Lesson

Objective:

Students will learn appropriate responses to bullying behavior that they can use for self-protection and to stop the bully. They will learn how to communicate their feelings assertively.

Materials:

Dealing with Bullies Handout
Assertive Communication Handout
Situation Cards for Assertiveness

Activities:

1. Review what bully behavior is: Actions, Words, Looks.
2. Briefly review the five defenses. Remind students of some examples discussed in session 2 as appropriate.
3. Begin discussion of assertiveness. Present the communication format for how to express their feelings. Elicit a definition of what assertiveness is and what it means versus aggression from the students. Give examples and encourage students to provide examples.

"I feel . . . when you . . . because . . . and I want you to . . ."

Use cue cards as you demonstrate this method of communication. These can be made by simply writing the cues on tag or poster board in large letters.

Have students draw situations from an envelope or box and give an assertive response following the cue cards. If necessary, the adult plays the roles to demonstrate. It is important for the student responding assertively to hear some very specific bully comments to make the experience more realistic. Solicit feedback and discussion from the class as this activity proceeds.

---

looking at the daily behavior of students, monitoring discipline referrals, and by listening to the students themselves.

The lessons require a minimum of eight weeks to present in sessions that are 40-45 minutes in duration. Shorter lesson times do not allow for adequate discussion by students. However, it is not inappropriate to lengthen the discussion period if time permits. The first series of lessons can be used when the program is being introduced to a school. The second series of lessons is designed for use as a review either later in the school year or the following year for those classes that have already covered the first series. Lessons are presented weekly on a set schedule so that students can look forward to the time for discussing their concerns and asking questions. While these lessons are not intended to be a counseling group, they do have the quality of a support group for many students. As the lessons progress it may be appropriate to offer actual small group or individual counseling sessions to some of the students. Some students in fact may ask for time to discuss individual problems they are having, and every effort should be made to respond to that need.

A critical component of this program is the time spent with staff. Unless all the staff are familiar with what is being taught and have the knowledge to respond in a supportive manner, this program will not be effective. Typically schools respond to aggressive behavior of students by calling forth other students as witnesses to the behavior. At this school, one of the main concerns expressed by everyone was that students who witnessed some behaviors were reluctant to come forth because of fear of reprisals by the bully. To address that, the school took the position that all reports of bully behavior from students would get a response. That response would be to help the victim utilize skills taught. It would also include intervention with the bully, which could be punishment, parent conferencing, and possibly counseling for that child. What this teaches the children is that what they have to say is important. They also learn that reporting behavior just to get someone in trouble is not appropriate.

METHOD

Participants, Materials, and Procedures

The lessons for bully prevention began with the third grade and progressed through the fifth grade on a staggered schedule with overlapping instruction. At the beginning of instruction at each class level the students were asked to complete a survey. The same survey was administered at the end of the school year. Questions were asked regarding the frequency and type of bully behavior they experienced or engaged in with peers. Sample questions include, "I worry that other kids will bully or bother me on the bus," "Other kids call me names," and "I see other kids being called names, teased, or hurt by what someone says."

Surveys were administered to 106 students in grades third through fifth. The entire group received the survey twice, before lessons began at the beginning of the school year and at the end of the school year. Surveys were tallied by grade level as well as totals for all students.

RESULTS

Results of the survey were evaluated using the chi-square technique. Changes in the reported frequency of the occurrence of bullying behaviors at all grade levels were significant, $X^2 (3, N = 106) = 7.81$, p < .05. The X^2 obt values were 31.27 for fifth grade, 10.39 for fourth grade, 27.73 for third grade, and 123.76 for all students. The results of the tallies and the chi-square evaluation are shown in Table 3. The X^2 obt results were significant and indicate that across all the categories, the frequencies are distributed in a manner that is significantly different from what would be expected in the population. Students were reporting far less bullying and fear or concern about being bullied after receiving instruction in prevention techniques.

Specific questions on the survey revealed a decrease in all bullying behaviors over the course of a year. There was a significant decrease in the number of students who reported feeling scared or nervous about going to school. Bullying in all settings at school decreased. These settings include the bus ride or walk to school, classroom, cafeteria, and playground. Physical aggression overall dropped. Verbal aggression also showed decline but continues to be an area of concern for students and staff.

The students were also asked whom at school they turned to for help in dealing with bullying. The majority who had indicated they were bullied stated they told no one and received help from no one. Those who sought help did so from parents or siblings. At the end of the year, the number of students who reported bullying and asked for assistance at school increased. As part of the program, students are encouraged to share with an adult either at home or at school their problems with bullies so that they can receive assistance in using the techniques they are taught in the program.

TABLE 3. Frequency of Bullying Pre- and Post-Instruction

Reported Incidents of Bullying	Never	Sometimes	2 Days Weekly	Most Days
Per-Instruction in Program				
Fifth Grade	4	12	15	6
Fourth Grade	13	13	2	7
Third Grade	10	9	7	8
All Students	27	34	24	21
Post-Instruction in Program				
Fifth Grade	29	7	0	1
Fourth Grade	21	11	2	1
Third Grade	24	10	0	0
All Students	75	28	2	2
χ^2 obt Values				
Fifth Grade	31.27			
Fourth Grade	10.39			
Third Grade	27.73			
All Students	123.76			

$\varsigma^2(3, N = 106) = 7.81, p < .05$

Qualitative Data

After completion of the initial series of lessons, six students in grades 3 and 4 were informally interviewed to elicit their view of the impact of the bully prevention lessons. All of the students stated that bullying had decreased in their classes. They related the decrease to two main factors. They said that teachers were now watching the bullies more carefully so they did not get away with the behavior as often. They also said that other kids were inviting them to play more often or letting them play if they asked to be included in a game. These are both specific skills taught as part of the bully prevention classes.

Two of the students who had previously been involved in bullying behaviors with peers have not been referred for aggressive behaviors since the lessons started. They both talked about playing with other peers. One of them stated that he had "found some other guys to play with who liked me because I don't get into so much trouble any more."

DISCUSSION

The initial series of lessons in the bullying prevention program showed a significant effect on the incidence of bullying behavior at this school site. Comments from staff and some parents were positive and encouraging. The lessons now are moving into the second phase. Students in the same three grades will receive a second set of lessons that will build on the initial concepts and techniques learned. Based on recommendations from the school site staff a series of lessons is also being planned for first and second grade students.

As the program progresses, further information will be gathered from the students about their experiences with peers as it relates to bullying and their emotional reactions to it. This preliminary feedback from the children involved as victims and aggressors provides information that makes it clear that these kids are sensitive to the reactions of adults, relieved to see adults becoming more alert to the problem, and also seem to be learning how to relate in a different manner to some of their peers.

It is important to recognize that children are capable of engaging in appropriate behaviors in response to bullying. These abilities need to be expanded and reinforced so that these children will be better able to develop their interpersonal skills. This bullying prevention program is one example of a potentially powerful tool to use with children.

REFERENCES

Atlas, R. S., & Pepler, D. J. (1998). Observations of bullying in the classroom. *Journal of Educational Research, 92,* 86-99.

Banks, R. (2000). Bullying in schools. *ERIC Review, 7,* 12-15. Retrieved October 24, 2001, from http://ericcass.uncg.edu/virtuallib/bullying/1036.html.

Bengtsson, H., & Johnson, L. (1992). Perspective taking, empathy, and prosocial behavior in late childhood. *Child Study Journal, 22,* 11-22.

Charlesworth, W. R. (1996). Co-operation and competition: Contributions to an evolutionary and development model. *International Journal of Behavioral Development, 19,* 25-39.

Chess, S., & Thomas, A. (1999). *Goodness of fit: Clinical applications from infancy through adult life.* Philadelphia: Brunner/Mazel.

Coie, J. D., & Dodge, K. (1998). Aggression and antisocial behavior. In W. Damon (Series Ed.), and N. Eisenberg (Vol. Ed.), *Handbook of child psychology: Vol. 3. Social, emotional, and personality development* (5th ed., pp. 779-862). New York: Wiley.

Colvin, G., Tobin, K., Beard, K., Hagan, S., & Sprague, J. (1998). The school bully: Assessing the problem, developing interventions, and future research directions. *Journal of Behavioral Education, 8,* 293-319.

Cowie, H., & Sharp, S. (1994). Empowering pupils to take positive action against bullying. In P. K. Smith, & S. Sharp (Eds.), *School bullying: Insights and perspectives* (pp. 46-94). London: Routledge.

Crick, N. R., & Bigbee, M. A. (1998). Relational and overt forms of peer victimization. *Journal of Consulting & Clinical Psychology, 66,* 337-347.

Dodge, K. A., & Frame, C. L. (1982). Social cognitive biases and deficits in aggressive boys. *Child Development, 53,* 620-635.

Dodge, K. A., Pettit, G. S., McClaskey, C. L., & Brown, M. M. (1986). Social competence in children. *Monographs of the Society for Research in Child Development, 51*(2 Serial No. 213).

Dodge, K. A., & Somberg, D. A. (1987). Hostile attributional biases are exacerbated under conditions of threats to the self. *Child Development, 58,* 213-224.

Dorsch, A., & Keane, S. P. (1994). Contextual factors in children's social information processing. *Developmental Psychology, 30,* 611-616.

Egan, S. K., & Perry, D. G. (1998). Does low self-regard invite victimization? *Developmental Psychology, 34,* 299-309.

Eisenberg, N., Fabes, R. A., Shepard, S. A., Murphy, B. C., Jones, S., & Guthrie, I. K. (1998). Contemporaneous and longitudinal prediction of children's sympathy from dispositional regulation and emotionality. *Developmental Psychology, 34,* 910-924.

Finnegan, R. Q., Hodges, E. V. E., & Perry, D. G. (1996). Preoccupied and avoidant coping during middle childhood. *Child Development, 67,* 1318-1328.

Guzman, L. D. (2001). *Bully Busters.* Las Vegas, NV.

Hodges, E. V. E., Boivin, M., Vitaro, F., & Bukowski, W. M. (1999). The power of friendship: Protection against an escalating cycle of peer victimization. *Developmental Psychology, 35,* 94-101.

Hodges, E. V. E., Malone, M. J., & Perry, D. G. (1997). Individual risk and social risk as interacting determinant of victimization in the peer group. *Developmental Psychology, 33*, 1032-1039.

Hodges, E. V. E., & Perry, D. G. (1999). Personal and interpersonal antecedents and consequences of victimization by peers. *Journal of Personality & Social Psychology, 76*, 677-685.

Hoover, J. H., & Oliver, R. (1996). *The bullying prevention handbook: A guide for principals, teachers, and counselors.* Bloomington, IN: National Educational Service.

Howard, K. A., Flora, J., & Griffin, M. (1999). Violence-prevention programs in schools: State of the science and implications for future research. *Applied & Preventive Psychology, 8*, 197-215.

Huesmann, L. R. (1998). The role of social information processing and cognitive schema in the acquisition and maintenance of habitual aggressive behavior. In R. G. Green & E. Donnerstein (Eds.), *Human aggression: Theories, research, and implications for policy* (pp. 73-109). New York: Academic Press.

Huesmann, L. R., & Guerra, N. G. (1997). Children's normative beliefs about aggression and aggressive behavior. *Journal of Personality & Social Psychology, 72*, 408-419.

Kochenderfer, B. J., & Ladd, G. W. (1996). Peer victimization: Cause or consequence of school maladjustment? *Child Development, 67*, 1305-1317.

National Resource Center for Safe Schools. (2001). New study reveals prevalence, harm of bullying. *The Safety Zone, 3*(1), 1-3. Retrieved January 22, 2002, from http://www.safetyzone.org/publications/zone8-story1.html.

Newman, R. S., Murray, B., & Lussier, C. (2001). Confrontation with aggressive peers at school: Students' reluctance to seek help from the teacher. *Journal of Educational Psychology, 93*, 398-410.

O'Connell, P., Pepler, D., & Craig, W. (1999). Peer involvement in bullying: Insights and challenges for intervention. *Journal of Adolescence, 22*, 437-452.

Olweus, D. (1991). Bully/victim problems among schoolchildren: Basic facts and effects of a school-based intervention program. In D. J. Pepler, & K. H. Rubin (Eds.), *The development and treatment of childhood aggression* (pp. 411-448). Hillsdale, NJ: Erlbaum Associates.

Olweus, D. (1992). Victimization by peers: Antecedents and long-term outcomes. In K. H. Rubin, & J. B. Asendorpf (Eds.), *Social withdrawal, inhibition, and shyness in childhood* (pp. 315-341). Hillsdale, NJ: Erlbaum Associates.

Olweus, D. (1993). *Bullying at school.* Cambridge, MA: Blackwell.

Park, L. C., & Park, T. J. (1997). Personal intelligence. In M. McCallum, & W. E. Piper (Eds.), *Psychological mindedness: A contemporary understanding* (pp. 133-168). Mahwah, NJ: Lawrence Erlbaum Associates.

Perry, D. G., Perry, L. C., & Kennedy, E. (1992). Conflict and the development of antisocial behavior. In C. U. Shantz & W. W. Hartup (Eds.), *Conflict in child and adolescent development* (pp. 301-329). New York: Cambridge University Press.

Saarni, C. (1999). *The development of emotional competence.* New York: The Guilford Press.

Safe Place. (2001). *Expect Respect.* Austin, TX: Safe Place.

Schwartz, D., Dodge, K. A., & Coie, J. D. (1993). The emergence of chronic peer victimization in boys' play groups. *Child Development, 64,* 1755-1772.

Schwartz, D., Dodge, K. A., Petit, G. S., & Bates, J. E. (1997). The early socialization and adjustment of aggressive victims of bullying. *Child Development, 68,* 665-675.

Schwartz, D., Proctor, L. J., & Chien, D. H. (2001). The aggressive victim of bullying: Emotional and behavioral dysregulation as a pathway to victimization by peers. In J. Juvonen, & S. Graham (Eds.), *Peer harassment in school: The plight of the vulnerable and victimized* (pp. 147-174). New York: The Guilford Press.

Skiba, R., & Fontanini, A. (2000). *Fast facts: Bullying prevention.* Bloomington, IN: Phi Delta Kappa International. Retrieved January 22, 2002, from http://www.pdkintl.org/whatis/ff12bully.htm.

Smith, P. K., & Sharp, S. (1994). School bullying: A cross-national perspective. In P. K. Smith, & S. Sharp (Eds.), *School bullying: Insights and perspectives* (pp. 1-13). London: Routledge.

Staub, E. (1999). The roots of evil: Social conditions, culture, personality, and basic human needs. *Personality and Social Psychology Review, 3,* 179-192.

U.S. Department of Education. (1998). *Preventing bullying: A manual for schools and communities.* Washington, DC: Author. Retrieved May 19, 2000, from http://www.cdi.ca.gov/spbranch/ssp/bulymanual.htm.

Zahn-Waxler, C., Radke-Yarrow, M., Wagner, E., & Chapman, M. (1992). Development of concern for others. *Developmental Psychology, 28,* 126-136.